Subconscious Acts, Anesthesias, and Psychological Disaggregation in Psychological Automatism

Pierre Janet's *L'Automatisme Psychologiue*, originally published in 1889, is one of the earliest and most important books written on the study of trauma and dissociation. Here it is made available, in two volumes, in English for the first time, with a new preface by Giuseppe Craparo and Onno van der Hart.

The second volume, *Subconscious Acts, Anesthesias, and Psychological Disaggregation in Psychological Automatism*, covers four main topics. Beginning with an examination of subconscious acts, Janet first assesses partial catalepsies, subconscious acts, and posthypnotic suggestions, then proceeds to a consideration of anesthesias and simultaneous psychological existences. This is followed by discussion of several forms of psychological disaggregation, including spiritism, impulsive madness, hallucinations, and possessions. Finally, Janet considers elements of mental weakness and strength, from misery to judgement and will. Janet's work, with its many descriptions of dissociative actions and the dissociative personality, will help clinicians and researchers to develop insight in trauma-related dissociation, and to become more adapt at relating to their patients' dissociative actions.

This seminal work will be of great interest to researchers and students of psychoanalysis, philosophy, and modernism, as well as psychotherapists and psychoanalysts working with clients who have experienced trauma. It is accompanied by *Catalepsy, Memory, and Suggestion in Psychological Automatism: Total Automatism*.

Pierre Janet (1859–1947) is regarded as one of the most seminal researchers, clinicians, and thinkers of the last two centuries. His work spanned the fields of psychotherapy, psychology, and philosophy.

Giuseppe Craparo, PhD, is a psychologist, psychoanalyst, and Associate Professor of clinical psychology at the Kore University of Enna, Italy.

Onno van der Hart, PhD, is a psychologist, former psychotherapist, and Emeritus Professor at Utrecht University, the Netherlands.

Subconscious Acts, Anesthesias, and Psychological Disaggregation in Psychological Automatism

Partial Automatism

Pierre Janet

Edited by Giuseppe Craparo and Onno van der Hart

Translated by Adam Crabtree and Sarah Osei-Bonsu

Routledge
Taylor & Francis Group

LONDON AND NEW YORK

First published in English 2022
by Routledge
2 Park Square, Milton Park, Abingdon, Oxon OX14 4RN

and by Routledge
605 Third Avenue, New York, NY 10158

Routledge is an imprint of the Taylor & Francis Group, an informa business

*L'automatisme Psychologique: Essai de Psychologie Expérimentale sur les Formes
Inférieures de L'activité Humaine* published in French by LIBRARIE FÉLIX
ALCAN, Paris, 1889.

British Library Cataloguing-in-Publication Data
A catalogue record for this book is available from the British Library

Library of Congress Cataloging-in-Publication Data
A catalog record has been requested for this book

ISBN: 978-1-032-05688-3 (hbk)
ISBN: 978-1-032-05689-0 (pbk)
ISBN: 978-1-003-19872-7 (ebk)

DOI: 10.4324/9781003198727

Typeset in Times New Roman
by Deanta Global Publishing Services, Chennai, India

Contents

Preface to the English edition

Giuseppe Craparo and Onno van der Hart

In 1889 the great French philosopher, psychiatrist, and psychologist, Pierre Janet published his master work, that is, his doctoral thesis in philosophy, *L'Automatisme psychologique: Essai de psychologie expérimentale sur les formes inférieures de l'activité humaine*. Over time, several unsuccessful attempts have been made to translate this still often-cited book into English. Finally, one hundred and thirty-two years after the publication of *L'Automatisme psychologique*, and eight years after the publishing of the Italian edition (2013; Francesca Ortu, transl.), the English edition (divided, for editorial reasons, into two volumes titled respectively *Catalepsy, Memory, and Suggestion in Psychological Automatism. Total Automatism* and *Subconscious Acts, Anesthesias, and Psychological Disaggregation in Psychological Automatism. Partial Automatism*), has materialized: this is an essential feat that now allows not only readers of the French language, but a much wider audience to benefit from Janet's paramount study on hysteria and dissociation, "hailed from the start as a classic of the psychological sciences" (Ellenberger, 1970, p. 361). With ten reprints by 1929, it played a major role in the psychopathology literature during the late nineteenth and early twentieth centuries: with the rediscovery of trauma-related dissociation in psychiatry and psychology in the fourth quarter of the last century, many scientists and clinicians felt increasingly called upon to refer to the original French edition. During its centenary, John C. Nemiah, M.D. expressed this praise when, in his Editorial for the *American Journal of Psychiatry*, he stated that "the French may yet take unalloyed pride in having produced one of the most seminal psychiatric clinicians and thinkers of the last two centuries" (1989, p. 1527). Nemiah concluded his *laudatio* by claiming that "[t]he advances in psychiatric knowledge during the 100 years since [*L'Automatisme psychologique*] was written have not improved on Janet's scientific method and vision" (p. 1529).

This book contains the fruits of experimental research performed by Janet between 1882 and 1888 in the psychiatric hospital of Le Havre – which eventually honored him by taking on his name. In these studies, he observed the "lower forms of human activity" in detail. In line with philosophers such as Maine de Biran, Henri Bergson, Hippolyte Taine, his uncle Paul Janet, and psychiatrists and psychologists such as Jacques-Joseph Moreau de Tours and Théodule-Armand

Ribot, Janet considered the concept of "activity" to lie at the core of psychic life, in relation to a hierarchical interpretation of the human mind as comprising different levels of consciousness; the higher levels include the function of reality ("the ability to act upon exterior objects and to change reality"; Ellenberger, 1970, p. 376), as well as presentification (experiencing the present as most real, as the center of one's history and expected future; cf. Janet, 1928), social and experimental actions, while the lowest level is the domain of automatism and reflexes.

For Janet, consciousness could not exist without action, nor could there be action without consciousness. Accordingly, Janet seemed to propose the construct of activity as lying at the intersection between mind, brain, and body, de facto overtaking the cartesian dualism (Descartes, 1637) separating *res cogitans* (thinking thing) from *res extensa* (extended thing): in this regard, Janet was in agreement with Spinoza (1670), for whom "The object of the idea consulting the human mind is the body" (Part II, Proposition XIII). With his mind/body model, Janet anticipated the current neuroscientific and psychological research on embodied cognition.

This premise is necessary to understand the psychodynamic processes of his patients suffering from hysteria, such as Rose, Lucie, Marie, and Léonie, the main subjects in this book. In these and other patients, Janet regarded hypnosis, possession states, catalepsy, somnambulism, successive existences, distractions, anesthesia, paralysis, and contractures as examples of what he called psychological automatisms: automatisms because they were regular and predetermined, and psychological because they were accompanied by sensibility and consciousness (Van der Hart & Friedman, 2019).

Contrary to the psychiatrist Prosper Despine (1880), who thought that psychological automatism consisted only of mechanical acts, Janet argued that it was determined by elementary forms of consciousness. He stated:

> The term automatic refers to a movement with two characteristics. First, it should have something spontaneous about it, at least in appearance, having its source in the object itself, which moves itself and does not need an impulse from without. A mechanical doll that walks by itself would be called an automaton; a pump which one operates from the outside would not be. Next, it is necessary that the movement remains very regular, operating under a rigorous determinism, without variations or caprice. Now the principle exertions of human activity possess precisely these two characteristics: they are induced and are not created by an outside force; they originate from the subject himself, and yet they are so regular that there can be no question here of free will, which higher faculties require. But there is also another meaning we often apply to the word *automatic,* one not so easily accepted. For some authors an automatic activity is not only a regular and rigorously determined one, but also one that is purely mechanical, without consciousness
>
> (Janet, 1889/2021, p. 1, vol. I)

Regarding automatisms, Janet distinguishes total automatism and partial automatism: in total automatism, the patient's consciousness is completely dominated by a reproduction of past experience, while in partial automatism only a dissociative part of the personality is occupied by it. For instance, his patient Lucie manifested as the dominant existence or part of her personality anesthesia, while another existence or part, Adrienne, felt pain when her arm was pinched.

Both "total automatism" and "partial automatism" involve a *désagrégation* or dissociation of the personality, which accompanies a "narrowing of the field of consciousness". Together, these phenomena stem from a "decrease of the personal synthesis" (lowering of the integrative capacity). As Janet stated, in psychopathologies such as hysteria, *"the power of psychic synthesis is weakened and lets escape, apart from personal perception, quite a considerable number of psychological phenomena: it is the state of disaggregation"* (p. 77, vol. II). He contrasted this "state of psychological misery" with a state of psychological health, including a high power of mental synthesis (integrative capacity); one in which *"all psychological phenomena, whatever their origin, are united in the same personal perception"* (p. 76, vol. II). In short, Janet regarded the fundamental character of hysteria and related disorders as consisting of two interrelated aspects, that is, a "psychological désagrégation" – not a repression of unconscious sexual drives – and a narrowing of the field of consciousness. It should be noted that, while Janet used in *L'Automatisme psychologique* the notion of disaggregation, in his previous and subsequent publications he mostly used the term dissociation, that is, in the sense of a structural dissociation of the personality, instead.

Moreover, it is important to underline that in Janet's view, *disaggregation* or dissociation *is not an active defensive mechanism* of the self. It is rather a *passive* falling away of higher mental functions ("psychological misery") consequent to vehement emotions evoked in situations, often of a threatening nature such as traumatizing events, with which the individual is unable to cope. As Janet stated in his Autobiography,

> These events, which had established a violent emotion and a destruction of the psychological system, had left traces. The remembrance of these events, the mental work involved in their recall and settlement, persisted in the form of lower and more or less conscious psychological processes, absorbed a great deal of strength, and played a part in the persistent weakening. Here still, if I am not mistaken, this notion has been fruitful and has given rise to a whole theory of neurosis and psychosis by the subconscious persistence of an emotional traumatism ...
>
> (1930, p. 128)

From Janet's clinical perspective, hysterical symptoms originate from vehement emotions (*"emotions véhémentes"* or *"émotions violentes"*) inherent in traumatic experiences which have a disintegrating effect on one's personality. There exists some misunderstanding in the literature with regard to Janet's emphasis on lowered integrative capacity in patients suffering of hysteria, that is, dissociation of the personality. This misunderstanding may be attributed to Breuer and Freud (1895/1975), who highlighted Janet's view on a constitutional weakness in this regard, which they contrasted with their emphasis on the pathogenic role of traumatic experiences (while eventually also recognizing the role of constitutional factors). Indeed, Janet was clear in his view that people are differently endowed with regard to the integrative capacity. However, he did notice the pathogenic or dissolving role of traumatic experiences in lowering this capacity. Still, being the careful researcher that he was, he was reluctant to generalize too easily, and noticed that extreme exhaustion and serious illness could also have this effect. In fact, in his books published between 1889 and 1904 (e.g., Janet, 1903), he determined traumatic experiences as an etiological factor in 257 cases out of 591 (the majority not suffering from hysteria but rather psychasthenia) (Crocq & De Verbizier, 1989).

Trauma-related disaggregation or dissociation of the personality manifested in dissociative "existences," which he also called "personalities," "parts of the personality," or "selves" – some of which he also labeled as subconscious "fixed ideas" (subsequently called "complexes" by, for instance, Jung). They remain isolated from personal consciousness and control of the presenting part of the personality, thus having a more or less autonomous life and development. In both total and partial automatism, these "fixed ideas" have their own, at least rudimentary "sense and idea of self" (*idée du moi*) and continue to exist at a subconscious level. From his patient Léonie, for example, Janet learned about her "successive existences" or, in modern parlance, alternating dissociative parts of her personality, and from Marie, that such a part was involved in her dissociative anesthesia. These "existences" all included their own subconscious memories. Thus, nowadays we would like to emphasize that the development of these "existences," "parts of the personality," etc., does not involve a mere falling apart of psychological elements but also a lower-order kind of integrative actions (Van der Hart & Rydberg, 2019): otherwise only chaos would remain.

It should be remembered that it was Janet (1910) who coined the term *subconscious* – not be confused with the notion of the Freudian unconscious. Indeed, unlike the Freudian unconscious, which is the seat of all drives, the Janetian subconsciousness has this fundamental characteristic: subconscious are all those mental functions and contents which exist outside the individual's personal consciousness. In traumatized individuals, these functions and contents outside their narrowed field of consciousness are dissociative in nature: they involve the existence of dissociative parts of the personality and their subconscious fixed ideas (cf. Bühler & Heim, 2009; Ellenberger, 1970).

We are delighted and immensely grateful that, finally, clinicians and researchers in the field of trauma and dissociation who are unfamiliar with the French language will be able to read this fundamental publication, written by Pierre Janet, the father of contemporary psychotraumatology, and be inspired by it.

References

Breuer, J., & Freud, S. (1895). Studies on hysteria. *S.E.*, 2, 19–305. London: Hogarth, 1975.

Bühler, K.-E., & Heim, G. (2009). Psychopathological approaches in Pierre Janet's conception of the subconscious. *Psychopathology*, 42(3), 190–200.

Crocq, L., & De Verbizier, J. (1989). Le traumatisme psychologique dans l'oeuvre de Pierre Janet. *Annales Médico-Psychologiuques*, 147, 983–987.

Descartes, R. (1637). *Meditations on first philosophy*. Cambridge: Cambridge University Press, 1986.

Ellenberger, H. F. (1970). *The discovery of the unconscious: The history and evolution of dynamic psychiatry*. New York: Basic Books.

Janet, P. (1910). Le subconscient. *Scientia*, 4(7), 64–79.

Janet, P. (1928). *L'évolution de la mémoire et de la notion du temps*. Paris: A. Chahine.

Janet, P. (1930). Pierre Janet autobiography. In: C. Murchison (Ed.), *History of psychology in autobiography* (Vol. 1, pp. 123–133). Worchester, MA: Clark University Press.

Nemiah, J. C. (1989). Janet redivivus: The centenary of *L'automatisme psychologique*. *American Journal of Psychiatry*, 146(12), 1527–1529.

Spinoza, B. (2005). (1670), *Tractatus Theologicus Politicus*, Hamburg: Heinrich Künrath.

Van der Hart, O., & Friedman, B. (2019). A reader's guide to Pierre Janet: A neglected intellectual heritage. In: G. Craparo, F. Ortu, O. van der Hart (Eds.), *Rediscovering Pierre Janet: Trauma, dissociation, and a new context for psychoanalysis* (pp. 4–27). London and New York: Routledge.

Van der Hart, O., & Rydberg, J. A. (2019). Vehement emotions and trauma-generated dissociation: A Janetian perspective on integrative failure. *European Journal of Trauma and Dissociation*, 3(3), 191–201. https://doi.org/10.1016/j.ejtd.2019.06.003

Acknowledgments

We are very much indebted to Sarah Osei-Bonsu and Adam Crabtree for their hard work and dedication to do as much justice as possible to the original text in their superb translation. Where others before them gave up in their translation attempts at some point, Sarah and Adam succeeded and hopefully have experienced what Janet called acts of triumph.

The realization of the English-language edition of this book is made possible by generous donations of the European Society for Trauma and Dissociation, International Society for the Study of Trauma and Dissociation, the Association Française Pierre Janet, the Institut Européen de Thérapies Somato-Psychiques (represented by its cofounders, Bernard Mayer and Françoise Pasqualin, President of AFPJ) and the following colleagues: Orit Badouk Epstein, Suzette Boon, Danny Brom, Martin Dorahy, Alessandro Lombardo, Sheldon Itzkowitz, Bessel van der Kolk, Andreas Laddis, Harriet Mall, Dolores Mosquera, Ellert Nijenhuis, Pat Ogden, Roger Solomon, and Kathy Steele – to whom we express our deep gratitude.

We wish to thank Gerhard Heim, Andrew Moskowitz, Francesca Ortu, Jenny Ann Rydberg, and Isabelle Saillot for their precious advice and comments. We are also very grateful for the support, including precious editorial work, we received from Jayanthi Chander and Susannah Frearson at Routledge during the production process.

Chapter 1

Subconscious acts

The psychological states which we have reviewed in previous studies, although very different from each other, had a common characteristic; they were a disposition, a way of being of the mind of the whole subject. The people observed were completely in a state of wakefulness, or somnambulism, or delirium, but they were never half in one state and half in another; also their consciousness, extended or restricted, whatever its nature, embraced all the psychological phenomena of the subject. The sensations, normal or abnormal, evoked by somnambulism or electricity, spontaneous or suggested acts, all were known by the subject. "I feel that I have an arm in the air, I feel that it moves, I see a bird." Such was the language of our subjects at the moment when one directed their actions or sensations. Is this always the case, and does the automatic life of mental phenomena always develop with a similar unity, in a manner which allows this unified consciousness to subsist? If this were the case, three quarters of the phenomena observed in states of illness or even normal states would be inexplicable.

All the psychological laws seem wrong if we look only to their application in the conscious phenomena of which the individual is aware. At every moment, we encounter facts, hallucinations, or acts that seem inexplicable, because we do not find their reason for being, their origin in other ideas that the conscious mind recognizes. In the presence of these shortcomings, the psychologist is too often willing to declare himself incompetent and to ask physiology for help, which it can hardly provide. Psychology cannot evolve if it remains incomplete and neglects phenomena whose knowledge is necessary to explain the problems it poses. If we consider in particular the question with which we are occupied, we will not take long to note that the laws of psychological automatism are often inadequate.

However, we believe that these laws are accurate and comprehensive, and that the challenges that are encountered can be overcome, provided we admit that these psychological laws, while remaining consistent, may in some cases apply in a quite distinct manner. Psychic automatism, instead of being complete, of governing all conscious thought, can be partial and govern a small group of phenomena separated from others, isolated from the total consciousness of the individual who continues to develop on their own account and in another manner.

DOI: 10.4324/9781003198727-1

It is therefore not new research that we undertake; it is a particular application of our previous studies applied to a new set of circumstances. In our review, we intend to follow the same structure, to demonstrate the simple automatism of sensations, that of more complete perceptions, and the constitution of memories and distinct personalities, as we have already done; but in these studies we will examine only those phenomena of which the subject who experiences them is unaware and which appear to be unconscious.

1.1 Partial catalepsies

We cannot, at the onset of our research, provide a clear and comprehensive definition of unconscious acts or those that seem to be such. For them to be observed and described, it is enough to accept this commonplace notion: what we mean by unconscious action is an act which has all the characteristics of a psychological act except one, namely that the very person who executes it is always unaware of it at the very moment that he executes it.[1] We do not consider the action that individuals forget immediately after making it as an unconscious act, for they knew and described the action while they were doing it. This act lacks memory, not consciousness, as we have demonstrated already. We shall now consider those acts of which the subject never admits to having had any consciousness. Acts of this kind may present in one of two ways. Sometimes the individual, at the moment when the act is performed, seems to have no conscious awareness either of the act or of anything else; they do not speak and show no expression. This is analogous to the cases of catalepsy that we have studied at length and will not revisit now. Sometimes, on the contrary, the individual keeps a clear awareness of all other psychological phenomena except of a certain act that they execute without knowing it. The individual then speaks with ease, but of matters other than their action; we can then verify, as the subject can themselves, that they are completely unaware of the action that their hands perform. It is this particular form of unconsciousness which is, it now seems to us, very important to well understand.

Unconscious acts of this kind have long been reported and studied from different points of view. Speculative philosophers have been precursors on this point and have maintained the existence of unconscious phenomena in the human mind, long before actual observations could have made them known. We know of the doctrine of Leibniz's small perceptions or deaf perceptions. "I grant to the Cartesians," he says, "that the soul is always thinking; but I do not grant that it perceives all its thoughts, because our great perceptions and our great attitudes which we perceive are composed of an infinity of small perceptions and small inclinations, all of which we cannot possibly perceive. And it is in these imperceptible perceptions that the reason of what happens within us is to be found, just as the cause of what happens in sensible bodies consists in unnoticeable movements."[2] And elsewhere: "Thus, it is good to distinguish between perception, which is the inner state of the individual representing external things, and apperception, which is the conscious or the reflective knowledge of this inner state – this latter state being one which is not given to all souls, nor always to the same soul."[3] Many philosophers, especially in Germany, have repeated ideas similar to those of Leibniz. One will find a more complete indication of these (which I cannot reproduce here) in the great treatise of Hartmann on the unconscious, in the introduction of the dissertation of Colsenet on the same subject, and in an article by Renouvier devoted to a discussion of these doctrines.[4] I would only like to point out a very interesting passage from Maine de Biran, where the illustrious French psychologist, on whose support we already depended in our discussion on catalepsy,[5] again seems to adopt and defend the ideas on the unconscious that we are going to explore: "By distancing ourselves from that which is absolute in the system of Leibniz, it is conceivable that the affections specific to the component monads or sensible elements can take place without being represented or perceived by the central monad that constitutes the self, or the principle of unity."[6] Cabanis, Condillac, Hamilton, and more recently Hartmann, Leon Dumont,[7] Colsenet,[8] and many others have expressed similar ideas.

All these philosophers have spoken about unconscious phenomena in a theoretical manner only; they demonstrated that, according to their methodologies, such facts were possible. At most they have tried to interpret some facts of daily observation in this sense. Those who have tried to observe in an experimental manner the existence and the properties of these ignored phenomena are far less numerous and less well known. During the old epidemics of possessions, the exorcists frequently had the opportunity to witness these facts; but needless to say, they were quite unable to understand them. In the more recent epidemics of convulsives, such as that of Saint-Médard, we find more interesting descriptions, such as this one from Carré de Montgeron: "It often happens that a succession of words issues from the mouth of the speakers independent of their will, such that they are witnesses to what they are saying and do not know what they are saying as long as they are speaking."[9] It must be admitted that there are adepts in one of the more curious superstitions of our time, the spiritualists, who, by their turning of tables and interrogation of spirits around 1850, drew the most attention to the unconscious phenomena. They have observed and even produced them in all their varieties. But the way they explain them is so strange, and their descriptions are so altered by their religious enthusiasm, that one cannot take their studies on the unconscious as a point of departure for research. It will be more natural to return to their descriptions when we have observed enough phenomena to be able to understand them and sometimes explain them. However, the problem raised by them was studied more precisely in the works of Faraday and Chevreul,[10] who were the first to demonstrate the intervention of truly unconscious psychological phenomena. These studies were, as we know, continued in the work that Richet recently dedicated to the illustrious centenarian,[11] and in the research of Gley on the same problem.[12] Since this period, investigations have been much more numerous, and we shall have to take account of them in our work.

Another question, which was raised around 1840, maintained that the hemispheres of the human brain acted as two independent bodies, functioning each on its own.[13] Since then, Wigan, Mayo, Laycock, Carpenter, Brown-Sequard, Luys, etc. have studied the facts, both favorable and unfavorable, to this hypothesis and found that in some cases human beings seem to be double, and to perform actions with one part which they are unaware of in the other. Some studies on hypnotism were led in this direction, finding dual-idea states affecting only one side of the body. Hemilateral catalepsies were studied and suggestions were made to two sides of a subject at the same time, in such a way as to simultaneously give them two thoughts and two expressions.[14] We shall not insist at length upon these phenomena, which it seems to us can be related quite easily to the preceding ones.

The simplest unconscious acts of all have been designated by Lasègue,[15] who was the first to report them, under the name of *partial catalepsies*, a very apt expression and the one we will use. These are indeed cataleptic phenomena quite identical to those we encountered early in our research in the complete cataleptic attack. The continuation of an attitude or movement, imitation, the association of movements – all these facts are found here again almost as we had described them. But now they are partial, that is, they exist only in one part of the subject's body, while the rest of the body is occupied with completely different acts and presents quite different characteristics. An arm, for example, behaves as if it were the arm of a person in catalepsy but the subject as a whole, far from being in this state, laughs and chats without worrying about what their arm is doing.[16]

Liébault[17] frequently points out incidents of this kind. Somnambulists keep their arms extended without seeming to be aware of it, all the while talking about something else. They even seem to be able to hold several fixed ideas at once. But these phenomena have been the subject of a careful study of Binet and Féré.[18] We can only summarise the observations which they have given and which we have been able to verify, merely insisting upon certain details which seem to us new and interesting.

These experiments are mostly performed on hysterics suffering from total anesthesia or partial anesthesia of the skin and muscles. They are particularly successful when one experiments on the side or limbs that are anesthetic and cannot be repeated without special precautions (which we will indicate later) upon the limbs which retain sensation. Consider persons of this type, Rose or Marie, who are complete anesthetics, or Léonie, who is anesthetized on the left, and let us take the precaution of hiding from the subject the arm or the leg whose movements we wish to observe. For that, it is sometimes sufficient to close the eyes of the subject. However, this process seems to us defective, because very often, in subjects of this kind, it produces a general modification of consciousness and even complete somnambulism, which we want to avoid. It is better to simply turn the subject's head and hide the arm with a screen. Now let us take the arm and put it in the air in any position. Very frequently, when the previous precautions are taken, the arm stays motionless in the position where we put it. If we impose a movement on the arm, the movement continues exactly with the regularity of a pendulum. These positions and movements can persist for a very long time. Binet and Féré have observed this for more than an hour, without there being any movement of the limb, nor any change in the breathing of the subject, which might indicate fatigue. These are precisely, as we have seen, the characteristics of general catalepsy. But we cannot insist upon this too much. The subject is not in a cataleptic state. They speak and are able to execute the movements they desire with their other limbs. What is happening is simply that they feel absolutely nothing that is happening in the arm that we put in the air and seem even to have forgotten of its existence. If we talk to them about this arm, of which they no longer appear to be aware, they can sometimes easily lower it, while sometimes they find themselves incapable of moving it voluntarily.

These movements, of which the subject is unaware, can be made more complicated and we can have them blow kisses or draw signs of the cross in the air. One can even, by putting a pencil in the hand, closing the fingers, and putting the arm over a sheet of paper, transmit the movements necessary for writing, have the hand write over and over the letter or even the word whose characters you had them produce. "It is difficult to immobilize the hand once it has started an unconscious movement of this kind; if we take away the pencil they will continue the movement."[19] One day, I wanted to stop a movement of Léonie's of this kind, and I squeezed her right hand. Then trembling started in her left hand, I stopped this one too and the movement passed to the left foot. Ordinarily, when the subject looks at their hand, they can stop immediately; but with certain subjects, such as Rose, the movement is prolonged for some time, even when she sees it and is trying to stop it.

The second phenomenon characteristic of the general cataleptic state was imitation or the repetition of acts and words. This is rare and difficult to observe in these partial catalepsies. However, we can observe imitations of this kind, that the subject carries out without any awareness, while they are speaking of something else. Despine cites a curious example: it was enough for him to touch with one hand the head of a subject and make a few gestures with the other free hand, so that all these movements were reproduced immediately. If one questioned this person, she answered: "Sir, I do not know, I do not want to do anything … I obey in spite of myself; it seems to me that the limb no longer belongs to me … I know I am doing something, but I could not say what it is, I am completely ignorant of it."[20]

I have recently observed a rather curious analogous fact, because it occurred during a delirium in a woman's last stage of pulmonary phthisis. She imitated almost all gestures made in front of her, without it interrupting her delirium. In many diseases, similar events have been reported, which we will not focus on now, because the anesthesia of the limbs which make the unconscious movements, which is the principal condition we are dealing with, does not always exist in those cases. On the contrary, I have observed with Léonie some phenomena which are far more comparable to the preceding ones and more clear-cut. If I stand in front of her during her complete waking state and if she does not look at her arms, she imitates my gestures with her left arm (which is anesthetic) and never with her right arm which has feeling.

During somnambulism, this unconscious imitation can be more complete. I was writing with my right hand next to Léonie who was in somnambulism, and when I touched her with my left hand I realized that her right hand trembled continually, though she claimed not to be aware of it. In fact, her hand was unconsciously repeating nearly every movement that mine made to write: it was enough to stop touching the subject to interrupt the phenomenon. I made other gestures with my right hand while touching her with my left hand, and these gestures were repeated. I ate and I drank next to her, and she repeated, without awareness, all my movements, even those of swallowing; this last point is all the more curious for if she wants to drink consciously, she cannot do it. In a curious circumstance, I even found a practical use of this unconscious imitation. Léonie has had recent attacks of violent hysterical asthma; during a somnambulism, she stopped breathing and began to suffocate. After various unsuccessful attempts to start her breathing again, I approached her, holding both her hands and I began to breathe very deeply and loudly. After a moment, she began to copy my breathing in the most singular way, coughing if I coughed, breathing quickly or slowly like me; I regularized my breathing, she did the same, and the bout of asthma was over.

We have seen that, during a true cataleptic state, movements become regular and give a harmonious expression to the whole body. We cannot expect to see here the phenomenon in such a complete way. However, Binet and Féré[21] describe something comparable when they say that among anesthetic hysterical patients, every motor phenomenon induced on one side of the body results in an analogous phenomenon, although weaker, on the other side. They do not talk about facial expressions occurring in these partial catalepsies and say they have not observed them.[22] However, I have twice had occasion to observe that a change in physiognomy can occur under these circumstances. When I placed Léonie's hands in a position of prayer, while taking precautions so that her hands were not visible to her, I saw her face take on an ecstatic expression similar to that which occurs during complete catalepsy, while her mouth spoke indifferently about other things. This expression was very imperfect and did not become generalized as it does in complete catalepsy. Another time, I put Lucie's hands in the position they took during the crisis of terror, which constitutes one of the periods of her great hysterical crisis. Her whole figure took a very marked expression of terror, though the words she spoke at the time had nothing to do with fear. I asked her if she felt any sense of fear: "Not at all," she said, "Why do you want me to be afraid?" But these expressions in partial catalepsy remain very rare, I have observed them only twice.

What is more common is the association or coordination of unconscious movements with each other and with the impressions that serve as their point of departure. If the two arms are pulled forward, the whole body lifts and the movements are coordinated to maintain a standing position,[23] without leaving the subject in doubt that they have stood up. If we disturb a movement that occurs unconsciously, sometimes the arm corrects the deviation and returns to the original movement.[24]

The anesthetic arm seems to understand the intention of the experimenter and, on the slightest impulse, pursue this or that movement. It is enough to make an initial impression for the movements to develop in a certain direction. In fact, if a weight is placed on the raised arm of the subject without them being aware of it, the arm does not bend under the added weight; on the contrary, the muscle tension adapts to the weight in order to maintain its position.[25] This was especially remarkable in Lem, a hysterical man that I studied at the military hospital with Dr. Pillet. I put on his extended arm sometimes a very light weight like a feather, sometimes a weight of several kilos, and the muscle tension adapted itself to each new weight unbeknownst to him, so that there was no change in the position of the arm. With Léonie, this adaptation goes a step further, for her hand grasps the weight and holds it so that it will not fall. If we put a pencil in her anesthetic hand, the fingers, as we have noticed, bend unconsciously and place themselves, unbeknownst to the subject, in the desired position for writing.

I will add that it is the same with any object. I put in Léonie's left hand (her left side is completely anesthetic) a pair of scissors and I hide this hand with a screen. Léonie, whom I question, can absolutely not tell me what she has in her left hand, and yet the fingers of her left hand have placed themselves into the scissor rings and are opening and closing the scissors. Similarly I put a lorgnette in her left hand; this hand opens the lorgnette and raises to bring it up to her nose. But, halfway there, it enters her visual field. Léonie, who then sees it, is stupefied. "Here," she says, "it is a lorgnette that I had in my left hand." These phenomena obviously present something contradictory: the hand we have said is anesthetic and feels nothing, yet Léonie feels the scissors and the lorgnette and adapts her movements to the nature of the objects. There is not only an unconscious act, there is also an unconscious sensation. Let us simply note this fact, which we will study in more detail later on.

We see, then, that all the phenomena of catalepsy can exist partially, while the ordinary consciousness of the subject in contrast seems to remain intact. Let us make some general remarks on all the circumstances in which these incidents occur, before attempting to interpret them. We will not speak here of the influence of this or that practitioner to produce these phenomena. The anesthetic limbs of the subject have their preferences and are obedient to one person and not to another. The analysis of this fact falls under the study of electivity, which we will discuss later. Let us note for now that for such phenomena to occur, there must be anesthesia. Partial catalepsies do not exist naturally without special procedures regarding the limbs which have preserved their sensitivity. More to the point, if, by such a procedure, an electrical current or metal plate or simply suggestion (when possible), I restore sensitivity to the arm of Rose or of Marie, the cataleptic state disappears, and their arm does not stay in the air, when I place it there. If sometimes, as in one of Rose's deep somnambulisms, the left arm is still in the air, even though it appears to have feeling, it is because the feeling/sensitivity is not complete, it is cutaneous and not muscular. The subject is able to appreciate more or less the position of her arm by the friction of her clothes, the folds of the skin, etc., but does not know if her muscles are contracted or not, something we can easily verify by inducing contractures of which she is unaware. There is always an anesthesia when there is a catalepsy of this type. Far better, when one induces a partial catalepsy in a subject with normal sensibility, it is accompanied by an identical anesthesia. Thus, Be has perfect sensitivity normally; but if Dr. Powilewicz, who was studying her, suggested that her arm should remain in any number of positions, the arm became cataleptic, and no longer had any feeling. I had no influence on her and could not make this suggestion to her in her waking state. When I placed her finger on a curved magnet of Ochorowicz, it caused anesthesia of her entire left side. This left side became cataleptic for me immediately, even though it was not originally. If one objects that there are cases where the arm stays in the air even when it retains feeling, I would say that then we have returned to the study of conscious suggestion made in the previous volume[26] and that it is not a case of partial catalepsy. The same phenomenon (and this is not always sufficiently appreciated) can present in many different forms.

This partial catalepsy is not unique to the waking state. It can occur when the subject is in other states which are very different from one another, provided that these two principal conditions are present: anesthesia of the limb and a certain unconscious electivity towards the operator. When a hysterical patient is placed into a mild somnambulic state, she usually retains her various anesthesias, and her limbs obey in the same way without her knowing it. Therefore there is a cataleptic state of the limbs in which the subject can speak and understand what is said to her. This partial catalepsy by anesthesia during somnambulism should not be confused with an attack of complete catalepsy.

These partial acts have been reported during general catalepsy itself, each subject's arm may perform a different gesture. So, with Léonie, her right arm can be throwing punches while her left arm stays in a position of prayer, and each of these actions brings its corresponding expression to a part of her face.

But I do not believe that anyone has reported this partial catalepsy during a hysterical crisis. When Rose is in a great hysterical crisis, at any stage, I can take possession (so to speak) of an arm or a leg by touching them lightly. The limb which I touch remains motionless for a few moments and does not take part in the tremors and convulsions of the rest of the body. If I lift the limb, it stays in the position where I put it or oscillates regularly, while the other limbs continue their convulsions. I have even (in these circumstances) put a pencil in her right hand and made her write an A and a B. The hand continued to write these two letters for almost a minute, while the body curved in an arch and the left hand hit the chest with a clenched fist. This occurrence is even more easily verified during hysterical deliriums and natural somnambulisms. In a word, whatever the state in which the principal part of consciousness finds itself at the time, these cataleptic actions can exist separately and live, so to speak, a life of their own.

How, then, should we interpret these new cataleptic phenomena? We return to all the hypotheses and all the discussions that have already been presented about complete catalepsy. We believe it is unnecessary to repeat them. Here once more, we believe that there is no valid reason for completely excluding the consciousness of these phenomena, considering that it alone can explain the unity and coordination that manifest themselves in these movements. These are muscular sensations that explain, under normal circumstances, analogous movements. We must believe that these are still muscular and tactile sensations which provoke and direct these movements of the same type.

But here there is one more difficulty that we did not initially encounter. There is already a consciousness in the subject that tells us: "I see, I hear, but I do not feel that my arm is moving." This consciousness, which is in the subject, is not the consciousness of cataleptic movements, since it declares itself unaware of them. Is it possible, then, that there is another consciousness in the mind of the same subject? Let us be content for the moment in demonstrating that this is not an absurd idea and see if there are other facts which can confirm this hypothesis. When we talked of consciousness during catalepsy, we admitted, along with Maine de Biran, that it must be very inferior, and that it consisted in sensations and images and not at all in perceptions. We have said that it was characteristic of these elementary images to not be united in the same thought, to not form a personality. They were conscious images without an idea of the self, so it is not surprising then that these images are not part of the normal consciousness of the subject who speaks to us, who says "I," and whose mind is very complicated. If images of this sort were able to exist alone in the mind, I do not see any absurdity in admitting that they may now exist separately, whilst the ordinary mind of the subject appears to function in a normal manner. We find in a passage from Dumont a full expression of this hypothesis: "The words consciousness and unconsciousness are taken sometimes in a relative sense and sometimes in an absolute sense. For example, we will say that a phenomenon is unconscious to express the idea that the self is not aware of it, but without saying that the phenomenon is not conscious in itself and on its own account. Physiology tends to confirm the fact that, in the human organism, an immense number of acts of consciousness occur which, for the self, seem to belong to other people, and even possess the additional disadvantage that they are not found linked with the faculties of expression."[27] Let us add that these phenomena, in the cases we study, being isolated and, for particular reasons, finding no resistance to their manifestation, behave according to the law of isolated psychological phenomena. They manifest, what is for them to exist and endure. Partial catalepsies show us the first germs of consciousness that we will see grow and become more exact in our other studies.

1.2 Distraction and subconscious acts

Anesthesia was the key condition of the preceding phenomena. Catalepsy normally existed only on the limbs without feeling and disappeared as soon as sensitivity returned. As it happens, every observer has noted that limbs with sensitivity sometimes participated in this state and remained, if only for a moment, in the position in which they were placed. I looked for the conditions of this new observation, and they seemed to me to be related to a momentary distraction of the subject. Indeed, as we have seen, distraction among hysterics is equivalent to anesthesia, even if it is only momentary.

Léonie is wide awake. I leave her to chat with another person and, during a moment when, lost in conversation, she no longer thinks of me, I gently raise her right arm. This arm stays in the air, continuing the movement it had begun, etc., behaving just as the left arm had done earlier. Nevertheless, there is a difference between the unconscious movements of the right arm and those of the left arm, in that there exists in those of the latter, even when Léonie is warned and pays attention to me (provided that the arm is hidden by a screen), the anesthesia of the left arm, which renders the distraction useless or rather is itself a sufficient distraction; while the unconscious movements of the right arm only exist if Léonie's attention is completely distracted by another object. When she stops speaking, she notices what her right arm is doing and stops it immediately. Theoretically, no doubt, the unconscious movement can be more easily simulated by the sensitive right arm than by the anesthetic left arm,[28] but we will not focus on this objection, which is too general and too vague and which applies to any kind of psychological experimentation. It is up to the observer to take precautions and to test the good faith of the subject in a host of preliminary experiments. The best evidence of the truth of these facts seems to us to be, as we have said, in their complication, in the connections that experiments have with each other. Most frequently, the subject does not understand what one is doing and simulates everything poorly.

If the previous distraction produced a momentary anesthesia of the tactile sense and muscle in the right arm, it can produce other anesthesias for the other senses. Here, to begin with, is a visual anesthesia obtained by this means. When Léonie's eyes are open and I do not use a screen, there is no unconscious movement; the movement that I initiate stops immediately. But, as soon as I begin to speak, her left arm lifts again, even though it is visible, and resumes the position that I wanted to give it. It had registered the order but could not execute it. At the first opportunity, that is to say, at Léonie's first distraction, it hastens to resume its position.

The same distraction will produce (without it being possible in this chapter to explain how) particular anesthesias of hearing, at least in regard to my own words. Léonie, with that easy tendency to distraction which we have seen among hysterics, will listen to other people who talk to her, but will no longer pay attention to me and will not hear me if I order something in that moment. This woman does not, like other subjects, present a great suggestibility in her waking state. If I speak directly to her and command a movement, she is surprised, argues, and does not obey. But when she is speaking with other people, if I speak in a low voice behind her, without her turning around, she cannot hear me anymore. Then she executes the commandments well, but without knowing it. In a low voice, I tell her to draw out her watch, and her hands do it gently, I make her walk, I make her put on her gloves and remove them, etc.; all things she would not do if she heard me order her directly. It is the same in her other states. In her first somnambulic state, which I will call "the state of Léonie," she is so little subject to suggestion that she always seems to act with independence, and, moreover, she boasts of it. In fact, you have to shout loudly and repeat the same sentence for a long time when you want to make a suggestion directly to her. But if we proceed differently, allow her to speak with another person, which distracts her much more than when she is in her waking state, and then speak softly, the orders that we give her are immediately executed without her being aware of the fact.[29] One day, in this state, "Léonie 2" was distracted, chatting, and she had completely forgotten about me. I ordered her in a low voice to make bouquets of flowers to offer to the people around her. Nothing was more curious than to see her right hand pick, one by one, imaginary flowers, put them in her left hand, bind them with a string and then offer them solemnly to those around her, all without "Léonie 2" being aware of it or interrupting her conversation. These same facts do not exist in the second somnambulistic state, the state of "Léonie 3", because, as we shall note later, she hears only me and can therefore no longer be distracted.

The same suggestions by distraction are very easily achieved with other subjects. It was with Lucie that I noticed them for the first time, during somnambulism and during the waking state, without fully understanding them. At first, she accepted my orders or else refused them and then did not execute them. To avoid these resistances, I ordered her in a low voice when she was not paying attention to me and then she always did what I said without protest. However, I was surprised to see that she was performing these acts unconsciously. I tell her to thumb her nose, and her hands position themselves at the top of her nose. When she is asked what she is doing, she always answers that she is doing nothing and continues to chat for a long time, without suspecting that her hands are busy at the top of her nose. I get her to walk through the room; she continues to talk and thinks she is sitting. Moreover, one day I tried another experiment without discussing it with her beforehand. I asked another person, M, to command something in my absence, but in my name. In the middle of the day, M stood behind her and said, "Monsieur Janet wants both of your arms to rise in the air." This was done immediately, and both arms remained contracted above her head. But Lucie was not in the least disturbed and continued what she was saying. When producing a permanent action, like a contracture of the arms, one could force her to become aware of it by ordering her to locate her arms, to look at them, to try to move them. Then she would become terrified, would groan, and would enter into a crisis if, by a word, the harm was not suppressed. But, once calmed, and with tears still in her eyes, she did not remember anything and went back to what she had been doing at the point where she had been interrupted. The unconscious suggestion once made, could oppose her conscious will, as it had previously with Léonie. When one or the other refused to do or to say something, it was enough to distract them and then to command them in a low voice. They obeyed without knowing it or suddenly pronounced a sentence in the middle of their conversation which they then resumed without noticing the interruption. For example, Dr. Powilewicz asks Lucie to sing something, she refuses energetically. I whisper behind her: "Come, sing, sing something." She stops her conversation and sings an air of Mignon, then resumes her sentence, convinced that she did not sing, and will not sing in front of us.

The majority of our other subjects present to us, in great number, phenomena that are identical except for insignificant variations. It is more interesting to examine the same facts in a subject of a completely different type. The preceding subjects are hysterical women, who have been frequently hypnotized. The following subject is a man, P, aged forty, that we have no reason to consider hysterical and who has never been hypnotized. P is admitted to the hospital under the care of Dr. Powilewicz for a subacute attack of alcoholic delirium. We have already described the suggestions that can be made to him by addressing him directly and that he executes consciously, but he also presented acts of another type.

While the doctor was talking to him and had him explain some details of his profession, I placed myself behind him and ordered him to raise his arms. At first, I had to touch his arm to induce the act, the unconscious obedience then occurred without difficulty. I had him walk, sit, and kneel, all without him being aware. I even told him to lie face down on the floor, and he fell immediately, but his head was still lifting to answer the doctor's questions. The doctor said to him, "Why are you in that position while I am speaking to you?" "But," he answers, "I am standing near my bed, I am not moving." "Do you not see how short you have become?" "Oh, I've always been shorter than you, but I am no shorter than usual." I could not believe that a man in his right mind, who was not delirious and was wide awake, could believe that he was standing when he was lying on the ground on his belly. In reality, there was a sort of hallucination that joined the unconscious to produce this singular result. The next day, when I wanted to resume the experiment, the disposition of the patient towards unconscious acts had significantly diminished. Two days later, all suggestibility was gone. The alcoholic delirium was over and, with it, these unconscious phenomena.

So far, we have only studied actions suggested without the subject's knowledge and when distracted. What would happen if we suggested hallucinations rather than actions? At first glance, this seems almost absurd because a hallucination cannot be unconscious. If we experiment, however, we will learn that a suggestion of this kind can be achieved in two completely different ways. One is quite simple or at least is easily related to the subconscious acts that we have just examined. The suggestion seems to run without the subject knowing anything about it, without awareness and manifests itself to us only by acts or facial expressions, as with all previous acts. Charles Richet has already demonstrated how a hallucination could be realized in this way and pointed out how curious the phenomenon is. He gave a glass of water to a subject suggesting that the water is bitter. While drinking, the subject makes all kinds of grimaces. When questioned and asked if the water is bitter and tastes bad, "No," she says, "the water is not bitter. However, I cannot help making faces as if it were bitter." The same subject, when told that there was a snake in front of her, recoils with gestures of terror, while saying that she sees nothing in front of her.[30] That is exactly how things happen with Lucie.

If I whisper to her (always by the same process of distraction and not by direct suggestion, which would elicit another result) that there is a butterfly in front of her, she follows with her eyes, makes gestures to catch it, etc. while speaking of something else, and, when asked if she sees it, she says that she sees nothing. This then is an identical phenomenon to the previous ones, things occurred in the same manner when Léonie was picking flowers without being aware of it.

But often, and with most other subjects, things occur differently. The command is not heard by the subject, the origin of the hallucination is unconscious, but the hallucination itself is conscious and enters all of a sudden into the mind of the subject. Thus, while Léonie is not listening to me, I whisper to her that the person she is talking to has on a frock coat of the most beautiful green. Léonie seems to have heard nothing and continues talking with this person, but suddenly interrupts herself and gives a cry of laughter: "Oh my God, look at how you are dressed, and to think that I had not noticed it before." I also whisper to her that she has a sweet in her mouth. She seems to have heard nothing, and if I ask her, she does not know what I am talking about, but begins making faces and exclaims, "Ah! Who put that in my mouth?" What seems most singular to me is that if I speak directly to the subject (who does not take direct suggestion well), and if I order a hallucination of this kind, she will resist me, say that it is absurd and in fact will not experience the hallucination unless I insist very strongly. Whereas if I make the command by means of distraction, Léonie will not know that I commanded her to do something, will not resist me, and will thereby experience the hallucination immediately. This phenomenon is very complex. It includes a mixture of unconscious elements and conscious elements which relate to a certain point of view and yet are separate from one another. We thought it necessary to mention here its existence so as not to leave a serious gap in the enumeration of suggestions by distraction. But we do not believe that we can show other varied examples and discuss them before first completing other studies, so we will continue with our examination later.

Let us go back to the phenomena that are uniquely and completely subconscious. A characteristic that is easy to identify is intelligence, which can demonstrate its presence with similar phenomena which are, nevertheless, separated from the normal mind of the subject.

We are no longer in the presence of a partial catalepsy where the acts are simply determined by a sensation or an image. We are rather, as we shall see, in the presence of partial somnambulism, in which acts are determined by intelligent perceptions. The subject does not repeat the words, they interpret them and execute them. Therefore, there is an intelligence present, which is easy enough to reveal in different ways.

Thus, I order Léonie to raise her arm, not immediately, but when I have clapped my hands ten times. I clap my hands, and, at the tenth clap, suddenly her arm rises. All of this was for her unknown: the command, the sound of my hands clapping, and the act itself. This is obviously a phenomenon of unconscious numeration. But we shall defer for a time the study of these unconscious calculations, as they have been studied more completely in connection with another problem. I give

Léonie another intelligent suggestion, that of answering my questions with a gesture, not verbally (which is possible, but would interrupt normal conversation), but by a sign of the hand. "You will squeeze my hand to say 'yes', and you will shake it to say 'no'." I take her left hand which is anesthetic; she does not notice and continues chatting with other people. Then I also talk with her, but without her seeming to hear me. Only her one hand hears me and responds to me with small movements very clear and very well adapted to the questions.

Let us go further: if we do not want to make her speak without her knowing it, we can instead have her write. I put a pencil in her right hand and her hand squeezes the pencil, as we have come to expect. But instead of guiding the hand and making it draw a letter that she will repeat indefinitely, I ask a question: "How old are you? Which city are we in?" And here is her hand moving and writing the answers on paper, without Léonie having paused in her conversation. I had her write out arithmetic operations, which were quite correct; I made her write long answers, which obviously showed a fairly developed intelligence.

This kind of writing is known as automatic writing, an apt enough expression if we mean that it is the result of the steady development of some psychological phenomena, but by which one must not understand, I believe, that this writing is without any kind of consciousness. Taine, in the preface to his book *Intelligence*, demonstrates very well the possibility and the interest of this singular phenomenon: "The more bizarre a fact is, the more instructive it is. In this regard, spiritual manifestations themselves put us on the path of these discoveries, by showing us coexistence at the same moment, in the same individual, of two thoughts, two wills, two separate actions, one of which the subject is aware, the other of which they are unaware and which is attributed to invisible beings … Here is a person who, while talking or singing, writes (without looking at her paper) coherent sentences and even entire pages, without being aware of what she writes. In my eyes, her sincerity is perfect; however, she states that at the end of her page, she has no idea of what she has put on paper. When she reads it, she is surprised, sometimes alarmed … Certainly here we see a doubling of the self, the simultaneous presence of two series of parallel and independent ideas, two centers of action, or, if you will, two active persons juxtaposed in the same brain; each has a task, and a different task, one on the stage and the other in the wings."[31]

Distraction already played a considerable role in ordinary suggestions performed consciously as we have studied in the previous chapter; but then they concerned only antagonistic ideas and allowed the consciousness of the suggested act itself to remain. We have just seen that distraction gives birth to another kind of suggestion. While the distracted consciousness is busy with indifferent ideas, the suggested act is also performed without the knowledge of the subject. In a word, distraction seems to split the field of consciousness into two parts: one which remains conscious, the other which seems to be ignored by the subject. The previously studied suggestions provoked phenomena belonging to the first part of the field of consciousness; those we focus on now determine actions that seem to stay in the second part and which retain absolutely the appearance of catalepsies which are partial and unconscious. Before explaining these facts further, we must see other examples and under different circumstances.

1.3 Posthypnotic suggestions: history and description

The persistence of the commands beyond somnambulism and their execution after the return to the normal state were phenomena so well known by the ancient magnetizers that their description can still be considered accurate today. "The magnetizer," says Deleuze, "may, after being accepted by them, be able to imprint during the somnambulistic state an idea or an intention that will influence them in the waking state, without their knowing the cause. So the magnetizer will say to the somnambulist: 'You will go home at such and such an hour; you will not go to the show tonight; you will cover yourself in such a way; you will not have any difficulty in taking a remedy; you will drink no liqueurs, no coffee; you will not occupy yourself with this subject; you will chase away that fear, you will forget something;' etc. The somnambulist will naturally be inclined to do what has been prescribed to him. *He will remember without suspecting that it is a memory*; he will have an attraction for what you have advised him, and a repulsion for what you forbade him."[32] Nevertheless this author, who knew so well the power of suggestions after waking, did not seem to recognize that there is a similar phenomenon in the action of his *magnetized water* which "sometimes purges and sometimes constipates according to need,"[33] and which "keeps its power for five years." Bertrand understands better the role of the posthypnotic suggestion in these phenomena, and he uses it to produce all the effects attributed to magnetism. He describes (being one of the first to do so) a very curious experiment that consists of ordering a subject during his sleep to return on a given day, at a given time. "It will not be necessary," he adds, "to remind him of his promise (when he is awake) to ensure that he will execute it; and, at the appointed moment, the desire to do what he intended in the somnambulism will spontaneously arise in him without him knowing the motive that drives him."[34]

Since, from this time (1823), the posthypnotic suggestion was in this way known and used, it is not surprising that all subsequent writers give us very clear and very curious examples of this phenomenon. Teste, who did not have the same scruples as Deleuze, performs genuine experiments and orders his subjects to light a fire the next day, embroider for an hour, etc.[35] He even proposes, with as much conviction as some hypnotists of today, "to regularize the mental and physical life of the subjects one puts to sleep and to work to improve them morally."[36] In this same way, Aubin Gauthier succeeded, he says, in changing the feelings of a young girl and, by suggestion, reconciled her with her mother; the touching scene he describes is quite singular.[37]

Charpignon is more precise in his experiments; he finds that a complex suggested hallucination of this kind (that of having received a wallet as a gift) persisted for two days after waking.[38] He also demonstrates the role of suggestion in induced sleep by sending magnetized tokens, showing that sleep occurs even if the tokens have not been magnetized, although the subject has been told during the previous somnambulism that they would be.[39]

Dupotet's *Journal of Magnetism* naturally contains a large number of occurrences of this kind. I note an interesting experiment on sleep induced at a given hour.[40] However, I believe that it is useful to quote a full summary, given by an interesting magnetizer that deserves to be better known, of hallucinatory phenomena on awakening as a result of posthypnotic suggestion. "It is often easy," writes Dr. Alfred Perrier,[41] "to give birth to this kind of neurosis (hallucination) in somnambulists and prolong it even into their waking state. We showed them, at our discretion, people who have been absent or dead for a long time. They talked about their drinks or the taste of the food we had assigned to them, their sense of smell, which included sensations of the most varied scents – all of which really existed only in our imagination. We have at this moment a somnambulist in whom the most perfect insensitivity and the illusion of taste persist for several hours after her return to normal life. Before *waking* her, we introduce some intention, and when she awakens, she experiences all the hallucinations of the senses which we have imposed. *One individual present remains for her perfectly invisible*; she sees another whose voice she does not hear; a third pinches her and she does not feel it. The liquids in her mouth have the flavors we desire; her hearing perceives the most varied sounds. Her perceptions are transfigured into images of our own thoughts … etc." It is difficult to give a more complete summary of all the hallucinations, even of those most recently referred to as negative hallucinations, which can be produced by suggestion. Liébault, in 1860, spoke of suggestions lasting 52 days and studied their execution.[42]

However, at that time there was such a puerile contempt for animal magnetism that all these psychological descriptions were completely forgotten, and it was believed to be a recent discovery when Charles Richet[43] published, in 1875, his observations on some suggestions executed upon awakening. It was difficult to believe that a woman, having forgotten all that was said to her during somnambulism, could nevertheless return after eight days at a given hour without knowing the reason. Yet in 1823 Bertrand already considered this experiment ordinary. It must be admitted that Richet's descriptions were more successful than those of Bertrand. They convinced more people, and since then the study of posthypnotic suggestion has been undertaken by a great number of observers, who have revived, one after another, all the facts noted by the magnetizers of old. We will not repeat the description of this phenomenon which is now well known. The preceding quotations may serve as a general description, and we will emphasize only the details, which will make us better acquainted with the functioning of the mind in these singular operations.

Note first that this persistence of an idea, despite the transition from one state to another, can also occur outside of hypnotism. "Typically," says Moreau (de Tours),[44] "dreams stop with sleep, although they sometimes persist in the waking state … An individual dreams that he can fly; upon waking, he feels the need to try it by jumping a ditch." "Another dreamed of his father who had died and sees his ghost. He continues to see the ghost when half-awake and even a little during his waking state."[45] "The delirium of many lunatics finds its inspiration in dreams while they sleep."[46] Crises of the nerves and ecstatic states show us phenomena of the same kind. Fontaine, one of the convulsionaries of Saint-Médard, announced (during a crisis) that for all the rest of Lent, he would only take one meal and he would take it as bread and water. After his convulsions, he did not remember anything, but he was impelled to fast and to carry out his prescription.[47] Liébault[48] speaks of a patient who dreamed that he had become mute and who, on waking, had really lost his voice. In the same sense, let us quote the ingenious technique of a lover who obtained permission to approach his beloved while she slept and to whisper his name into her ear. This young person afterwards had much tenderness for him, in the form of a kind of recurring dream.[49] Finally, Charcot quotes a hysteric who, after a crisis where he believed he was bitten by animals, examines his arms to look for traces of the bites he thinks he has suffered,[50] and Maudsley speaks of a doctor who thought he had a white horse which he had dreamed of during the delirium of typhoid fever.[51] All these phenomena are obviously identical to those that occur after hypnotic sleep, but they are neither so clear nor as accessible to experimentation.

1.4 Execution of suggestions during a new somnambulistic state

We already know under what circumstances a suggestion of the kind that we are studying now ought to be made: they do not differ in this respect from those which were studied in the previous chapter. The subject must be normally or artificially in an incomplete psychological state where the phenomena in consciousness, limited in number, and not offer sufficient resistance to the ideas suggested to them. But under what circumstances are such suggestions successful? It is here that things are no longer so simple. Indeed, if we awaken the subject, to use the usual expression, we bring them back into a psychological state which differs from the previous one in two points. First, the nature of the predominant images being no longer the same, the memory of somnambulism and the memory of the suggestion itself seem to be completely lost. Then, since the number of simultaneous phenomena is ordinarily considerably more, *the subject is no longer actually suggestible*. One wonders, then, how this suggestion can be present in the mind of the subject and how it can have and other memories do not have at that moment. The answer to these questions is quite difficult, because the mechanism of posthypnotic suggestion is far from being the same in all subjects.

Let us start by setting aside subjects who have no real somnambulism, that is to say, who do not have a second life quite distinct from their first. Some people, like Blanche, whom I have talked about,[52] or a hysteric whom I have often put to sleep, G, keep the same state of sensitivity when they are awake or asleep and therefore retain an almost complete memory of their second state. In addition, the field of their consciousness varies little, being always strongly restricted, and they are as suggestible in one state as they are in the other. There is no real change. Their sleeping or their waking states are but a simulacrum obtained by suggestion. In similar subjects (which are numerous enough), the posthypnotic suggestion is the same as one of those previously studied, ordinary suggestions with a point of reference. If I tell G, while she sleeps, to go around the room when I clap my hands, this idea remains consciously in her mind and is realized at the given signal. If I wake her up before the execution of the suggestion, what does it matter, since for her the memory of somnambulism persists almost completely. (It is true that she remembers suggestions more easily than other words; this is probably because she has attached more importance to them.) Awake, she says to me: "I know what you have just told me, you told me to go around the room." As she is very suggestible when she is awake, she does not know how to resist this idea any more than any other, and, at the given signal, she gets up saying as if to explain her action to herself, "You really do have funny ideas ... it is very boring ... finally, because you insist ... You know, if I did not want to go around the room, I would have stayed in my chair ... it is because I want to." Her ideas are actually a little more numerous and come faster than in her previous state, and also she has some sense of resistance and of freedom. This sense is not absolutely wrong, since she could actually resist this type of suggestion. I told her one day to thumb her nose at me once she is awake. I wake her up, she still remembers the suggestion and says, "You think I am going to thumb my nose at you ... ah! but no ... I am not so silly." And sure enough she does not do it. Besides, we know well that a subject can resist even during somnambulism; there is nothing new here. This only confirms our finding that there are subjects in whom the states of wakefulness and somnambulism are almost identical and execute posthypnotic suggestions in the same way as ordinary suggestions.

We will arrive at a similar conclusion when we consider subjects who, in appearance, are very different. I want to discuss now those who experience true somnambulism, separated from their waking state in all respects, with complete loss of memory upon awakening. We will carefully examine their psychological state after and during the execution of a posthypnotic suggestion. A very important initial fact was discovered by Beaunis: regardless of how they executed the order, once the action was accomplished, they lost their memory of it completely. They do not know what they did, even though they had acted during the waking state. I tell N to go embrace Mrs. X on awakening. She gets up, performs this action quite deliberately, even jokes as if she was completely awake. A moment later, I asked her why she got up and what it was that she had wanted. "Ah! I do not know," she said, "simply to walk a little." "Did you say anything to Madame X?" I ask. "Nothing at all, it has been half an hour since I've spoken to her." This is almost always the case and it has been so often described that I will not spend any more time on it. Let us move on to a second fact, described for the first time, I think, by Gurney, which is at least as important as the previous one. If one questions a subject while performing a posthypnotic suggestion, one will note that they have, at that moment, the memory of all their previous somnambulisms, although ordinarily they have completely lost these memories. "We give him some news during the hypnotic state; when he awakens, he does not remember, but when he carries out a suggestion, he remembers the news he was told during the hypnosis."[53] I have verified this characteristic, especially with Mary, in the clearest way.

A third characteristic, naturally linked to this one, is indicated in an article by Gurney and was verified by us in an interesting manner. If we give a suggestion to a subject when he is in a state in which he is insensitive and if he is woken up in another state where he is normally sensitive, he becomes insensitive at the moment when he executes the suggestion.[54] I have observed a fact which confirms this, although it seems in appearance to be quite the opposite. Rose was normally completely anesthetic, but in a certain somnambulistic state she gained sensitivity to her right side and became hemi-anesthetic (on her left). Upon awakening, she consistently lost that sensitivity and became completely anesthetic again. In this particular somnambulism, I order her to look for an object on a table and to come and show it to me. Then I wake her up completely; a few moments later, she gets up, walks a little about the room, goes to the table, takes the object, and brings it to me. When she passes near me, I pinch her right arm; she cries out and turns around, which she never did when she was in her waking state. The next moment, she had lost the memory of having shown me the object and the sensitivity to her right side. Marie does not present, in her first general somnambulism, large variations in sensitivity; she is a complete anesthetic in her waking state. But here is a detail which I have consistently noted: her right eye (she was then completely blind in her left eye) had, in her waking state, a very weak visual acuity, one-eighth of Wecker's chart. During somnambulism, if you have her open her eyes, the visual acuity of her right eye always increases (by a quarter or a third) without any suggestion. During this somnambulism, I suggested she take a broom and sweep the room when she had awakened. Some time after waking, she took the broom and swept, "because it is dirty," she said. I then placed her, without removing the broom, in the same position as before, five meters from the chart, and had her read it. Her visual acuity was a third. Some time later, the broom being removed, I measured the right eye; the visual acuity was an eighth. In short, she resumed, at the moment of executing the posthypnotic suggestion, the sensory state she had had during somnambulism. We believe that this is how one must interpret the observations of certain authors according to whom a particular anaesthesia characterized the execution of posthypnotic suggestions. This only happens if the state in which the suggestion was made was itself a state of anesthesia. In a word, among the subjects in this category, the state of the sensitivity at the moment a suggestion is executed is the same as when the suggestion was received.

Finally, Gurney points out another fact which we will note as a fourth point. If we take a subject who is not suggestible in the waking state, but who is clearly suggestible during the somnambulistic state, they will resume, at the moment of executing a posthypnotic suggestion, the disposition towards suggestion which they did not have during the normal waking state. "During this execution, we can impose on the subject a new command which would be regarded as a joke if the subject were awake and which is then executed as if it were given during the hypnotic state."[55] I tested this new fact, but I do not find that my observation has much value because the subject on which I performed it was quite strongly suggestible even during the normal waking state. It will be necessary to repeat this experiment, because Gurney's observation remains a very interesting one.

Therefore, in summary, one can in certain cases observe four important psychological characteristics at the time of the execution of a posthypnotic suggestion: (1) forgetfulness of the act after it has been accomplished; (2) memory at the moment that the suggestion is completed of previous somnambulisms; (3) variations of the sensitivo-sensorial state; (4) increase of suggestibility. The connection seems obvious now and these four characteristics are precisely those which distinguish the somnambulic state from the waking state. Certain subjects, when they execute posthypnotic suggestions, return to a somnambulic state identical to the one during which the suggestion was received. This idea has already been expressed by Fontan and Segard[56] and by Delboeuf, who gave it (at least in my opinion) too general an application, for it had not been sufficiently demonstrated. In fact, that author insists upon a variation in the physiognomy of subjects, a wildness in the eyes at the moment when they execute a posthypnotic suggestion. The choice of this characteristic seems to me unfortunate, for somnambulists do not necessarily have wild eyes. As we have said, and as we now are ready to reaffirm, there is no specific physical sign of somnambulism. But the psychological phenomena are very characteristic and show that, in certain cases, subjects are again in a somnambulistic state when they perform the suggestion.

But can we say that this observation, however interesting it may be, resolves completely the problem of posthypnotic suggestion? Obviously not. First, it is essential to note that these things do not happen for all subjects, and it is quite rare to observe all four characteristics that I have emphasized, during the execution of a posthypnotic suggestion. There are subjects who have neither the memory nor the sensitivity of somnambulism when they execute a suggestion; thus they do not fall back into a hypnotic state. Furthermore, even in subjects who conform with the preceding description, these phenomena are far from having been explained. If the suggestion is carried out immediately after the apparent awakening, we can say with enough likelihood that they didn't actually wake up. But if, as is common, the suggestion is executed much later – two days or a hundred days later – there is still an essential fact to explain: why do they return to the sleeping state at that moment?

There is no point in saying (and it would hardly be accurate to say) that any posthypnotic suggestion is equivalent to this: "You will go back to sleep at this time and you will do this particular thing," because the posthypnotic suggestion of sleep is just as difficult to explain as any other. After waking up, the subjects completely forget that they have to go back to sleep and they do not think about this suggestion until the moment when they must execute it. Why does this forgotten memory assert itself at this time? After their sleep, they are no longer suggestible. We can, as noted by Beaunis,[57] make them believe that a suggestion was made while they were in a sleeping state. But if the suggestion was not actually made during somnambulism, this idea is not enough and the suggestion is not carried out. Why does this idea of sleep, in preference to other ideas, have the power to be carried out? This is not explained, even if we admit that every suggestion is carried out during a new somnambulism. To advance in the study of this problem we have to look at other subjects that present, in a clear and regular fashion, another way of carrying out suggestions. The new phenomena that we will see in these subjects already existed in others, but in an unspecified manner, mixed in with other facts. It is better to examine them separately before returning to more complex phenomena.

1.5 Subconscious execution of posthypnotic suggestions

A hysterical woman whom I had the opportunity to study presented in the highest degree, and in an extremely clear way, an important phenomenon that exists in all other subjects in a more or less concealed manner. It is one of those noteworthy cases of which Bacon speaks, which it is necessary to understand before passing on to others. It concerns Lucie, a young woman of nineteen who had grand crises of hystero-epilepsy every day, whom I had put to sleep for the first time in the middle of an attack. After having studied her reactions to typical suggestions during the hypnotic state (which were remarkably successful), I gave her orders to be carried out after waking, and I was struck by the singular way in which she performed them. She had, at that time, the most natural appearance, and spoke and behaved with full awareness of all the acts which she spontaneously performed. But, in the middle of all these natural acts, she carried out, as though *by distraction*, the acts which she had been ordered whilst asleep to do. Not only, like most subjects, did she forget the suggestions after having carried them out, but she did not seem to be aware of them at the very moment when she executed them. I tell her to raise both arms in the air after waking up. Hardly has she returned to her normal state than she raises both arms above her head, but she is not bothered by it. She comes and goes, chats all while holding her two arms in the air. If we ask her what her arms are doing, she wonders at such a question and says very sincerely: "My hands are not doing anything at all, they are just like yours." By this process, I make her thumb her nose, I make her walk across the room, I order her to cry and when she wakes up she really sobs, but she continues in the midst of her tears speaking of very happy things. Once her sobs have ended, there is no trace of this grief, which appears not to have been conscious. I even begged her one day to make every effort to resist me. She did not seem to understand very well, for she did not recall her obedience. She assured me, laughing, that she would certainly not carry out any order that I was going to give. I order something during an instant of sleep and my command is immediately executed upon awakening, but she keeps laughing, saying, "Go ahead and try to order me. I will not do anything at all." In a word, everything related to the posthypnotic suggestion seemed to no longer penetrate her consciousness.

Things were a little different when it was no longer an action, but a hallucination which was prescribed after awakening. The command was also ignored, but the hallucination itself was, or seemed to be, conscious. That is to say that it suddenly invaded Lucie's consciousness without her seeming able to know where it came from. "You are going to drink a glass of cognac," I said to her. Once awake, she said she had not heard anything and wanted to talk about something else. But her arm automatically rises, her hand approaches her lips, Lucie seems to taste something and, when asked, says that she drinks cognac, which she is very happy about because the doctor had forbidden it.[58] Oblivion is also very fast and you have to question her quickly enough to observe the fleeting awareness of the hallucination. Apart from these cases, in which the suggestion was carried out with a certain perception, consciousness appeared to be completely abolished.

Once convinced of this unconsciousness which, no doubt, has already been noted by many observers, but which I had not yet observed to this degree, I tried to figure out how far it extended, that is to say which acts and psychological phenomena could exhibit this characteristic. At the same time, I tried to shed some light on a small psychological problem which had been previously reported about posthypnotic suggestion.

Paul Janet, in the articles he published on hypnotism[59] and by which he made philosophers aware of curious and often neglected phenomena of human thought, raised some doubts about a particular type of suggestion. Richet and Bernheim, like most of the old magnetizers, had cited examples of suggestions that the subject was to carry out upon awakening, not at a given time indicated by a signal, but after a certain number of days: "I told S," said Bernheim, "during a somnambulistic state that he would come back to see me after thirteen days. Awake, he does not remember anything. On the thirteenth day, at ten o'clock, there he was."

Paul Janet writes about this: "I admit that these ignored memories, as Richet calls them, may reappear at a certain time, according to this or that circumstance. I would also understand the return to a fixed moment of these images and those acts which follow on from them, if the operator associates them with the appearance of a vivid sensation. For example "the day you see Mr. so and so, you will embrace him," the sight of Mr. so and so serving as a stimulant to the return of the idea. But what I absolutely do not understand is the return on a fixed day with no connecting point but the progress of time, for example, in thirteen days. Thirteen days is not a sensation; it is an abstraction. To make sense of these facts, we must suppose an unconscious faculty of measuring time. Now, this is an unknown faculty." Richet replied with a few words;[60] but, unless I am mistaken, he did little more than confirm the accuracy of the fact and linked it rather vaguely to others of the same kind. "Intelligence," he said, "can operate outside of the self, and since it operates, it can measure time. This is obviously an easier operation than that of finding a name, making a verse, solving a geometry problem – all things that it can accomplish without the participation of the ego."

Since then, Bernheim has attempted an ingenious explanation. This measuring of time, he says, took place really and consciously. From time to time, the memory of the suggestion came back into consciousness and, from time to time, the subject counted the days gone by, but that thought passed quickly through his mind and he forgot it. "He no longer remembers that he remembered."[61] It is the same when we go to bed with the intention of waking up the next day at a fixed time; from time to time we wake up, check the time, then go back to sleep, and, "when we awaken we do not remember having thought all night long about not missing the time, and we believe that the waking up was spontaneous and unconscious."[62] The assumption is interesting and it had already seduced several philosophers. We found it in Jouffroy's article on sleep[63] and in Charma's work on the same subject: "Intelligent acts, the precautions taken in sleep, occur, in reality, in a waking instant which separates two immediate periods of sleep and which are forgotten afterwards. This is why we wake up to a noise that interests us and not to another, because after another, we go back to sleep without the memory of having done so."[64] This explanation would have the advantage of simplifying things and of substituting a phenomenon of forgetting for a phenomenon of unconsciousness. I believe, however, that it is still insufficient. First of all, this theory would not explain to us why the memory of the suggestion, which appears not to exist, returns from time to time and what impels the subject to take these precautions. Furthermore, the assumption does not seem to me to be in accordance with the facts. If we seriously examine the mind of a subject in all the moments preceding the execution of the suggestion, we will not find a moment when he really remembers it. Here we have, not an oversight, but a true unconsciousness, as Beaunis[65] remarked when discussing the supposition of Bernheim.

To clarify this question a little, I must admit that I would not pose it in the same way as Paul Janet did. "This is a new fact," he said,[66] "of a completely different order from the preceding ones and which, if it were true, would have us enter into the domain of the mysterious and unknown faculties of animal magnetism, second sight, presentiment, etc." I cannot share this feeling. The somnambulist whom we suggest perform an act after thirteen days does not need a particular and mysterious faculty to measure time. He is influenced by the same conditions we all are, he sees day and night, he sees the time on the clocks, and I do not know why he would measure time in a mysterious way, when nothing prevents him from measuring it in the ordinary way. But, it will be said, he has no memory, no consciousness of the suggestion. This does not prevent the days and nights from making an impression on him, and to execute the suggestion at the appointed hour, he has only to *count* them. It is true that this counting has to be done unconsciously, since the subject, in his ordinary consciousness, does not know he has an action to execute in thirteen days. But, in any case, this is only a faculty for unconsciously counting perfectly real things and not a mysterious faculty of measuring time which seems to me useless here. Having said that, I find Paul Janet to be perfectly right on the other hand, in distinguishing this operation from ordinary memory, and this particular kind of suggestion from all the others.

When we make an ordinary suggestion ("As soon as you see Mr. X, you will embrace him"), the somnambulist, once awake, retains nothing in consciousness, or rather he retains a latent association of ideas which he does not need to evoke a psychological phenomenon. We do not all know ourselves the latent associations which are in our minds. The sight of a particular person may perhaps awaken in us a sad or cheerful idea of which we are unaware. The awakened somnambulist has an additional latent association in his mind, the sight of Mr. X will awaken in him the idea of embracing him. There is nothing here that departs from the most normal psychology. But, in the second case, when we said to the subject, "You will perform this act in thirteen days," his mind cannot entirely forget the suggestion upon awakening. It cannot remain latent until the thirteenth day, because this thirteenth day not being in itself different from the others would not evoke in him the suggested idea more than the twelfth or fourteenth day. It would be necessary that, from the time he was woken up and throughout the entire interval. He should be thinking without interruption, "Today is the first day, or the second …" until, when he thinks "this is the thirteenth," the association would be made. Now, it is obvious to everyone that somnambulists who have woken up have no such memory even for an instant, and are not conscious of making these observations and this enumeration. Nevertheless the enumeration must be made. Here we do not have an association, that is to say a pure possibility persisting in a latent state, but a real psychological phenomenon, observations, enumerations – in a word, judgments which persist for thirteen days in the mind of an individual (without his being conscious of it); an unconscious judgment is something quite different from a latent association.

The problem thus reduced to terms which seemed simpler to me, I have attempted above all to verify the reality of the fact in question. The person of whom I had charge presented, like the others, many examples of latent associations. I had made the suggestion that she fall asleep as soon as I raised my arm and I put her to sleep in this way with the greatest of ease. I questioned her one day in the waking state to see if she was aware of the procedure I used for putting her into a somnambulistic state; she was absolutely unaware of it. I spoke to her of the sign, of the raised arm; she believed it was a joke and yet the sight of my raised arm immediately put her to sleep. This is a well-known occurrence which Bernheim had already noted: that if, during the somnambulistic state, the subject was made to understand that the magnet produced the transfer, once awakened he would retain no memory of what had been said to him in this regard. "However, if I repeat the transfer experience made during somnambulism with suggestion, the same phenomena will happen, again to their amazement, proof that the brain had kept in the waking state the unconscious memory of suggestive phenomena induced during the hypnotic state."[67] Thus, there are latent associations in the mind of the subjects, but are there also unconscious judgments that the subject can take note of without being aware of the fact?

On one occasion, when Lucie was in an observable state of somnambulism, I spoke to her using a suggestive tone, "When I have clapped twelve times, you will go back to sleep." Then I talk to her about something else and, five or six minutes later, I wake her up completely. The forgetting of everything that had happened during the hypnotic state and my suggestion in particular was complete. This forgetting, which is the important piece here, was guaranteed, firstly by the previous sleep state which was a real somnambulism with all the characteristic signs. Secondly by the agreement with all those who have dealt with these questions and all who have recorded that similar suggestions were forgotten by the subjects upon waking up. Finally, by the sequence of all the preceding experiments performed upon this subject during which I had always noted this lack of consciousness. Other people surrounded Lucie and spoke to her about different things, I remained a few steps away, I clapped my hands five times fairly weakly and at rather long intervals. Noting then that the subject was not paying attention to me and was engaged, I approached and said to her, "Did you hear what I just did?" "What was it, I was not paying attention." "And that?" (I clap my hands). "You just clapped your hands." "How many times?" "Only once." I withdraw and continue to clap weakly from time to time. Lucie, distracted, no longer listens to me and seems to have completely forgotten me. When I have clapped six more times, bringing it up to a total of twelve, Lucie stops immediately, closes her eyes and falls back asleep. "Why are you sleeping?" I asked. "I do not know, it came on all of a sudden." If I am not mistaken, this is Richet and Bernheim's experiment, but reduced to greater simplicity. The somnambulist must also have had to count, for I made a point of clapping the same way each time and the twelfth hand-clap did not differ from the preceding ones; but, instead of counting days, which has led to the belief that calculating time was involved, she had counted sounds. There was no new faculty involved. All the claps were easy to hear, although she claimed to have heard only one: she must have heard them and counted them, but without knowing it, unconsciously. The experiment was easy to repeat and I did it again with many variations. Lucie counted unconsciously up to 43, and the claps were sometimes regular, sometimes irregular, without her ever making a mistake on the total. One of the most striking experiments was this: I order, "After the third clap your hands will rise, on the fifth they will fall, and on the sixth you will thumb your nose, on the ninth you will walk around the room, on the sixteenth you will fall asleep in an armchair." There was no memory upon waking and all these acts were carried out in the correct order, while, all the time, Lucie responded to questions that are addressed to her, and had no awareness of the sound of my claps, or that she has thumbed her nose or walked around the room.

After repeating the experiment, I had to think about varying it, and I attempted to obtain in this way very simple unconscious judgments. The general form of the experiment remained the same. Suggestions are made during a well-noted hypnotic sleep; then the subject is woken up completely; the signals and the execution take place in the waking state. "When I say two letters which are the same, one after the other, you will remain stiff." After waking up, I whisper the letters "a ... c ... d ... e ... a ... a". Lucie remains motionless and fully contracted, this is an unconscious judgment of resemblance. Here are judgments of difference:

"You will fall asleep when I say an odd number," or else, "You will start to wring your hands when I say a woman's name." The result is the same. As long as I whisper even numbers or men's names, nothing happens. The suggestion is only executed when I give the sign. Lucie therefore unconsciously listened, compared, and appreciated these differences.

Then I attempted to further complicate the experiment in order to see the extent of this unconscious faculty of judgement, "When the sum of the numbers I am about to recite totals 10, you will blow kisses." The same variables are present; she is awake, absence of memory is observed and, far from her, while she is chatting with others (who distract her as much as possible), I whisper "2 ... 3 ... 1 ... 4," and the movement is made. Then I try with more complicated numbers or other operations, "When the numbers I am going to recite, in pairs, subtracted from each other, equal a remainder of six, you will make the following gesture," or multiplications or even very simple divisions. Everything runs almost error free, except when the operation becomes too complicated and could no longer be done in her head. As I have noted already, there was no question of a new faculty, but of ordinary phenomena being executed unconsciously.

It seems to me that these experiments relate quite directly to the problem raised in the *Revue Littéraire* and, in general, to the problem of intelligent execution of suggestions that appears to be forgotten. The reported facts are perfectly correct; somnambulists can count the days and hours that distinguish them in the execution of a suggestion, although they have no recollection of that suggestion itself. Apart from their consciousness, we do not know how there is a memory that persists, an attention always alert, and a faculty of judgment capable of counting the days, since they can perform multiplication and division. But it is nonetheless true that these phenomena are, at first glance, strange and that it is necessary to try to continue their study, in order to better understand the phenomenon of posthypnotic suggestion and perhaps the general nature of conscious life.

In order to make some progress in this study, we had to try to penetrate this unconsciousness, to reveal these psychological operations, which were outside of the normal mind and of which, thus far, we have only observed the results. How was one to make them manifest, by a sign, or through language? Since spoken words were revealing nothing, we tried a different type of sign: writing. "When I clap my hands," I said (always keeping the variables of the experiment consistent), "you will take a pencil and paper from the table and write the word 'Hello.'" At the given sign, the word is written quickly, but legibly. Lucie was not aware of what she was doing; she acted through pure automatism, which showed no great intelligence. "You will multiply in writing 739 by 42," I said. Her right hand wrote the numbers clearly and she completed the operation, without pausing until it was finished. During this time, Lucie, fully awake, told me about her day and did not stop talking as her right hand was (correctly) writing out the calculation. I wanted to give more independence to this singular intelligence. "You will write out a letter of some kind." Here is what she wrote without being aware of it, once awakened: "Madame, I cannot come Sunday, as planned. Please accept my apologies. It would be a pleasure to see you, but unfortunately I am unable to come that day. Your friend, Lucie. P.S.: please give my love to the children." This automatic letter is correctly written and indicates some reflection. As Lucie was writing the letter, she was talking about other things and responded to several people. Moreover, she could make nothing of this letter when I showed it to her and maintained that I had copied her handwriting. Oddly enough, when I wanted to repeat this experiment, Lucie wrote the same letter a second time without changing a word; it was as though a machine had been programmed and could not be altered. The handwriting in these letters is interesting. It is similar to Lucie's normal writing, but not identical. The style slants and the words are written very loosely; the words tend to be elongated. Charles Richet, to whom I showed these fragments of automatic writing, advised me that this characteristic occurs frequently in the writings of mediums (whom we will discuss later) and that in their letters, a word often filled a whole line.

After having Lucie write several automatic letters of this kind, I had the idea of questioning her at the moment when I made the suggestion and of ordering her to answer me through writing. I began my questions during the sleeping state; then I woke her up completely in order to be more certain of the absence of memory and lack of consciousness. At an agreed-upon signal, Lucie took up the pen and wrote the answer without being aware that she did so. I was not slow to realize that there was no need to put her into the sleep state for each question. It was enough to suggest to her, during her initial sleep, that she would answer my questions in writing, so that, when awakened, she always responded in the same automatic way. At this point Lucie, although awake, seemed to no longer consciously see or hear me. She did not look at me and spoke to everyone, but me. If I addressed a question to her, she answered me in writing and without interrupting what she said to others. I had to change my tone entirely and even take her hand to force her to listen to me again in an ordinary fashion. Then she would tremble slightly and seemed a little surprised to see me again. "Oh, I forgot that you were there." But as soon as I walked away a little, she forgot me and started to answer me in writing again.

We cannot study more thoroughly at this point these conversations by means of automatic writing and the intelligence which manifests in them. We can do so only after reporting other phenomena. But before we go any further, we have to slightly modify our previous statements concerning the unconsciousness of these acts executed by posthypnotic suggestions. This expression, applied to the preceding facts, no longer has much meaning. What is an unconscious judgment, an unconscious act of multiplication? If speech is for us a sign of the consciousness of others, why should writing not also be a characteristic sign? These phenomena seem to belong to a particular consciousness below the normal consciousness of the individual. This is probably not an explanation but the observation of a fact, however bizarre it may seem. We will only summarize these observations by calling them subconscious facts, indicating a consciousness below normal consciousness, period. Once we have come to know them better, we will take up the question as to their nature with more precision.

This particular way of executing posthypnotic suggestions in the form of sub-conscious acts has also been encountered in other subjects, although generally in a much less clear-cut manner than in Lucie's case. During somnambulism, I ordered Léonie to take off her apron when she awoke and then to put it back on again. Once fully awake, Léonie led me to the door and asked me what time I would return the following day. As she spoke, her hands gently untied the knot of her apron, and she removed it entirely. With a gesture, I drew Léonie's attention to her apron. "Here!" she said, "My apron fell off," and suddenly, this time consciously, she put it on and tied it up again, and then spoke about something else. Now her hands start their operation over again, untying the cords and completely remov-ing the apron. Since this time Léonie was not looking at her hands after having removed the apron, she took it up and put it back on again, very neatly. The sug-gestion, it seems, had not been fully executed the first time, since Léonie had put the apron back on herself and her hands wanted to start the operation over again. This time, moreover, the act having been completed, nothing more occurred, the subject had not had the least awareness of all these acts.

On another subject, N, I performed some experiments (more complicated than those which had been so striking with Lucie), calculated to come into play at a given moment. N added up the figures without being aware of it and without even hearing them. Besides which, she too presented automatic writing by posthypnotic suggestion. "If I speak to you," I said to her while she slept, "you will answer me in writing." Once fully awake and chatting with several other people, I asked in a low voice, behind her, "How old are you?" Her hand took a pencil and wrote, "Thirty years old." I asked, "Do you have children?" She wrote, "Yes, two boys and a girl." If I interrupted her and asked, "What are you writing?" she replied, astonished, "I am not writing anything." She looked at the paper and said, "Who wrote this?" No need to cite more examples. I was able to reproduce with this subject almost all the experiments that I have reported in the previous study with Lucie.

However, these subjects do not resemble one another in every respect. N is similar to the type of subject which we described at the outset of this study of posthypnotic suggestion. She sometimes executes an order with what seems to be complete consciousness, although admittedly with a loss of consecutive memory. Léonie, by contrast, resembles the second type; she has a tendency to fall asleep completely when executing a suggestion, and it is sometimes necessary to wake her up entirely after an act of this kind, as after a somnambulistic session. Only certain acts are executed by these two subjects in the manner in which we have just described.

The study of these phenomena with these new subjects allows us to make another important observation. When there are several different and successive somnambulisms, as with Léonie, the posthypnotic suggestion can be transferred from one somnambulistic state to another (as happens between somnambulism and the waking state) and it maintains the same characteristics. So let us suppose that Léonie is in the final somnambulism that we described, the state of "Léonie 3." I order her to look for a scarf and put it on, then I wake her up, that is to say I bring her from this deep state into another state which is still somnambulism, but in which the memory of "Léonie 3" is completely forgotten. In this state, "Léonie 2" does not remember the order given and speaks of something else, but her hands look for the scarf and puts it around her neck without being aware of doing so. The action happened subconsciously, as if the subject was in a waking state in relation to the second somnambulism. It is the same with Lucie. Although we did not observe it initially, the suggestions made to "Lucie 3" are executed unconsciously during the first somnambulism. We can even say in general that the suggestions always seemed to address this third order group of phenomena, since they were rarely known during the first somnambulism. These remarks on the execution of suggestions are therefore general, they apply not only to the transition from somnambulism to the waking state, but to all changes of state. One suggestion given in a more profound state takes the form of a subconscious act when the subject is brought to a different state and, above all, one which is less profound.

It is, then, to the persistence of a subconscious thought that I would link the action of most posthypnotic suggestions with a therapeutic effect (on which latter fact we do not insist). The formation of a red mark on the skin in the form of a star, whether it takes place after waking up or during somnambulism, as in the preceding cases, equally cannot be explained only by a thought. It is not enough to say that this redness is due to the excitation of a vasomotor nerve, since there is no nerve which extends precisely at this place in the form of a six-pointed star. It is a partial and systematic excitation of several nerves that I cannot explain without the intervention of a thought which coordinates these excitations. During somnambulism, the subject directly expressed this thought and told us, "I keep thinking of your poultices." When she was fully awake (immediately after the suggestion), she seemed not to think any further about it, nor to be conscious of anything. But something must have been thinking about it in her in the indicated manner, albeit without her knowledge. We sometimes see this therapeutic thought manifested through subconscious acts. Rose had, among her various hysterical symptoms, quite prolonged uterine hemorrhages. We could not succeed in stopping them by direct suggestion (by simply ordering her not to have them). She said during a somnambulism that she had already stopped a similar incident by drinking an ergotine potion. So I ordered her, "Every two hours you will drink a spoonful of an ergotine potion." I woke her up and I refrain from talking to her about the suggestion. Every two hours, Rose acted out a curious scene; her right hand clenched as if she were holding a spoon, then brought it to her mouth which opened and a rapid movement of swallowing took place. In vain she was asked what she was doing, but she maintained that she had not moved. The most curious aspect of the experiment is that the hemorrhaging stopped, the subconscious thought having clearly manifested in this case.

We admitted at the start of this study that not all posthypnotic suggestions are executed in the same way among all subjects, as some of them remained in the normal waking state to execute the suggestion while others would return to a genuine somnambulism. On the basis of the new studies we have recently completed regarding subconscious acts, let us return for a moment to our first descriptions and complete them. We will not dwell on the subjects who remain in a normal waking state with recollection of the suggestion and its execution. These, as we have said, were not hypnotized; they were simply suggestible in their normal state. But let us demonstrate that the second group, those who sleep at the moment of the execution of the suggestion, differ little from those who execute suggestions unconsciously and that there is only a slight degree of difference between them.

Léonie executes suggestions subconsciously, we have said, but in order to do so they must not be too complicated. By a complicated suggestion, I do not mean simply one which involves a large number of successive acts. In this case, as we have already noted,[68] each part of the act appears to the mind of the subject successively and gradually, and there is no real complication. Rather, I am talking about delicate acts that require an intellectual effort, like a calculation or a thought. The suggestion is more difficult to execute, one can appreciate, when it has been insufficiently or badly explained, or when it has not been verbally explained, as in the case of mental suggestion, which I have had the opportunity to deal with. In these cases, the subjects are troubled without knowing why; they sense an effort within themselves, an intense labour of which they are unaware. They try in vain to resist. The subconscious effort increases, taking to itself all the strength of thought, and ordinarily the conscious individual faints. The suggestion is then executed in a complete somnambulistic state, which frequently occurs with Léonie. But here again this bout of somnambulism is but secondary. If there had not been preliminary subconscious work, one could not explain why the subject falls asleep without any reason precisely at that moment.

It is therefore only in appearance that posthypnotic suggestions present different characteristics. In reality, these phenomena always contain a common element. The idea that was suggested during somnambulism does not go away after waking up, although the subject seems to have forgotten it and retains absolutely no consciousness of it. It subsists and develops outside and below normal consciousness. Sometimes it comes to its complete realization and brings about the execution of the act suggested without ever having entered this consciousness. Sometimes at the end of its development, during the execution, it enters into thought for a moment, modifies it, and brings back the initial somnambulistic state (more or less completely). The essential thing is the existence of subconscious thinking which the posthypnotic suggestions (more than any other phenomena) come to reveal to us, since they cannot be understood without it.

1.6 Conclusion

By examining partial catalepsies and suggestions affected by distraction, we were led to think that they must depend, as do ordinary suggested acts, upon an image and a perception which develop automatically. But as this image or this perception seemed completely absent from the subject's mind, we were forced to assume that it existed outside of consciousness. The study of posthypnotic suggestions seems very appropriate in confirming this supposition. If one does not admit to a thought which retains the memory of the somnambulism, in spite of awakening and which persists below normal thought, these suggestions cannot be explained. But until this point we have only seen this second consciousness manifest itself through acts. Now, the study of acts is appropriate in revealing a consciousness, but not in explaining it. To understand this new thought, it is necessary to study the sensations or the images which it contains and add to the study of subconscious feelings, subconscious acts.

Notes

1 This chapter and that following contain a number of studies that we have already published in the *Revue Philosophique* under these titles: *Les Acts Inconscients et le Dédoublement de la Personnalité*, 1886, II, 577. *L'Anesthésie Systématisée et la Dissociation des Phénomènes Psychologique, ibid.*, 1887, I, 449. *Les Actes Inconscients et la Mémoire pendant le Somnambulisme, ibid.*, 1888, I, 238. We are revisiting these studies to complete them and relate them to more general theories.

2 Leibniz, *Edition Dutens*, II, 1715, 214.

3 Leibniz, *Principes de la Nature et de la Grâce*, 1714, § 4.

4 Renouvier, *Critique Philosophique*, 1872, I, 21.

5 Cf. Volume 1, *Catalepsy, Memory, and Suggestion in Psychological Automatism.*

6 de Biran, *Œuvres Inédites*, II, 1859, 12.

7 Dumont, *Théorie Scientifique de la Sensibilité*, 1875, 102.

8 Colsenet, *La Vie Inconsciente de l'Esprit*, 1880.

9 Carré de Montgeron, cited by Bérillon, *De la Dualité Cérébrale*, 1884, 103.

10 Chevreul, *Lettre à M. Ampère sur une Class Particulière de Mouvements Musculaires, Revue des Deux-Mondes*, 1833. *De la Baguette Divinatoire, du Pendule dit Explorateur et des Tables Tournants, au Point de Vue de l'Histoire, de la Critique et de la Méthode Expérimentale*, 1854.

11 Richet, *Revue Philosophique*, 1884, II, 653, and *Des Mouvements Inconscients*, in Homage to Chevreul, 1886.

12 Gley, Société de Biologie, Juillet 1884.

13 See Bastian, *Le Cerveau*, II, 1888, 127. – Ribot, *Les Maladies de la Personnalité*, 1885, 114.

14 Cullerre, *Magnétisme et hypnotisme*, 1887, 286, 296.

15 Lasègue, *Études Médicales*, 1884, II, 35.

16 Saint-Bourdin, *Traité de la Catalepsie*, 1841, 29 and 59.

17 Liébault, *Du Sommeil et des États Analogues*, 1860, 72.

18 Binet and Féré, *Archives de Physiologie*, 1st October 1887.

19 *Ibid.*, 351.

20 Despine, *Etude Scientifique sur le Somnambulisme*, 1880, 193. – Cf. Barety, *Magnétisme Animal*, 1886, 390. – Hack Tuke, *L'Esprit et le Corps*, 1886, 41, who both note a phenomenon similar to unconscious imitation.

21 Binet and Féré, *Op. cit.*, 353.

22 *Ibid.*, 342.

23 *Ibid.*, 342, 326.

24 *Ibid.*, 342.

25 *Ibid.*, 343.

26 Cf. Volume 1, Chapter 3.

27 Dumont, *Op. cit.*, 102.
28 Binet and Féré, *Op. cit.*, 333.
29 Charpignon had already noted an analogous fact when he said that if somnambulists refuse to carry out an act consciously, one may get them to execute it automatically, without their knowing it. *Physiologie, Médecine et Métaphysique du Magnétisme*, 1851, 379.
30 Richet, *Revue Philosophique*, 1886, II, 326.
31 Taine, *De l'Intelligence*, Preface, 1870, I, 16.
32 Deleuze, *Instruction Pratique*, 1825, 118.
33 Deleuze, *Histoire Critique du Magnétisme Animal*, 1813, I, 125, *Instruction Pratique sur le Magnétisme Animal*, 1825, 65.
34 Bertrand, *Traité du Somnambulisme*, 1823, 199.
35 Teste, *Magnétisme Expliqué*, 1845, 341.
36 *Ibid.*, 435.
37 Gauthier, *Histoire du Somnambulisme Chez tous les Peuples*, 1842, II, 361.
38 Charpignon, *Physiologie, Médecine et Métaphysique du Magnétism*, 1841, 82.
39 *Ibid.*, 94, 362.
40 Dupotet, *Journal du Magnétisme*, 1855, 181.
41 Perrier, *Recherches Médico-Magnétiques. – Journal du Magnétisme*, 1854, 76.
42 Liébault, *Du Sommeil et les États Analogues*, 1860, 153.
43 Richet, *L'Homme et l'Intelligence*, 1884, 251.
44 Moreau (de Tours), *Du Hachisch et de L'aliénation Mentale*, 1845, 252.
45 *Ibid.*, 230.
46 *Ibid.*, 261.
47 Gasparin, *Tables Tournantes*, II, 1854, 62. – Regnard. *De la Sorcellerie*, 1874, 178.
48 Liébault, *Revue Hypnotique*, I, 145, and *Du Sommeil et les Etats Analogues*, 1860, 157.
49 Liébault, *Proceed.*, S. P. R., 1882, 287.
50 Charcot, *Maladies du Syst. Nerv.*, III, 1877, 262.
51 Maudsley, *Pathologie de l'Esprit*, 1883, 219.
52 In Volume 1, Chapter 3.
53 Gurney, *Problems of Hypnotism. Proceed.*, S. P. R., 1884, 273.
54 *Ibid.*, II, 265.
55 Gurney, Peculiarities of certain post-hypnotic states. Proceed., S.P.R., 4, 1887, 271, 273.
56 Fontan and Segard, *Eléments de Médicine Suggestive*, 1887, 158.
57 Beaunis, *Le Somnambulisme Provoqué*, 1886, 208.
58 This is a complex phenomenon analogous to those which we have reported above.
59 Paul Janet, *Revue Littéraire*, 26 July, 2, 9, 16 August 1884.
60 Richet, *Revue Littéraire*, 23 August 1884.
61 Bernheim, *De la Suggestion*, 1884, 174.
62 *Ibid.*, 172.
63 Jouffroy, *Mélanges Philosophiques*, 1875, 233.
64 Charm, *Du Sommeil*, 1852, 26.
65 Beaunis, *Op. cit.*, 243.
66 Paul Janet, Response to Richet, *Revue Litteraire*, August 23, 1884.
67 Bernheim, *Revue Philosophique*, 1885, I, 312. – Cf. *De la Suggestion*, 161.
68 De Rochas, *Les Forces Non Définies*, 1887, 215.

Chapter 2

Anesthesias and simultaneous psychological existences

We come now to a study which is very important and, let us point out, very difficult. All the problems we have studied have brought us back, one after the other, and as though by necessity, to the same point. Upon what does somnambulism, and the forgetfulness that characterizes it, depend? On the disappearance, upon awakening, of a certain dominant sensitivity during the second state, that is to say on anesthesia. How do we explain obedience to suggestions without voluntary consent? By a contraction of the field of consciousness which manifests in part through a complete and lasting anesthesia and in part by a transitory and systemized anesthesia. What are the conditions for partial catalepsy and distraction by suggestion? A complete and lasting anesthesia of a limb for the first, and a distraction, that is to say, a temporary and systematized anesthesia for the second. Finally, what is the most important characteristic of the execution of posthypnotic suggestions? That the subject thinks about the suggestions without realizing it and performs them without awareness; that is, that subjects are, for their part, truly anesthetic. Everything brings us back to the psychological study of this singular anesthesia that we have so often reported and which consists, not in the lesion of a sense organ, but in the abolition of a true mental faculty, of all its powers and of all the memories which it had acquired. The study of this problem is all the more delicate since, if I do not deceive myself, it has scarcely been approached from this point of view up till now. There are numerous and excellent studies on hysterical anesthesia considered from the physical point of view, in its localization and in its supposed lesions. But we find few authors who consider this phenomenon from a psychological point of view, who seek the mental ramifications which it can have and the intellectual problems upon which it depends. The importance of the problem in our studies on automatism forces us, however, to engage with it. The observations and experiments which we report, and which may be of some interest, will serve to justify the attempts at explanation that follow from them.

2.1 Systematized anesthesias: historical overview

Anesthesia presents itself to us in two forms. Sometimes it is general and deprives the subject of the totality of sensations ordinarily furnished by a sense. Sometimes

DOI: 10.4324/9781003198727-2

it is *systematic and removes only a certain number, a certain system of sensations or images, whilst allowing the knowledge of all the other phenomena provided by this same sense to reach consciousness.* It is this latter form that we will examine first, because it is easy to artificially reproduce and study it, thanks to a very curious experiment that has been familiar for a long time under the name of *suggestion of negative hallucination* or *suggestion of systematized anesthesia.* Indeed, thanks to suggestion, one can forbid something to somnambulists, just as easily as a positive order can make something happen. When sensations are forbidden, an artificial deafness or blindness can be produced, just as a positive command can produce a hallucination. This prohibition is especially interesting, since it does not take away from the subject the vision of every object, but only a certain object, which remains invisible, while every other object is clearly distinguishable.

Facts like these have been reported for a very long time. "We often take advantage of the period of somnambulism," said Deleuze in 1825, "by making patients take a remedy for which they had a strong aversion. I saw a woman who had horror of leeches allow them to be applied to her feet while in a somnambulistic state and say to her magnetizer, 'Now forbid me to look at my feet, when I am awake.' Indeed, she never suspected that leeches had been applied at all."[1] Bertrand, in the same period, wrote, "I have seen someone who magnetizes somnambulists tell them when they were asleep: 'When you wake up, I want you not to see any of the people in the room, but to see this or that person,' whom he designated and who often was not present. The patient opened her eyes and, without appearing to see any of the people surrounding her, spoke to those she thought she saw."[2] Here is a curious story shared by Teste, "Mrs. G is asleep, M makes two or three large longitudinal passes over some people present. Mrs. G is awakened and only sees herself and myself. All the rest of the room, in which she seemed persuaded that she was alone except for the two of us, seemed to her filled, she said, with a whitish cloud: 'It is amazing,' she said, 'I hear voices speaking to me ... but where are these gentlemen, and Mrs. X, what has become of her? There is no mistake that I hear them, tell them to show themselves, please, I am scared.'"[3] What is most singular is the way Teste explains the phenomenon: "It is the magnetic fluid, an inert vapor, opaque and whitish, hanging like a fog where the hand deposits it, hiding objects from the somnambulist." I must cite a whole passage from Charpignon,[4] where, despite the falsity of these kinds of theories, one finds a quite precise psychological description: "The ability to make the memory of what has taken place during the somnambulistic state pass into the ordinary state extends to modifications which are applied to the functions of the senses. So, having presented to some somnambulists three oranges, only one of which had been magnetized and surrounded by a thick layer of fluid with the intention that it remained invisible, this orange actually was invisible when the somnambulists were restored to their normal state. In vain we told them that the tray was carrying three oranges, they laughed at us and showed us the two oranges which they picked up. Finally, groping around with their hands, they find an object which they pick up; the spell is broken, and the three oranges become visible. (This last detail forms an interesting observation which we have occasionally verified.) I asked another somnambulist if she could see the little table which was in the middle of our living room, and she answered yes. I then proceeded to surround the feet of the table in fluid and she was astonished to see a tabletop suspended in the air. Upon awakening, her astonishment cannot be described. This lady presses this aerial table on all sides, she finds it solid and leaves feeling very worried. We have varied these experiments in a thousand different ways, and believe them to be not well known. They have always been successful, when we were dealing with a very lucid somnambulist." However, one need not attribute to all the magnetizers of old this somewhat puerile explanation. Bertrand, as we know, supported a theory quite analogous to that of Braid. In 1843, Braid said: "The suggested impression has so taken hold of the patient's mind that one can, under its influence, suspend the functions of sight, render him blind to an object placed in front of him, or induce the thought that the object has been transformed into another."[5] This theory of the phenomenon is also found with few modifications in the work of Philips[6] and in that of Liébault.[7]

Bernheim, who takes up again the study of the same phenomenon, distinguishes with precision ordinary or positive hallucination from this suppression of sensation, which he calls *negative hallucination*. "I suggested to a lady from my household, G, that when she woke up, she would no longer see me, would no longer hear me – that I would no longer be there. Awake, she looked for me, I shouted in her ear that I was there, but with no success. I pinched her hand and she recoiled abruptly without discovering where the pinch had come from ... This negative hallucination, which I had already produced with her in other sessions, but which only lasted five to ten minutes, persisted in this instance for the twenty minutes that I stayed with her."[8] Bernheim cites other facts, but with little variation to the experiment. We criticized Bernheim for the name he chose to designate this phenomenon. This is not a hallucination, we said, but the suppression of the perception of a specified object while leaving intact the perception of other objects. It is a phenomenon analogous to systemized paralysis of movement, loss of particular movements with the conservation of movements of another kind. It is a *systematized anesthesia*.[9] No doubt, the phenomenon in question resembles anesthesia more than hallucination, and it is, as we shall see, of the same nature as the paralyses. The two words *negative hallucination* thus form a fairly inaccurate association; short of calling general anesthesia a total negative hallucination (which is not the normal usage) it seems more natural to designate this phenomenon by the expression *systematized anesthesia*, which was adopted by Binet and Féré. However, Bernheim is right not to consider this phenomenon a genuine anesthesia, a genuine suppression of sensation. He says, "I did not produce a paralysis of the eye, the subject sees all objects except that which was suggested to be invisible to her. I erased in her brain the sensory image; I neutralized or rendered negative the perception of this image. I call that a negative hallucination.[10] The phenomena which we have studied confirm this opinion of Bernheim, and, if we adopt this new word, it is because it seems to us more accurate to designate by an analogous term the general anesthesias of hysterics and these partial anesthesias which are, as we will show, of the same type.

The most recent authors who have made a special study of this phenomenon are, I believe, Paul Richer[11] and Binet and Féré. The latter indicate that they have made several very precise experiments on the subject.

(1) If it is suggested to a somnambulist that a person, Mr. X, had disappeared, the somnambulist can no longer see him anywhere in the room where he is standing. However, if we add an object to Mr. X, a hat for example, since it was not included in the suggestion, it remains visible and seems to float in the air. On the other hand, if Mr. X takes a handkerchief from his pocket, this handkerchief remains as invisible as he. I have had the opportunity to observe, as the authors themselves point out, that these two phenomena and others of the same kind are quite variable. For one somnambulist, any object added to Mr. X also becomes invisible, to another the object is still visible. I once observed a person who saw half of the object, as if cut in two, when it was held both by the invisible person and by a visible person.

(2) The person or the object which has been made invisible actually hides or covers the objects which it blocks from view, but the somnambulist supplements the vision of these objects by a hallucination which replaces them. This is what we do every day for objects which are situated in the blind spot of the retina. This hallucination can go very far; I once saw a subject, to whom I had suggested that he could not see the room, replace it with the hallucination of another apartment, which I had not mentioned.

(3) The invisible object must actually be perceived, because it sometimes produces a consecutive image of a complementary colour which itself is visible. We make a red paper disappear; the somnambulist does not see it, but, after a while, will see a greenish colour in its place. I have not observed this phenomenon in a clear enough manner, but the physical and mental conditions upon which somnambulism depends are so complex that one should never be surprised if one does not encounter exactly the same phenomena as other observers.

(4) "Among ten cards of a similar appearance, we designate one for the somnambulistic patient which alone will be invisible. When she awakens, we successively present to her the ten cards, only one is invisible: the card which singled out to her during somnambulism. If the patient is wrong sometimes, it is because she loses her point of reference and the cards are too similar. Similarly if we only show her a small corner of the cards she will see them whole."[12] This experiment is, in my opinion, essential and it shows us the true position of the question. It is no longer a matter, in fact, of either a complete or partial paralysis of the retina: "the subject must recognize this object so as not to see it … Recognition of the card which requires a very delicate and very complex operation, ends nevertheless in a phenomenon of anesthesia. It is therefore

probable that this act takes place entirely in the unconscious ... There is always an unconscious reasoning which precedes, prepares and guides the phenomenon of anesthesia." Not only is this likely; it is necessary. Awake, the somnambulist no longer remembers what we ordered her to do; she does not know that there is an object that she must not see, nor what the object is. When we show her the card, however, this memory must be evoked again, and she must recognize this card by certain signs, although she is not aware of that fact. It seems to me that there is some analogy between this question and one of the problems we studied in the previous chapter. How does a somnambulist whom we ordered to return in eight days count those eight days when she has no recollection of the suggestion? How does she recognize a sign which she does not remember and which she even seems not to see? These two problems are identical, and if the observation of the subject of which we spoke, Lucie, allowed me to bring some light to bear upon the first point, perhaps it will allow me to somewhat clarify the second one.

2.2 Persistence of sensation despite systematized anesthesia

The authors of the previous experiments say that their experiences make "probable" the existence of an unconscious recognition of the sign. Let us first of all replicate them with precision. During full hypnotic sleep, I put five white paper cards on the lap of a somnambulist, two of which are marked with a small cross. "When you are awake," I say, "you will no longer see the cards marked with a cross." I wake her up as completely as possible ten minutes later, and she has no memory, either of my order or of what she did during the somnambulism. As she is surprised to see cards on her lap, I ask her to count them and give them to me one by one. Lucie takes the three unmarked cards, one by one, and gives them to me. I persist and ask for the others. She claims that she cannot give them to me, because there are no cards left. Her expression does not seem altered and she seems fully awake. She can speak freely and recall all that she had done, even her replying that there were only three cards on her lap. I take all the cards and spread them on her lap, upside down, so as to conceal the crosses. She counts five and gives them all to me. I replace them leaving the crosses visible; she only takes the three unmarked cards and leaves the other two. That is the experiment of Binet and Féré, and it seems natural to conclude from it, as they did, that the crosses are seen and recognized in some manner. We can make this assumption even more convincing by making the experiment more complicated. I put the subject back to sleep and put twenty small numbered cards on her lap. "You will not see," I say, "the cards which bear numbers with a multiple of three." Lucie, upon awakening, experiences the same lack of memory and astonishment in seeing the cards on her lap. I ask her to give them to me one by one; she gives me fourteen and leaves six, which she was careful not to touch (the six remaining cards are marked with multiples of three). No matter how much I insist, she does not see the others. Was it not necessary here that she remember that it was a question of multiples of three and that she should see the numbers in order to recognize them? We can finish with this pleasantry: suggest to a subject that she will be unable to see the card on which is written the word "Invisible," and in fact it is this card that she will not see.

The seemingly invisible object is therefore seen. This is probable. We know (and we are not alone in noting this) that the subject is sincere when she says that she does not see it. The vision of these objects must be of the same kind, of the same level as the subconscious acts which we were describing earlier. Let us demonstrate this: I say to Lucie during somnambulism (I will not repeat the arrangement of the experiment, which is always the same) that Dr. Powilewicz, then present, has just left the room. When she awakens, she no longer sees him and asks why he has left; I tell her not to be concerned. Then moving behind her as she chatted (as indicated, with suggestions by distraction), I say to her in a low voice: "Get up and go give the doctor your hand." She gets up, walks over to the doctor, and takes his hand; however, her eyes continue to search for him. She is asked what she is doing and to whom she has given her hand, and she replies laughing – "You can clearly see, I'm sitting on my chair and I am not giving my hand to anyone." As she thought she was seated and motionless, she probably did not feel any reason to move and remained standing with her hand outstretched. It was necessary to order her in the same way to return to her seat. Naturally, Lucie had no memory of having risen and offered her hand, but she remembered everything else, especially the disappearance of the doctor. A subconscious act had taken place; but we note that the subconscious vision of the doctor had remained attached to this act, despite his apparent disappearance for Lucie.

The same experiment can be performed in a different way. Now it is the person who is not visible who gives commands and tells her to get up, to thumb her nose, etc. Everything runs perfectly, although Lucie still claims not to see or hear this person. I also made this observation with another subject, Marie. People whom she did not know well, who were unable to make any suggestion to her when seen and heard normally, take on a power analogous to that of the magnetizer when they had thus disappeared. Therefore, they had power over a group of subconscious phenomena less resistant than the group of conscious phenomena. It is to phenomena of this kind that we must relate the observation of Beaunis, that people who have thus disappeared can put the subject to sleep by means of magnetic passes.[13] This is quite natural, since they are still connected to these subconscious phenomena of which somnambulism is, as we will see, the greatest development. Besides, by an order addressed directly and forcefully to the subject, we can make them recall all of those orders which they were supposed not to have heard. In general, one can, by suggestion, restore the memories of all the sensations that seem to have been suppressed by systematized anesthesia. But we will shortly meet again, in the context of general anesthesia, this question of the memory of subconscious phenomena.

According to these observations, which are now sufficient, it is therefore most likely first of all that the suppressed sensation still exists, and then that it is related in some way to the subconscious acts. The use of automatic writing, which we have already mentioned, will provide a definitive verification. Let us return to our earlier experiments. Lucie sees neither the cards marked with a cross, nor cards with numbers that are marked with multiples of three, and has not given them to me. At this moment, I move away from her, and, taking advantage of a moment of distraction, I order her to take a pencil and write down what is on her lap. The right hand writes, "There are two cards marked with a small cross." I ask, "Why did Lucie not give them to me?" "She cannot; she cannot see them." Or else she writes, "On my lap there are six small cards." I ask, "And what is on these cards?" "Numbers 6, 15, 12, 3, 9, 18. I can see them clearly." The same experiment was repeated with multiples of two, then multiples of five. I then put cards in front of her marked with a letter and I made the vowels or consonants disappear. Following this, I used cards marked with several lines and made those which had three lines disappear. Finally, showing her coloured cards while she was sleeping, I ordered her not to see the colour red. The results of these experiments were exactly the same as those of the previous ones. Lucie did not see the suppressed objects at all, but the group of subconscious phenomena (which we do not yet know how to designate otherwise) replied by automatic writing that the objects were seen clearly.

It remained to be seen whether more extensive anesthesias would present the same characteristics. During sleep, I suggest that upon waking she will be completely blind, and upon waking, she is completely blind. Fortunately this does not frighten her too much, because she assumes (as an explanation) that the lamp has gone out and that we are all in the dark. A strong light projected directly into her eyes does not even cause her to avert her gaze. Ordinarily, under such circumstances, she hides her eyes in terror and even falls into catalepsy. This is similar to an experiment of Binet and Féré, who, by suggestion, made a gong disappear, the noise of which was no longer heard by the patient and no longer caused catalepsy. Despite Lucie's apparent blindness, I question (using the typical method) the unconscious, which claims to see very clearly and designates in writing all the objects that were shown.

I am not talking about other experiments of systematized anesthesia affecting the sense of hearing or the sense of smell (by removing an odor or the sound of the voice of a person who is no longer heard consciously but who can still command unconscious acts). These experiments always yield the same results. It seems to me more interesting to focus for a moment on the same observations applied to the sense of touch. Systematic anesthesia of touch can be observed in one of two ways: either we say to the subjects that they will not feel the contact of a particular object among a group of others, and the experiment unfolds as before, or we indicate a part of the subject's body (which usually has feeling) and declare that this part no longer feels anything, while the rest of the body remains sensitive. This is the experiment that Charpignon[14] was conducting when he boasted that he could, at will, make a hand or an arm insensitive. I remember my amazement when Gilbert showed me that one could draw a circle on Léonie's right arm and make this area insensitive, while the rest of the arm remained normal. Here one may be more ready to believe it is a real anesthesia. Anesthesia in this case could not be said to be systematic; it could be considered partial – a nerve no longer feels anything, just like an eye or part of the retina may not feel anything. I do not think that this is the case however. The anesthetic circle or star that we trace on the arm does not exactly correspond to the area of superficial distribution of a cutaneous nerve. It is not a single nerve which has been anesthetized, it is a segment of one, as well as a segment of many others.

This intelligent distribution of anesthesia in the manner of drawing a circle or a star can only be made with a conscious idea. In order to answer me correctly, when I prick her arm and question her, the subject must know, even without looking, when the pinprick enters the circle. Consequently, she must feel it. We are therefore not surprised that the unconscious responds to us, by automatic writing, that it is very much aware of what we do and that it can discern a pinprick, a touch, a hot or cold object, even within this anesthetized area.

Having thus determined the existence of a new kind of consciousness during systematic anesthesia, I wanted to examine the extent of this consciousness, that is to say the number of phenomena that it could contain. Let us return to the first experiment. It is not dramatic and has the disadvantage of entertaining neither the public nor the somnambulists, but it is very specific. While sleeping, I again put five cards on her lap and repeat the same command, "You will not see the cards marked with a cross." When she wakes up, I do not question Lucie, as I had previously, and I do not order her to give me the cards she sees. It is the group of subconscious phenomena which I now question first, and it is by subconscious acts that I am receiving the cards that were placed on her lap. Her eyes drop for a moment and the hand passes me two cards, both marked with a cross. I insist further; the hand does not move; finally the hand writes, "There are no more." I appeal then to Lucie, "Give me the cards that are on your lap." She looks and gives me, without hesitation, the three remaining cards. So all the cards were seen and handed over, but some by Lucie and others by a personage below which she seems to be unaware of. However, neither has seen all of the cards.

If the previous remark is true (and I admit that the experiments were, on this point, neither as numerous nor as precise as on the previous one), this must follow: any phenomenon artificially added to the second group will be removed from Lucie's normal consciousness (made up of the first group), so we must ascribe a systematized anesthesia to Lucie, which produces, in the subconscious group, a positive phenomenon. Let us try this (whether during sleep or waking is of little consequence): I address the subconscious personage by the process of suggestion during distraction. "You will see," I said, "the cards marked with a cross, the multiples of three, etc." The result is exactly the same as before. Lucie, questioned first, no longer sees these same cards. I have noted that the secondary personage did not make use of the eyes to write and in general did not see.

I suggested that the eyes be used in order to see clearly. This is what took place: immediately Lucie exclaims, "What is going on, I cannot see anymore." I have to put her back to sleep to ease her trouble. Note that, when studying post-hypnotic suggestions, we have already seen facts similar to this. Subconscious acts thus obtained have a general, obvious, and even necessary character: they are accompanied, if not constituted, by a systematized anesthesia of the type which we now study. I tell Léonie to snub her nose at me; upon waking she lifts up her hand and puts it on her nose without being aware of it. It is an unconscious act: she does not see her hand which is in front of her eyes. I tell N to raise her right arm; once awake she raises it, but she does not feel her arm in the air. However, she does not ordinarily have a loss of muscular sense in this arm. I clap as I count behind them, and they don't hear; however, they are not deaf. Here is an even clearer example: I had suggested one evening to Lucie, during somnambulism, to come the next day to Dr. Powilewicz's office at two o'clock. When she arrived the next day, I could not convince her of where she was; she maintained that she was still at home. This, without doubt, is an unconscious act by posthypnotic suggestion, but it is also a beautiful example of systematized anesthesia. Lucie had seen neither the road, nor the house, nor the office where she found herself. She made up for this absence with a hallucination. We know that that is the rule, but the principle fact remained as a visual anesthesia. I had just suggested an act to the subconscious personage and therefore knowledge of the road, house, and office at the same time. Without knowing it, I had removed this knowledge from Lucie under this law of mental disaggregation which increasingly seems to characterize subconscious phenomena.

All these experiments, which have been conducted on all the senses, either by directly evoking anesthesia by suggestion, or by evoking it indirectly by ordering a posthypnotic action, lead us to this conclusion: *with the suggestion of systematized anesthesia, sensation is not suppressed and cannot be suppressed: it is simply displaced. It is removed from normal consciousness, but can be found as part of another group of phenomena, of some other type of consciousness.*

2.3 Systematized electivity or esthesia

One will no doubt be surprised to see me examine the following phenomenon, which is the subject of this section, because we are not accustomed to comparing somnambulists' *electivity* to their systematized anesthesia. However, these two phenomena seem to me related or, to put it better, they are (in my opinion) one and the same thing, considered from two different points of view.

Somnambulists are always or almost always elective; such is the observation that has been made consistently since the time of Mesmer and Puységur. By that we mean that, *in this particular state of somnambulism, the subjects do not feel all sensations indifferently, but they seem to choose from among the different impressions that fall on their senses, and perceive some and not others.* Most subjects, once asleep, can hear their magnetizer and chat with him, but seem to hear no other person, no other noise, not even that of a pistol being fired near them, as in Dupotet's experiments. "The very sounds of a piano are only heard if the magnetizer touches it."[15] "Sounds are only heard if they are magnetized. The magnetizer must touch the air or the piano keys for the somnambulist to hear the notes that will be played."[16] "A bouquet only has a scent if it has received the breath of magnetizer."[17] "A subject does not feel the pins sunk into his skin, although he ordinarily has a very fine tactile sense."[18] "A subject will feel the pencil that has been touched by the magnetizer, but will not feel it if it has been touched by another."[19]

This link with certain people or certain objects, which allows subjects to sense some to the exclusion of others, has received the name of *magnetic rapport*. We put a person in rapport with subjects when you force the subject to see or hear them. This outcome of the magnetic relationship is very interesting and very easy to observe. It exists to a greater or lesser degree in most of the subjects I have studied. Léonie in the first somnambulism hardly presents this characteristic at all: she hears and sees everything. She presents this feature much more strongly in second somnambulism, because then she hears only me, and only when I touch her. She has greater electivity in all states when it comes to suggestion, because she always obeys only me. Marie and Rose are generally more elective than Léonie. From the instant they fall asleep, they seem to lose the notion of the outside world. They seem to see, hear, or smell only the one who put them to sleep. Marie retains for other people only a slight sensitivity of touch, if you can call it that, because she experiences a very marked sense of suffering and repugnance when she is touched by an unknown person who is not in rapport with her. Rose never feels anything like it. I am not mentioning Lucie, who has very little electivity and distinguishes me from other people only when it is a matter of obeying me.

This isolation manifests itself in different ways. One of the most curious and the best known is this: if I raise their arm in the air and place it in a particular position, it remains motionless, and I can move their arm easily just by touching it. But if another wants to move the arm, it suddenly becomes stiff and violently resists the movement that one wants to impose on it. If you force a change in position, the arm returns as if by elasticity, as soon as it is let go, to the position where I had originally placed it.

We know that this electivity can be different in the different parts of the subject's body. The right side can obey one experimenter, while the left side obeys another. Neither can cross the centerline of the body and enter the territory reserved for the other. I have not often repeated this experiment, which (at least from what I observe) tires the subjects enormously.

This electivity can be modified using different methods, which allows one observer to be substituted for another, according to the somnambulist's preferences. To achieve this result, some use touching of the top of the head, others use passes, while some succeed simply by speaking. This substitution between magnetizers is sometimes easy, sometimes difficult. Among the subjects that I have observed, the magnetizer who most often puts them to sleep is the one who most easily captures and maintains this influence. When I am frequently putting a subject to sleep, no other observer can take my place, and I can easily regain my influence, even if someone else began the somnambulism. When a subject has been put to sleep often by different people, these substitutions are easy. However, generally speaking in these cases, electivity does not take long to disappear.

The ease with which one can make somnambulists hear another person with whom one wants to put them into rapport, without losing control of them, varies. With Rose, this is very difficult. You have to firmly order the somnambulist to hear Mr. such and such, and, even then, a rapport established in this manner does not last long. With Marie, on the contrary, it is very simple; all that is required is an introduction. She resembles a reserved young person who is waiting to chat with strangers once they have been presented to her. You only have to say to her, "Marie, here is a gentleman who comes to say hello to you," and she receives him and continues to hear him for the rest of the session. Curiously, this simple introduction is sufficient for her to no longer fear this interaction. With Léonie, in the second somnambulism, you must take her hand on one side and the hand of the unknown person on the other. Léonie then claims to hear a distant voice which passes through my body; "It is like a telephone," she says.

In some more complex cases, this relationship can be established by means of the *magnetic chain*, as has been described by the operators of old. I myself formerly wrote of an example of this kind.[20] Several people hold hands, and the magnetizer, hidden and unbeknownst to the subject, touches or does not touch the last person. In this case, these people then are or are not in rapport with the subject. The difficulty here is to understand in what manner the subject learns that the magnetizer touches or does not touch the people in the chain. As to the phenomenon of the rapport itself, it is identical to the previous examples.

I do not pretend to explain all of these details, the study of which does not belong entirely within our discussion. These details contain hallucinations, memories, habits, perhaps even (I take care not to deny it) very particular physical phenomena thus far poorly understood. Let us remember the principal fact, which is that the subjects do not hear, see, or even feel when touched, except for a small number of people who, depending on the circumstances, may change; they seem to be deaf, blind, and insensitive to all others.

We find similar facts during natural somnambulism that we cannot disregard without citing, although they are very well known. During a naturally occurring crisis, a patient, of whom Paul Richer speaks, can hear and feel only one person.[21] I recently obtained a very credible account of a similar instance. Mr. X had the opportunity to render a great service to an individual suffering from severe hysteria. One day he found him in the grip of a great attack of nerves, during which he could not hear any of the people present. Taking him by the arm to support him, the patient stopped and, with his eyes still closed, spoke, "Ah! It's you … I owe you everything, I must not resist you … You want me to be calm, well! I will not move anymore." As soon as Mr. X let go of his arm, the convulsions began again and no one else could stop them. I have already reported similar incidents regarding the hysterics that I have studied, but this one is far more interesting, because Mr. X had not thought of hypnotizing this patient, and no somnambulistic influence can explain this electivity due to recognition alone.

The electivity of natural somnambulists does not generally relate to people, but to objects. Just as the magnetized subject only hears a certain person, the natural somnambulist seems to see only certain objects, while they are completely unaware of others. Who does not know the description so often quoted of the somnambulist Castelli, who was only illuminated by his own candle and who believed himself in the dark when it went out?[22] There is no observation more curious nor more complete, from this point of view, than that of the automaton studied by Mesnet. During his attacks of somnambulism, this individual seemed to have only the sense of touch, by which he steered and received all kinds of information from surrounding objects. No other sense could be awakened in him; he could neither see nor hear. But when, through the sense of touch, his attention had been attracted to an object, he could see that object very well. "The sense of sight did not awaken except when an object was touched and its application was limited solely to objects with whom he was currently in contact."[23] "The patient," says the author, "sees certain objects and not others. The sense of sight is open to all personal objects which are in rapport with him through the impressions of touch and (on the contrary) closed to things which are external to him … he sees *his* match, he does not see *mine*."[24] One of the subjects I studied, Lucie, repeatedly presented phenomena of a similar nature during certain attacks of natural somnambulism. She woke up one night with the fixed idea of cleaning; it was one of the habits she had during somnambulism and in waking. She lit a lamp, carried it out of her room, and began to dust and put everything in order. Someone who had followed her tried in vain to be seen or heard. Lucie did not seem to see anything that this person put in front of her eyes, until the lamp carried by Lucie began to dim, and straightaway the somnambulist hurried back upstairs. She did not see those in attendance who were trying in vain to get her attention, but she noticed immediately that her lamp needed to be tended.

These phenomena of electivity do not differ from systematic anesthesia except in one point, that they are or appear to the inverse. Instead of the subject previously becoming blind towards a certain person, for a specific object, while continuing to see all others, they now seem to see only one specific object while remaining blind to everything else. We can easily move along from one case to another. Suppose that the subject originally hears all the people present and that I forbid them to hear Mr. X. That would be systematized anesthesia. If I continue and forbid them to hear Mr. Y, Mr. Z, etc. until they can only hear me, that would be electivity. This last phenomenon is, in effect, merely a (quite notable) type of systematized anesthesia, in which the suppressed phenomena are more numerous than the preserved phenomena, and, to express this analogy, one could designate it by a word already used by some authors, that of *systemized esthesia*.

If this is so, is it not natural to push the comparison further and to find out whether the supposedly missing psychological phenomena are really absent? Simple reflection shows us that this is not likely. Since the subject hears me and sees me, they do not have paralysis of hearing or sight. Because they hear and feel me alone, it is because they distinguish my voice and my touch from all others. This is not very difficult. A person can easily be recognized by their voice or by a touch, but the subject must still hear and feel the others in order to make this distinction and this recognition, and must therefore possess the seemingly suppressed sensations.

This is a natural assumption that has been noticed by many authors. "Deep sleepers," says Liébault,[25] "who seem isolated, nevertheless have sensations, although they seem to ignore them. They can remember them later as if by intuition." "The isolated somnambulist," says Ochorowicz,[26] "cannot hear strangers, but we are wrong if we believe that auditory sensations remain completely inactive. They enter the brain, and then produce a phenomenon which I will readily call latent hearing: this can combine with others and give results which, at some point, can appear among the other more intense states."

These assumptions can, in some cases, be fairly easily verified. A young man, H, who, during somnambulism, had seemed not to hear two people who tried to talk to him, could repeat to me later, at my request, everything they told him, noting that at the time he could not answer them. Sometimes you have to be firm when ordering the subject to remember something, so that the memory of these seemingly unperceived phenomena will come back completely, although other subjects discover this memory faster and more easily. It is enough that we put them in rapport with a person involved, so that this operation has some kind of retroactive effect and makes them remember everything that has been said previously. Marie absolutely does not hear and does not see Mr. X who is speaking to her. After a few minutes, I present Mr. X: "Marie, look at this gentleman who comes to see you." She sees him now and hears him, and from that moment she remembers her previous conversation and responds to it. Am I not right to say she had heard him?

As before, the person who appears not to be heard can give suggestions that are executed unconsciously. If Mr. X says to Marie, "Raise your arm," she raises her arm although she does not hear Mr. X, who has not yet been presented. Finally, another, N, who, in somnambulism, claims to be unable to hear anyone but me, is sometimes mistaken in a very unique way. She hears other people and answers them, but she calls them by my name and takes them for me. It is only by mistake that she answers them and that she is aware of hearing them, but this error is only possible because the words of strangers were actually heard. Unfortunately, I have not had the opportunity to use automatic writing to verify this real, albeit subconscious, hearing of people who are not in rapport. Lucie, who demonstrates automatic writing to a high degree, did not present any natural electivity. But the preceding remarks seem to me sufficient to establish the similarity between the phenomenon of electivity and that of systematic anesthesia, and to explain them in the same manner. *The sensations of which subjects appear to have no awareness have not disappeared but still exist in them in another way.*

2.4 Complete anesthesia or natural anesthesia of hysterics

The anesthesias previously studied were incomplete: they suppressed the perception of this or that object, while allowing the perception of this or that object to subsist. It seems that the results of observation should be quite different when we examine the complete anesthesia which occurs much more frequently in the course of natural hysteria. [27] Indeed, in this case, the subject seems to have completely lost a certain kind of sensitivity. Instead of choosing among the objects to see, hear, or feel, while some are no longer sensed, she seems to sense nothing. The ear is deaf to all sounds, the eye blind to any light, the skin insensitive to all contact. Can we not say that here anesthesia is altogether different and that it is due to a state of the organ itself? Can we not believe that there is no longer any means to support the persistence of sensation, which has in effect disappeared?

There are undoubtedly differences between complete anesthesia in hysterics and systematized anesthesia, but one should not assume an absolute opposition between these two phenomena, which are comparable in many ways. I will report first a small and singular detail which had escaped my observation, and which was pointed out to me by my brother, concerning a patient at the Hôtel-Dieu. Sometimes there is electivity even in these natural anesthesias, and the patients who seemingly have completely lost all sensitivity can still recognize some specific objects. Here are the facts. A hysterical woman, M (who was seriously ill), seemed to have completely lost all skin sensitivity, at least in both hands and arms (the only parts of her body that were placed before me for regular observation). She felt no pain, recognized no object, did not perceive any temperature. However, she recognized perfectly, upon contact, certain familiar objects from her toilette. She knew, by touching her ear, if she had or did not have her earrings. She recognized her ring and knew when she was wearing it and when it had been removed, without the need to look closely. At first, I thought that these gold jewels had a particular influence on her sense of touch. So I put a gold coin in her fingers, but she could not feel it and persisted in saying that she had nothing in her hand, whereas she immediately felt her earring. Besides, she also felt in her hair her iron or tortoiseshell pins which she could locate by touch and remove or put back, even if they had been moved. One must recognize that this is a case, during normal wakefulness, of elective anesthesia completely identical to what happens during somnambulism. M feels her pins and does not feel a gold coin, just as Lucie in natural somnambulism sees her lamp dimming and does not see the people around it. This experience is likely not rare among hysterics, and I think I have discovered it in Marie. At a time when she feels nothing with her hands, she can comb her hair without a mirror and feel if the position of her hair has been disturbed. Full anesthesia is similar to systematic anesthesia.

Secondly, complete anesthesia, that is to say relating to all exterior objects, is rarely general. It seldom extends to the whole body or even to a whole sensory organ. Skin anesthesia does not occur on all of the skin, but on only a few parts, often on half of the body, and then most often on the left half. Sometimes it also occurs on irregular plaques scattered over the limbs and on the trunk. Anesthesia of taste, smell, and even sight is also rarely complete. It occupies portions of the tongue and nasal mucosa, and leaves the other parts sensitive.[28] It spreads irregularly on the retina, sometimes narrowing the visual field concentrically, sometimes cutting it in half, sometimes forming irregular scotomas, that is to say spots of insensitivity, in the middle of a retina which remains normal.[29] It seems to me that there is in this singular distribution of insensitivity something analogous to the phenomena of systematic anesthesia. This distribution is in no way explained by anatomical or physiological characteristics of the organs, it does not correspond in particular to the distribution on the surface of the body of the cutaneous nerves, nor to the distribution of arteries. In some cases, when a limb has hysterical paralysis, the anesthesia, says Charcot,[30] is terminated by a circular line perpendicular to the axis of the limb. This is perhaps quite logical, because things happen in such a way that the ill imagine that their limb has been surgically severed, but it suffices to look at an anatomy chart to see that it does not match any clear physiological notion. I saw a hysteric whose arm was divided naturally for a few days, in a series of parallel zones, alternately sensitive and insensitive. This is something that is hardly anatomical, but which singularly recalls the squares and circles that one could, by suggestion, render insensitive on the skin of Léonie. Many current psychologists are inclined to believe, with Wundt, that a "local nuance of tactile sensation or feeling of pressure varies continuously from one area of the body to another,"[31] and that, therefore, "every area of our epidermis has a special way of feeling, and the quality of the sensation varies with the region of the skin."[32] If so, and considering the advantages that this hypothesis has to explain many problems, for my part, I am almost certain of its truth. One should not say that some hysterics have lost the sensitivity of a region of the skin. Rather, it should be said that they have lost certain groups of tactile sensations of a certain nuance, a certain quality, and they have retained other tactile sensations of another nuance. This is a reflection which brings us much closer to the previous observations, because it is always about keeping a particular sensation when you have lost another particular sensation. These two sensations do not differ by the organ which receives them, since the same nervous branch innervates the sensitive plaque and the insensitive plaque. These two sensations differ only in quality. It is the very same person who, with the same eye, always sees Mr. X no matter where he stands, and never sees Mr. Y. This distinction, as we have shown, can only be made if the two persons, the two groups of tactile sensations, are actually felt. The study of partial anesthesia leads us to the same conclusion as the study of systematized anesthesia.

Yet the anesthesia can be quite general, can extend over the entire surface of the skin, and can completely suppress an eye or an ear. This was the case with Lucie, who had no tactile sensitivity on any region of her body. Also with Marie, who sees nothing with the left eye and is in complete darkness when you close her right eye. Here again we could, perhaps by a little subtle reasoning, still speak of systematized anesthesia, because the tactile sensations differ in quality from those of the hearing sensations which are retained. The sensations of the left eye are not qualitatively the same as those of the right eye, and the patient still shows in this anesthesia some electivity. The analogy, I admit, is a bit remote, and to arrive at the same conclusions in regard to general anesthesia as for previous insensitivities, it must be submitted to new observations.

All the observers who have dealt with this partial blindness of hysterics (who seem to have had the sight of one eye completely removed), have noticed with astonishment a very singular fact: patients claim to see absolutely nothing with their left eye and to be plunged into the darkest night when you close their right eye, yet when we tell them to leave both eyes open, they see, without suspecting it, both with their left and right eyes. The observations made on this point are summarized in an article published by Bernheim,[33] and in the book by Pitres.[34] The experiments are very conclusive and easy to repeat. Here is one of the simplest ones, which I borrow from Pitres' book: "Now let us conduct the screen experiment. I write on the board a series of letters, a cardboard screen is placed vertically in front of the middle of the patient's face who sits in front of the board. With her right eye closed, she declares that she is unable to distinguish the characters written on the board. Left eye closed, she reads without hesitation the letters placed on the right of the screen. With both eyes open, she reads all the letters, both those to the left of the screen and those to the right." Other experiments have been conducted in quite large numbers and have all come to the same conclusion, which Pitres expresses thus: "Hysterical amblyopia corrects itself, because it is its nature to exist only in monocular vision. As soon as both eyes are open and they are acting synergistically, the amblyopia disappears and vision becomes normal." Which is to say, the hysteric is blind in the left eye when she tries to see with it, but at the same time believes that only this eye has the capacity for sight. However, she is no longer blind at all in that eye when she does not think about it and when she thinks she is seeing everything with her right eye.

Pitres' proposal summed up the previous comments well, but I believe that we must go much further and find new and more significant facts. I claim that the hysterical amaurotic sees perfectly with her left eye even when the right eye is closed, that this amblyopia does not even exist in the monocular vision, and that in general even the most complete hysterical anesthesia does not suppress any sensation. Let us stick to the facts without trying to understand now how this singular contradiction is possible. To verify this sensitivity of the anesthetic parts, do not directly question the subject and wait for an immediate response. Instead, you must employ somewhat indirect procedures, here focusing on two principle methods: the memory test and the study of subconscious acts.

If there is one point that is acknowledged in psychology, it is that memory is only the conservation of sensations. All sensation may, for different reasons, not become a memory, but all memory has been a conscious sensation. If our subjects do not actually feel the impressions made on the anesthetized parts of their body, they obviously will not keep the memory of it. What then do we make of the following experiments? Marie's right eye is carefully closed. She claims, as we know, to be in complete darkness. Regardless of what she says, I pass a small drawing several times in front of her left eye, and then remove it. The drawing depicted a tree with a snake climbing around the trunk. I then allow her to open her right eye and I question her; she claims to have seen absolutely nothing. A few minutes later, I apply to her left temple an iron plate (which is her preferred metal). Tingling is felt on the left side of the head, and the eye, as we have seen, resumes ordinary sensitivity for some time. I then ask her if she recalls what I had shown her. "Why yes," she says, "it was a drawing, a tree with a snake climbing around it." A few days later, I repeated the experiment as follows. I show a drawing to the left eye only (which had become anesthetic again); it is a large star drawn in blue pencil. Then, when both eyes are open, I show her a dozen small drawings among which is the star. She recognizes none and claims to be seeing them all for the first time. I apply the iron plate to her temple, sensitivity returns, and Marie takes the card with the blue star and says to me, "Except this one however, which I have seen once before."

The same experiment can be made with the tactile sense. One day I placed in the completely anesthetic hand of the same subject a small object (it was a rosebud) and I left it there for a few moments, taking all the precautions so that it was not seen. I ask her if she has anything in her hand; she searches carefully and assures me that she has nothing in her hand. I do not insist and I remove the rosebud without her noticing. Some time later, with the application of an iron plate, I return tactile sensitivity to this hand. Hardly has the tingling stopped (which signals for her the return of sensitivity), when she says spontaneously, "Ah! I was wrong, you put a rosebud in my hand, where is it?"

I have repeated this experiment several times with this subject and with three other anesthetic hysterics, and I have modified the experiment in various ways. Sometimes it suffices, as with systematized anesthesia, to order the subject to remember, so that the memory comes back while also bringing back sensitivity. In other cases, we can suggest the return of sensitivity which then brings back memory. Finally, we must sometimes employ an electric current using metal plates (proper to the particular subject), to return sensitivity. Once, I left an interval of two days between the moment when I placed an object onto the anesthetic hand and the moment that I brought back sensitivity. The result has always been the same. When the sensitivity became conscious again, the memory of the sensation which, in appearance, had not existed, reappeared completely.

Finally I thought of doing the same experiment with Rose, using the muscular or kinesthetic sense. I place her arm (which is anesthetic) in an arbitrary position: I point two fingers in the air and close the others, or I have her make a threatening gesture. Rose is not aware, because I have hidden her arm behind a screen. I now lower her arm and place it back on her lap. Then, by means of a weak electric current (suggestion cannot return sensitivity to this subject), I return complete sensitivity of the skin and muscle to Rose's arm. She can now tell me the positions that her arm was in and consciously repeat the gestures.

We have already studied analogous experiments with regard to the memory of somnambulists, in which case the return of sensitivity brought back the memory of a sensation that was actually recognized by the subject at the time it took place and had simply been forgotten. Here however the sensation has never been recognized by the subject, but it must have taken place, since it can be remembered using the same methods. We could speak of unconscious physiological recording, although that is far from clear. How then can a physiological phenomenon, which did not bring a sensation at its onset (when it was at its strongest), bring about a conscious memory two days later (when the trace of it is obviously weaker)? This is certainly in contrast to the idea that we usually have of memory. I prefer, for my part, to suggest that this sensation, the memory of which can be so lasting and so clear, actually existed and was a conscious phenomenon.

Let us consider things from another point of view to confirm our supposition. We know that acts are the continuation and manifestation of conscious states. Let us examine the acts which follow these impressions, apparently unfelt by the anesthetic limbs. I am not discussing here (to avoid complicating the question) those reflex acts which subsist in large numbers despite the disappearance of conscious sensation; we are used to considering them (wrongly I believe) as purely physiological phenomena. Let us take, as the object of our studies, complex acts which can only take place following a conscious, precise, and intelligent phenomenon. Lucie or Léonie is blindfolded and several people, without making any noise, raise her completely anesthetic left arm and then let it go; the raised arm falls heavily without the subject noticing anything. I in turn lift the same arm (whilst the subject continues to be unaware) and the arm remains in the air in a cataleptic state. There is nothing marvelous there; the arm obeys because it is me, it is a suggestion with a reference point. But it is still necessary that the anesthetic arm distinguished, by touch, the contact of the different people who raised the arm. Lucie does not feel the contractions of her muscles: why then, when I close her fist without her being able to see it, does her face take on the expression of anger? I tell Marie to touch her ear with her left hand, she misses and touches her hat, then corrects her movement and descends to her ear; she pretends not to have felt her hat, and I want to believe it, but why did she correct her movement? One day I made Rose believe that I was electrifying her leg and I purposely used a device that did not work and gave no current. After placing a screen which blocked her sight, I applied the electrodes to her skin which is anesthetic, and muscle contractions occurred. It is a suggestion, but why then did the contractions stop suddenly as soon as I lifted the electrodes, and why do they start again as soon as (without warning) I gently reapplied them to the skin? A list of similar facts would be endless. Certainly other observers have noticed many. Let us move on to still more decisive observations.

We have pointed out, in previous studies, the curious phenomenon of automatic writing; we have seen how it is produced and how it allows us to penetrate into regions of consciousness that the subject is not aware of. Since this phenomenon is quite pronounced in Lucie, it is her that we will now consider. While she is chatting with other people, I pinch her left arm hard. Lucie, as I have known for a long time, does not frown, but her right hand in which I have placed a pencil suddenly writes, "Did you pinch me?" I ask questions of this subconscious writing while Lucie talks of other things: "Which finger am

I touching?" I ask. "The little one ... the second one," writes the right hand. "What do I put in your left hand?" I ask. "A small pencil ... a penny." "Where has your arm been placed?" "It is up, you have extended it ... you put my hand on my head ... Now it is touching my ear," the hand writes. One might expect this result; it would naturally follow what preceded. I was, however, very surprised, as I was accustomed to considering this person absolutely anesthetic. Out of curiosity, I measured this subconscious sensitivity with an aesthesiometer and, although Lucie was unable to feel even a strong sudden burn, automatic writing showed that she could sense the spacing of the two points of the instrument as well as a healthy person. On the underside of the wrist, the minimum spacing that we were able to put between the two points (so that the writing still indicates, error-free, two punctures), is 22 millimeters on the right, and 30 millimeters on the left. The same observation, made on normal people, gives me figures varying between 25 and 35. The sensation, despite the apparent anesthesia, is therefore very fine. We never really penetrate a person's consciousness; we only appreciate it according to the external signs that it gives us. If I believe Lucie, who tells me that she cannot smell, why should I not believe her when, through her writing, she tells me that she can smell? Writing is as complex as speech; when she responds to questions, she manifests just as much intelligence and consciousness, and I see no reason not to believe one type of manifestation over another.

We note above all that these observations on the various types of anesthesia are absolutely in agreement. Whether it is a matter of systematized anesthesia obtained by suggestion, systematized esthesia, or the electivity of somnambulists, plaque anesthesia of hysterics, their blindnesses, or their general anesthesias, the results are exactly the same. Note also that these observations are in complete agreement with those of Bemheim, Pitres, and many others on the unilateral amaurosis of hysterics. Just as they found, in many cases, that the hysteric sees with her blind eye although she believes the opposite, in the same way I have shown that she frequently feels what she imagines she does not feel. Let us look at the facts, even if we cannot understand them. In the same way, just as there are a large number of complicated unconscious acts that the subject can perform intelligently without awareness, *so too are there many sensations that can be experienced and remembered, and which can be reasoned about, without there being any conscious awareness.*[35]

2.5 Different hypotheses concerning the phenomena of anesthesia

We encounter very few hypotheses that have been proposed to explain the facts that we have just reviewed, because hysterical anesthesia has rarely been presented in this way, and, in particular, it has rarely been compared to systematized anesthesia (of which, however, it is only a particular case).

We will not accept the simplest and most banal hypothesis which comes naturally to mind when considering such matters: that they pretend not to feel, and yet, as we can demonstrate, they can feel perfectly well; so the subjects have lied and are simply feigning. We have used and abused hysterical simulation to suppress problems that we did not understand, and this simplistic assumption makes no sense. First of all, we cannot simulate anesthesia: "all it takes is a little attention to thwart the deceptions," as Pitres[36] has shown in connection with an individual who professed himself to be an insensitive man and who had learned to suppress manifestations of pain. Next, we must not forget that these subjects do not boast of their anesthesia, but most often are unaware, and it is we who reveal it to them. Finally, do not take all hysterics for ignorant people and attribute to them simulations that are absurd and clumsy. The first subject that came along would know that if they simulate blindness in the left eye, they should not read the letters on the left side of the screen. Marie, who is not foolish, would know very well, if it was simulated, that one should not recall the drawings shown to her left eye, and yet we have seen that she consistently remembers. Let us not insist otherwise.

We will not study further the physiological or anatomical suppositions that have been made, first, because they are not within our competence, and next, because they seem to us to be just a roundabout way of introducing psychological hypotheses. Thus Pitres explains the general anesthesia of hysterics by a functional inertia of the basilar centers of the brain, that is to say cell groups of the protuberance and the peduncle.[37] Why this hypothesis? It is because it represents anesthesia, from the psychological point of view, as being a lesion, not of intelligence or perception, but of raw sensation, and that these basilar centers are considered today as the organs of raw sensation. Let him be led to make another psychological hypothesis, and the author will indicate another anatomical location. After having noticed the curious phenomena relating to the unilateral amaurosis of hysterics, Pitres affirms the multiplicity of the cortical centers of vision[38] and will suggest that the lesion occurs in these centers. It is here that he saw, without stating it clearly, that the modification is found in the perceptions and not in the raw sensations. There is nothing surprising in this parallelism between the anatomical and psychological hypotheses. It would even be desirable, for the progress of the two sciences, that it should have been pushed much further. But, as is natural, we will only deal with the psychological hypotheses in themselves, not speaking about the anatomical translation that it is always possible to make.

We have just pointed out a first psychological hypothesis which seems, at first sight, to be very natural and to simply interpret the facts. It suggests that anesthetic individuals present no psychological disturbance other than their insensitivity; they reason well with what they know. They do not present (with regard to the preserved sensations) those disturbances of interpretation and recognition so characteristic in verbal blindness and verbal deafness. The patient who presents an intellectual disorder in "the organs of the psychic development of sensations" sees and hears in reality, but does not recognize or understand well what they see or hear. Hysterical anesthesia does not have this characteristic. It suppresses such or such sensation purely and simply; *it is a lesion of the raw sensation.*

We cannot share this opinion. From a theoretical point of view, the intellectual development of phenomena descends lower than the authors seem to suppose. The development which makes it possible to understand language or writing and the lesion which causes verbal deafness or verbal blindness is a superior development, below which there are several others. And such modifications of an elementary development, while respecting the raw feeling, can very well prevent a person from having the personal consciousness of what they see or hear. From an experimental point of view, the facts are in complete opposition to this theory and consistently show us that the raw sensation has not been destroyed. In the case of monocular anesthesia, Pitres himself recognizes that the sensations of the blind eye are not definitively eliminated and that the subject can perfectly appreciate them given certain circumstances. Experiments on systemized anesthesia show that, in certain cases, the subject can be convinced that they do not see an object, while we know that they must necessarily see it to recognize it. Finally, the experiments that I have indicated (and which are sometimes easy to reproduce) demonstrate that one can always find the sensation, seemingly erased, and demonstrate its existence.

Not only do natural or experimental anesthesias not seem to suppress the sensation, but they do not even succeed in modifying it. Here is some research that I did on the subject. During somnambulism, I forbid Lucie to see the colour red; upon awakening, she does not perceive this colour, but the subconscious character declares, through automatic writing, that she sees it very well. Now, we know that the colour white is formed by red rays and greenish-blue rays. A person whose tired retina no longer distinguishes red rays only sees green rays within the colour white and sees it as green; at least this is the explanation that we give consecutive images of complementary colour. If anesthesia changes sensations, as with retinal fatigue, Lucie, who can no longer distinguish red, must therefore also see a white paper with the colour green. I show her white paper, and she finds it absolutely white; the red alone is invisible and its disappearance has no influence on the other colours that are seen normally (with confusion for some due to a slight achromatopsia that existed prior to the experiment). On the other hand, if the second consciousness sees red, it should with the colour white distinguish the red rays, which it does not do, because it does not recognize a white paper. We would find the same fact, I believe, in natural achromatopsia; a hysteric who no longer recognizes red, however, continues to see the colour white without modifications. From these experiments, it seems to me that we can draw the following conclusion, which confirms our previous remarks: anesthesia does not change raw sensations in any way. It is therefore not in the study of sensations in themselves that we can find the reason for these insensitivities. We must seek it higher, within the mechanism of elementary perception; there is no real verbal blindness or verbal deafness there. Bernheim, however, is correct in saying, "These phenomena are due to an illusion of the mind ... the blindness of hysterics is a psychic blindness."[39]

It is necessary, however, to examine beforehand another theory which is not, as far as I know, clearly stated by an author, but which will be someday, because it presents enough of a likelihood. Could one not explain anesthesia or the subconscious by the weakness of certain images, in the same way as one might want to explain conscious suggestion by the force of certain others? Could we not say, for example, that the visual image of the drawing shown to Marie's left eye is very weak and that the metallic applications result in increasing its force and making it perceptible? We have already explained Binet's hypotheses regarding suggestion, and our opinion has not so far been modified by these new facts. I see no reason to say that the sensation produced on the anesthetic organs is a weak sensation. This feeling is precise. It allows the subject to recognize very small details of the object that is shown to her and to point them out later by memory or immediately through automatic writing.

When can we say that a person has a lively and strong sensation (given that this term has any meaning) if not when they appreciate the minute details of the impression evoked by these senses? We measure visual acuity with the reading of small letters, we measure the acuity of the tactile sense by distinguishing between close tactile sensations, that is to say, sensations that are almost the same. There can be nothing more in a strong sensitivity, except a mixture of painful phenomena foreign to the sensation itself, which are modifications of nature and not of the quantity of the sensation. Now these anesthetic organs discern very delicate things. Marie's left eye, as I have confirmed, recognizes my drawing even when it is small and placed at a distance. Lucie's hand recognizes the spacing of the points of the aesthesiometer at an interval where many people, who have a supposedly strong sensitivity, do not appreciate it. The unconscious acts of Léonie show that she recognizes my hand by simple contact, which is not the mark of a weak sensation. On the other hand, if subjects failed to recognize the sensations impressed on their anesthetic organs because of their weakness, they should not be aware of any other weak impressions. We do know, however, that a subject can be anesthetic in one sense and have another sense which is very refined; Rose, who does not feel the prick of pins on her limbs, becomes angry because, far away outside, she hears someone singing out of tune. It is therefore not the smallness or the weakness of these sensations that prevents the subject from being aware of them.

The best study of these phenomena that I know of is that of Bernheim titled, "Of Hysterical Amaurosis and Suggestive Amaurosis."[40] The author declares that two very important points have been demonstrated: (1) the complete analogy between natural hysterical anesthesia and systematized anesthesia produced by suggestion: it is indeed, in both cases, a certain sensation, distinct from the others not by the organ which produces it, but by its psychological quality which does not manage to enter into the consciousness of the subject; (2) The sensation actually exists with all its psychological characteristics; the visual or tactile image is completely real and conscious. We fully share the author's opinion on these two points and we believe we have made a few observations which help to strengthen it. The author, however, seeks to explain the phenomenon in a language that seems to me to lack full precision and clarity: "Having perceived the visual image, the hysteric unconsciously neutralizes it with her imagination ... Psychic blindness is blindness by imagination; it is due to the destruction of the image by the psychic agent." Pitres, who quotes this theory, does not seem, in my opinion, to attribute sufficient importance to it. "I do not understand," he says,[41] "how the hysteric can subconsciously neutralize, with the imagination, the monocular perceptions and not also unconsciously neutralize the binocular perceptions, or, at least, the part of the binocular perceptions which come from the amblyopic eye." Bernheim would no doubt reply, if I may allow myself to speak for him, that the hysteric does not neutralize binocular perceptions, because she does not present as blind in both eyes, but only in the left eye; neither does she neutralize part of these binocular perceptions, because she does not know that these perceptions come from the left eye, because she thinks she sees everything through the right eye. If one points out to her, during experiments, that a particular object can only be seen by the left eye, she will no longer see it.

For my part, I will make another criticism of Bernheim's formulation: I find that the image is neither neutralized nor destroyed, because it still exists and it manifests its existence through subconscious acts and automatic writing. In addition, this image did not need to be neutralized, because it was never in the consciousness of the subject. One cannot say that Marie begins by seeing my drawing, then ceases to see it; she has no such negation to make, because she has never seen this drawing. Finally, the role which Bernheim attributes to the imagination hardly corresponds to its ordinary definition. Its role of representation and combination of images seems to have the task of evoking them, rather than denying them. Finally, we do not hope to have much more success than Bernheim in explaining these delicate and complex phenomena clearly, and perhaps we will actually express a theory which on many points is similar to his own.

2.6 Psychological disaggregation

The phenomenon which occurs in our consciousness following an impression made on our senses and which is communicated by these expressions, "I see a light ... I feel a sting," is a phenomenon that is already very complex. It is not only made up of simple raw visual or tactile sensations, but entails an operation of active synthesis and at each moment links this sensation to the group of previous images and judgments constituting the self or the personality. The seemingly simple fact which translates into these words, "I see, I feel," even without speaking of the ideas of exteriority, distance, or location, is already a complex perception. We have previously insisted on this idea when studying automatic acts during catalepsy. We adopted the opinion of Maine de Biran, who recognized in the human mind a purely affective life of mere sensations that are conscious, but not attributed to a personality, as opposed to a perceptual life of unified sensations, systematized and attached to a personality.

We can, while attaching to these representations only a purely symbolic value, represent our conscious perception as a two-step operation.

(1) The simultaneous existence of a certain number of conscious tactile sensations like TT'T", muscular sensation like MM'M", visual sensations like VV'V", auditory sensations like AA'A". These sensations exist simultaneously and in isolation from each other, similar to a quantity of small lights that would light up all the dark corners of a room. These primitive conscious phenomena, anterior to perception can be of different species – sensations, memories, images – and can have different origins. Some may come from a current impression made on the senses, others can be brought about by the automatic interplay of association following other phenomena. But, in order not to complicate an already complex problem, let us first consider, in this chapter, only the simplest and let us now suppose that all these elementary phenomena are simple sensations produced by an external modification of the sense organs (see Figure 2.1).

(2) An operation of active and current synthesis by which these sensations are linked to each other, aggregate, merge, and fuse in a unique state. In this way, a main sensation attains its nuance, but it probably does not resemble, in a complete way, any of the constituent elements. This new phenomenon is perception P. As this perception takes place moment by moment the result of each new grouping contains memories, as well as sensations. It forms the idea that we have of our personality, and from now on we can say that a person feels the TT'T" MM'M" images, etc. This activity, which thus synthesizes the different psychological phenomena at each moment of life and which forms our personal perception, should not be confused with the automatic association of ideas. This association, as we have already said, is not a *current* activity. It is the result of an old activity which formerly synthesized some phenomena in a single emotion or perception and created a tendency for them to reoccur in the same order. The perception we are talking about now is the synthesis occurring at the moment it is formed, at the moment when it brings together *new* phenomena into a unity at each *new* instant.

We do not have to explain how these things happen; we only have to note that they do happen this way. Or, if we prefer, to suppose it and to explain that this assumption makes it possible to understand the preceding characteristics of hysterical anesthesia.

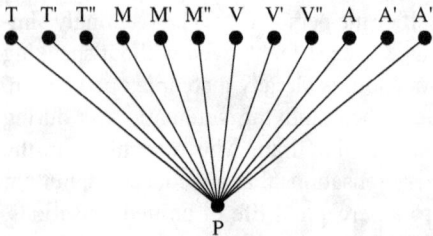

Figure 2.1 TT'T", elementary sensations of touch; MM'M", of muscular sense; VV'V", of vision; AA'A", of audition; P, perception.

In a theoretical person (such as probably does not exist), all the sensations included in the first operation TT'T", etc., would be united in perception P, and this person could say: "I feel ..." about all the phenomena that occur in them. It is never so, and even in the ideal person there must be a multitude of sensations which are produced by the first operation and which escape the second. I am not speaking only of sensations which escape voluntary attention and which are not understood "with perfect clarity." I speak of sensations which are wholly unattached to the personality and of which the self does not possess any awareness, because, indeed, it does not contain them. To represent this, suppose that the first operation remains the same, only the second one is modified. The power of synthesis cannot be exerted at every moment of life, but only on a determined number of phenomena, on five for example and not on twelve. Of the twelve supposed sensations, TT'T", MM'M", etc., the self will only be aware of the perception of five, of TT'MVA for example. Regarding these five sensations, it will say: "I felt them; I was aware of them." But if we discuss with it the other phenomena (T'V'A', etc., which in our hypothesis were also conscious sensations), it will answer that "it does not know what we are talking about," and that "it has no knowledge of that." Now, we have carefully studied a particular state of hysterics and neuropaths in general that we have called the narrowing of the field of consciousness. This characteristic (following our hypothesis) is produced precisely by this weakness of psychic synthesis which is pushed further than usual and which does not allow subjects to connect within the same personal perception a large number of the sensory phenomena which are actually occurring within them (Figure 2.2).

This being the case, the sensory phenomena which occur in the minds of these individuals are naturally divided into two groups: (1) the group TT'MVA, which is united in perception P and which forms their personal consciousness; (2) the remaining sensory phenomena T"M'M"V'V"A'A", which are not synthesized in perception P. We are only dealing with the first group for the moment.

In most cases, the phenomena that fall into the first group, that of personal perception, while being limited in number, can however vary and do not always remain the same. The operation of synthesis seems to be able to select and to connect to the self and consequently to personal consciousness, at times one group

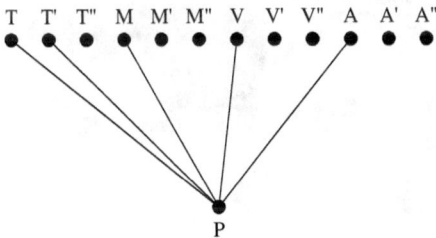

Figure 2.2 Perception based on narrowed field of personal consciousness.

of sensations, at times another, which may include tactile sensation, as well as visual. At one time the group perceived can be TT'MVA, at another, it can be MM'V'AA' (see Figure 2.3).

When things happen this way, there are indeed, at each moment, phenomena which are ignored and remain unperceived (like M' in the first moment, or V in the second). However, these ignored phenomena are not perpetually unconscious; they are only momentarily so. Alternatively, these phenomena (which are unconscious) do not always belong to the same sense; they are sometimes muscular sensations, sometimes visual sensations. This description seems to me to correspond to what we have observed in a particular form of narrowing of the field of consciousness by distraction, by electivity, or by systematized esthesia: in a word, in all anesthesia with variable limits. The distracted hysterical subject who hears only one person and does not hear the others (because she cannot perceive so many things at once), if she synthesizes the auditory and visual sensations which come to her from a person, can do nothing more. The hypnotized individual who hears everything said by her magnetizer and knows everything he does, without being able to hear or feel any other person, and the natural somnambulist, who sees her lamp and feels her own movements but is not aware of the other visual sensations forming in her mind, are striking examples of this first form of weakened and restricted synthesis. In these people, in fact, no sensation is perpetually unconscious; it is so only for the moment. If the subject turns to you, she will hear what you say to her. If I put you in rapport with the hypnotized person, she will speak to you. If the somnambulist dreams of you, she will see you. In addition, the sensations which have disappeared do not always belong to the same sense and, if the subject is questioned by a person successively on each of the senses,

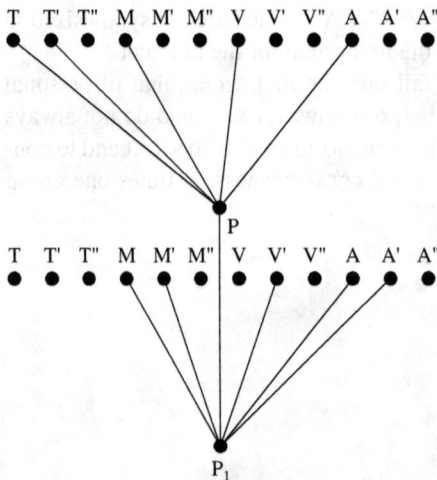

Figure 2.3 Perceptions based on alternation of two divided groups of sensations.

she will prove to him that she senses everything quite well and does not appear to be in real anesthesia.

It is among this type, which I am least disposed to believe, that we must categorize hysterics without anesthesia. They are very rare. Pitres says he has observed two, but I have not had a chance to encounter any. These hysterics must still have the essential character of their illness: the narrowing of the field of consciousness, the diminution of the power of perceptual synthesis, but they have retained the power to successively exercise this faculty over all sensible phenomena, whatever they may be.

Why do they perceive this group of sensations at one time rather than another? There is no voluntary choice here as there is with attention, because, for such a choice to be possible, there must first have been a general perception of all sensitive phenomena, then a purposeful elimination. The electivity is due to the automatic development of this or that sensation which is repeated more frequently, and which associates more readily to this or that other group. When a hysterical person looks at someone, she will hear the words of one person rather than the words of another, because the sight of the speaking mouth, gestures, and attitude are associated with the words that this person pronounces and not with the words of another. A somnambulist who does her housework will notice her dimming lamp more readily than she will see a stranger in the room, because the sight of the lamp combines with the sight of other household objects and fills this small field of consciousness, without leaving room for the image of the stranger. In other cases, a sensation remains dominant and draws in those related to it, because it has dominated in a moment of even greater narrowing of the field of consciousness and is reduced almost to unity. At the beginning of hypnotism, the semi-cataleptic subject can only perceive one sensation; that of the magnetizer dominates because he is present, he touches the hands, he speaks to the ear, etc. The field of consciousness widens a little, but it is always the thought of the magnetizer which retains its supremacy and which directs associations towards this or that other sensation. In all these cases, systematized esthesia is a form of this automatism which unites in the same perception the sensations which have some affinity, some unity among them. Current activity, through a kind of sluggishness, does little more than continue or repeat the syntheses already established in the past (Figure 2.4).

But things can happen in a completely different way. The weak power of synthesis can often be exercised in the same direction, uniting in the perception, sensations of the same type and losing the practice of bringing others together The subject no longer uses visual images and only rarely addresses images of touch. If her power of synthesis decreases, if she can no longer unite more than three images, she will totally reject perceiving the sensations of this or that type. At first, the loss is momentary and she can, if need be, find them. But soon the perceptions which enabled her to know these images are not being made. She can no longer, even if she tries, connect to the synthesis of the personality the sensations which she has let escape. She therefore renounces, without realizing it, the sensations that come from a part of the skin's surface, or the sensations from an

T T' T" M M'M" V V' V" A A' A"

P

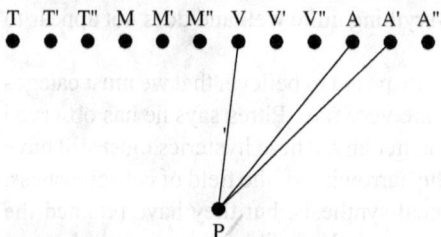

Figure 2.4 Perception based on narrowed field of personal consciousness.

entire side of the body, sometimes the sensations of an eye or an ear. It is still the same mental weakness, but this time it results in a much clearer and more material symptom, a permanent anesthesia with fixed limiting of the arm, the eye, or the ear. The subject you are questioning can only tell you what she perceives and cannot speak to you about the sensations which are happening within her without her knowledge, since she does not perceive them anymore.

Why is anesthesia localized in certain ways? We suspect the reason in some cases; we can hardly guess at it in others. Hysterics more readily lose tactile sensitivity, because it is the least important, not psychologically, but practically. At the beginning of life, the tactile sense is used to acquire almost all notions. But later, thanks to acquired perceptions, the other senses almost always replace it. Hysterics tend to lose sensitivity on the left side rather than the right, probably because they use it less often. I thought I noticed that there are parts of the body, the fingertips, the lips, etc., in which they retain sensitivity longer than others, probably because the sensations they provide are particularly useful or pleasant. A hysterical person I observed had lost sensitivity to the limbs, but retained sensitive bands in all the joints: this perhaps favoured her movement. But if we consider the scattered islets of anesthesia that certain subjects have on the skin, we do not know enough of the variations of local sensations, their similarities and their differences, to understand the reasons for these bizarre distributions.

The sensations produced by these anesthetic parts always exist, and it only takes the smallest thing for the perception which has lost the habit of grasping them to recover them once more, if I may express myself this way. Force someone to think of a visual image usually linked to a tactile image. Tell Marie that a caterpillar is walking on her arm, and the whole arm becomes sensitive again. This, however, cannot last, for the field of consciousness has remained very small: it has moved, but it has not grown, and it will have to return to the most useful sensations for this subject who does not have enough psychic force to allow a richness of perception. It is the same for the sensations of both eyes, which are coupled together and function reciprocally. No matter how weak their power of perception, these subjects cannot stop at half a word when the neighbouring sensation presents the whole word. The sensations of the right eye, which are kept in the center of the small field of perception as useful and essential, bring about the perception of the images provided by the left eye, as soon as there is some reason to recover them, as with the image of a caterpillar on the arm which returns the tactile sense of the arm. But there is no longer (in the restricted field of perception), an evocative image, whether the right eye is closed, or is looking at an object arranged so that it can be seen entirely with that eye. Here the sensations provided by the left eye, too neglected by perception, are not taken up. If I am on Marie's right and if I speak to her, the people who approach from her left are not seen, although she has both eyes open; if I move to her left, drawing her attention with me, she continues to see me with the left eye. Anesthesia in this case seems to have a fixed limit, but, since there is no absolute separation between these various kinds of anesthesia, it behaves in many cases like systemic anesthesia with variable limits. It is the power of the dominant perception which changes the sensation and which brings to light, according to the needs, such or such image (since none had really disappeared).

Perhaps the metal plates, the currents, the passes act in the same way. It is possible, but, before committing myself, I will admit to some doubt. These processes, which in the end can bring about the last somnambulism (that is to say a complete widening of the field of consciousness), seem to me to directly increase the force of perception. But, for whatever reason, the self now contains the sensations it had lost, it finds them as they were with the memories recorded in its absence. She recognizes a drawing that she has not seen, she remembers a movement that she did not feel, because she gathered in the sensations that had seen this drawing and felt this movement. Complete anesthesia which covers an entire organ therefore differs from systemized anesthesia only to a degree. The same weakness of perception, which causes one person to neglect a particular image, leads another to almost entirely neglect the images provided by the left eye (except when they are necessary to supplement those of the right eye), and leads a third person to definitively neglect (so that they can no longer be found) the sensations of an arm or a leg.

Undoubtedly, this is only a way of representing things, an attempt to bring together apparently contradictory and therefore unintelligible facts. This assumption has obvious advantages from this point of view. It explains how certain phenomena can both be known by subjects and not known by them; how the same eye can see and not see, because it shows us that there are two different ways of knowing a phenomenon: impersonal feeling and personal perception (the only one that the subject can indicate with conscious language). This hypothesis also explains to us how the impressions made on the same sense can be subdivided, because it teaches us that it is not always all the raw sensations of a sense which remain outside of personal perception, but sometimes only some of them, while the others can be recognized. These explanations seem to summarize the facts with some clarity and that is why we are ready to consider *systematized or even general anesthesia as a lesion, a weakening, not of the sensation, but of the faculty of synthesizing the sensations in personal perception, which brings about a real disaggregation of psychological phenomena.*

2.7 Simultaneous psychological existences

Let us refer once again to the symbolic image which enabled us to understand anesthesia and let us now study it from another point of view. Instead of examining the three or four visual or auditory phenomena VV"AA' (see Figure 2.5, below) which are united in personal perception P and whose subject owns the consciousness. Let us now consider in themselves the remaining sensations TT'T"M, etc., which are not perceived by the subject but which nevertheless exist. What becomes of them? Most often they play a hidden role; their separation, their isolation makes for their weakness. Each of these facts contains a tendency to movement which would be carried out if it were alone, but they mutually destroy each other and above all they are stopped by the stronger group of other sensations synthesized in the form of personal perception. At most they can produce these slight tremors of muscles, these convulsive tics of the face, this trembling of the fingers which give many hysterics a particular stamp, which make them easily recognizable, as we say, an excitable person.

But it is quite easy to promote their development. It suffices to remove or reduce the obstacle that blocks them. By closing her eyes, by distracting the subject, we decrease or divert in another direction the activity of the main personality, and we leave the field free for these subconscious or non-perceived phenomena. It is then enough to evoke one of them, to raise the arm or to move it, to put an object in the hands, or to pronounce a word, so that these sensations bring (according to the ordinary law) the movements which characterize them. These movements are not known by the subject herself, since they occur precisely in that part of her person which for her is anesthetic. Sometimes they are produced in limbs of which the subject has completely and consistently lost sensation, sometimes in limbs with which the distracted subject is not occupied at this moment; the result is always the same. We can move Léonie's left arm without any other precaution than hiding it behind a screen, because it is always anesthetic; we can move her right arm by diverting her attention elsewhere, because it is only anesthetic by accident. But, in both cases, the arm will move without her knowing it. Speaking as a rule, these movements determined by non-perceived sensations are not known by anyone, because these disaggregated sensations, reduced to the state of mental

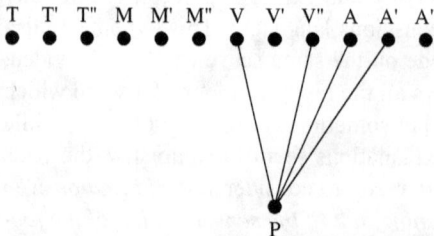

T T' T" M M' M" V V' V" A A' A"

P

Figure 2.5 Perception based on narrowed field of personal consciousness.

dust, are not synthesized in any personality. These are indeed cataleptic acts determined by conscious, but not personal, sensations.

If things sometimes happen this way, it is not difficult to see that they will often be more complex. Subconscious acts do not always manifest simple impersonal sensations. Sometimes they obviously show us memory. When you raise the arm of a hysterical anesthetic for the first time to check for partial catalepsy, you must hold it in the air for some time and specify the position you wish. After a few attempts, all you have to do is raise the arm a little so that it takes the desired position on its own, without having to be shown. If an act of this kind has been executed in a specific context, it will repeat itself a second time when the same context occurs. I showed an example of the subconscious acts of Léonie to Mr. X: I had her left hand snub her nose without her being aware of it. A year later, when Léonie sees the same person again, her left hand raises to her nose and she snubs it. Certain subjects, like Marie, are content, when one guides their anesthetic hand, to repeat the same movement indefinitely, to continuously write the same letter on a sheet of paper. Others will complete the word that they had started to make. Others write the word dictated to them when they are distracted and do not hear because of a sort of systematized anesthesia. Finally there are some, like N, Léonie, or Lucie, who will respond in writing to the question put to them. This subconscious writing contains reasonable reflections, detailed accounts, calculations, etc. The nature of things has changed, they are no longer cataleptic acts determined by simple raw sensations. There are perceptions and intelligence. But this perception is not part of the normal life of the subject, of the synthesis which characterizes it and which is represented by P in our figure, because the subject is unaware of the conversation being carried out by her hand, just as much as she is unaware of partial catalepsies. It must of necessity be assumed that the sensations which have remained outside of normal perception have in turn been synthesized into a second perception P'. This second perception is probably composed (it will have to be verified) of tactile and muscular T'M' images, which the subject never uses and which she has definitively abandoned, and of an auditory sensation A" which the subject can catch hold of (since, in some cases, she can hear me) but which she has temporarily put aside because she is focused on a conversation with another person.

A second psychological existence was formed, at the same time as the normal psychological existence, by these conscious sensations, which normal perception had abandoned in too great a number (Figure 2.6).

What is, in fact, the essential sign of the existence of a perception? It is the unification of these various phenomena with the notion of personality which is expressed by the words "I" or "me." Now this subconscious writing uses the word "I" all the time. It is the manifestation of a person, exactly as happens in the normal speech of the subject. There is not only secondary perception, there is secondary personality, a "secondary self" (as some English authors have said, when discussing the experiments on automatic writing that I have published in the past). No doubt this "secondary self" is very rudimentary at the beginning and can hardly be compared to the "normal self", but it can develop in a very remarkable way.

T T' T'' M M' M'' V V' V'' A A' A''

P   P

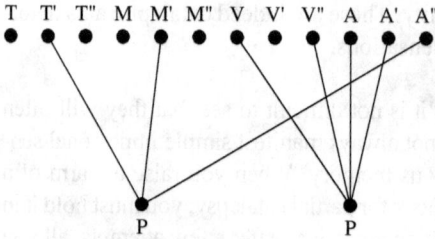

Figure 2.6 Two simultaneous perceptions, each with its own narrowed field of personal consciousness.

Having noticed, I admit with some astonishment, the secondary intelligence which was manifested by Lucie's automatic writing, one day I had the following conversation with her while her normal self was chatting with another person. "Do you hear me?" I say to her. (She answers in writing), "No." "But in order to answer, you have to hear." "Yes, absolutely." "So how do you do it?" "I do not know." I ask, "Does someone have to hear me?" "Yes." "Who is that?" "Someone other than Lucie." "Ah! Someone else. Do you want us to give them a name?" "No." "Yes, it will be more convenient." She responded, "Well then, Adrienne."[42] "So, Adrienne, can you hear me?" She responded, "Yes." No doubt it was I who suggested that she name this personage and thus gave her a sort of individuality, but one can see how far she had already developed in that direction spontaneously. These namings of the subconscious personage greatly facilitate experiments. Moreover, automatic writing almost always takes a name of this kind, without anyone having suggested anything, as I have seen in automatic letters spontaneously written by Léonie.

Once baptized, the unconscious personage is more determined and sharper. It displays its psychological characteristics better. It shows us that it is mainly aware of those sensations neglected by the primary or normal character. It is the one who tells me that I am pinching her arm, or that I am touching her little finger, though Lucie had long since lost all tactile sensation. It is the one who sees the objects that the negative suggestion has taken from Lucie's consciousness, who notices and marks my crosses and my numbers on the papers. It uses those sensations that have been abandoned to it to produce its movements. We know indeed that the same movement can be executed, at least by an adult, in different ways, thanks to visual or kinesthetic images. For example, Lucie can only write by visual images; she leans over and continuously follows her pen and paper with her eyes. Adrienne, who is the second simultaneous personality, writes without looking at the paper; in this way she uses kinesthetic images of writing. Each has its own way of acting, as well as thinking.

One of the first characteristics manifested by this "secondary self," one which is visible to the observer, is a marked preference for certain people. Adrienne, who obeys me very well and who willingly chats with me, hardly responds to anyone else. If others examine this same subject in my absence, as has happened, they will notice no partial catalepsy, no subconscious acts by distraction, no automatic writing, and they will tell me that Lucie is a normal person, very distracted and very anesthetic. They are observers who have seen only the first self with its lacunae and not encountered the second. According to the observations of Binet and Féré, it is not enough that a hysteric is anesthetic for her to present partial catalepsy. Without a doubt, this condition requires one additional condition beyond anesthesia: a sort of connection between the experimenter and the subconscious phenomena. If these phenomena are very isolated, they are caused by the experimenter. But if they are grouped in a personality (which happens very frequently in hysterics who are seriously ill), they show preferences and do not obey just anyone.

Not only does the secondary self not obey, it resists those it does not know. When I raise the arm of Lucie, or that of Léonie, who exhibits the same phenomenon, and put it in a cataleptic position, nobody can move them. If one tries to move it, the arm seems contracted and resists with all its strength. If one bends it with effort, it goes back, as if by elasticity, to its first position. When I touch the arm again, it suddenly becomes light and obeys all impulses. We must remember this characteristic of electivity, which belongs to the subconscious personage, this will help us later to better specify its nature.

This personality usually has little will; it obeys my slightest orders. There is no need to emphasize this already well-known quality. Suggestion is the explanation in this case, as in the circumstances previously studied. It is produced here, as always, by the smallness, the weakness of this personality, which is grafted onto the first and which is even narrower than it. We already know the only fact to remember is that these suggestions are carried out (in typical cases, the only ones that we are considering now)[43] without the subject herself being aware. It is a second individual, even more suggestible than the first, who acts alongside and without the knowledge of the subject we are studying, but who acts according to the exact same laws.

However, just as the most suggestive individuals have shown themselves capable of resistance and spontaneity, so the secondary personage is sometimes very uncooperative. I had quite amusing quarrels with the personage Adrienne, so docile at the beginning, who, while growing, became less and less so. She often answered me in an impertinent manner and wrote, "No, no", instead of doing what I ordered. One day she was so angry with me that she completely refused to answer me. Partial catalepsy, unconscious acts, automatic writing – all these had disappeared simply because of Adrienne's bad mood. How can we, as some authors do, consider cataleptic phenomena in the waking state to be purely physiological and muscular phenomena, when we see them suddenly disappear as a result of an anger manifested in automatic writing? I was at that point forced to chat with the normal personage, with Lucie, who, completely ignorant of the drama that was going on inside herself, was in a very good mood. When I managed to reconcile with Adrienne, the cataleptic acts started again as before. Such phenomena are far from rare, and I have observed them in several other subjects.

These resistances of the secondary personage help us to understand more easily its spontaneous acts, as I have been obliged to note in similar cases. Another subject, Léonie, had learned to read and write fairly well, and I had taken advantage of her new knowledge to have her write a few words or a few lines unconsciously the previous day. But I had sent her away without suggesting anything more. She had left for Le Havre more than two months prior when I received the most singular letter from her. On the first page was a brief letter, written in a serious tone: she was indisposed, she said, "suffering more each day than the next, etc.," and she signed with her real name, "Woman B." However, on the other side began another letter in a completely different style (which I was permitted to copy by way of a curiosity): "My dear good sir. I am here to tell you that Léonie – true, all too true – is making me suffer a lot. She cannot sleep. She is really hurting me. I am going to destroy her. She annoys me. I am sick also and very tired. All this is from your devoted Léontine." When Léonie returned from Le Havre, I naturally asked her about this strange missive. She had kept a very precise memory of the *first letter* and could still repeat the contents. She remembered sealing it in the envelope and even details of the address, which she had written with difficulty, but she had no memory of the *second letter*. I can explain this forgetting: neither the familiarity of the letter, nor the freedom of style, nor the expressions used, nor, especially, the signature, belonged to Léonie in her waking state. On the contrary, all this belonged to the unconscious personage who had already manifested itself to me by many other acts. At first, I thought there had been a spontaneous somnambulistic attack between the time she finished the first letter and the time she sealed the envelope. The secondary personage of the somnambulism, who knew the interest I took in Léonie and the way in which I often healed her from her nervous crises, would have appeared for a moment to call to me for help. The situation was already very strange, but since then, these subconscious and spontaneous letters have multiplied, and I have been able to study their formation better. Fortunately, I was able to surprise Léonie once when she was performing the following singular operation. She was near a table and still held the knitting she had just worked on. Her face was very calm, eyes looking up in the air with a little fixedness. But she did not appear to be experiencing a cataleptic attack; she sang a country round in a low voice, while the right hand wrote briskly and almost secretly. I began by removing the paper without her noticing and spoke to her. She turned around, immediately awake, but a little surprised, because, in her state of distraction, she had not heard me enter. "I spent the day knitting", she said, "and I sang because I thought I was alone." She had no knowledge of the paper she had been writing on. Everything had happened exactly as we have seen with unconscious acts by distraction, the difference being that no suggestion had been made.

This form of subconscious phenomena is not as easy to study as the others. Being spontaneous, it cannot be subjected to regular experimentation. Here are just a few comments that chance has allowed me to make. First of all, the secondary personage who writes these letters is intelligent in its spontaneous manifestations (as in its provoked manifestations). In what it writes, a great deal of memory is in play (a letter that was written told the story of Léonie's childhood). It shows common sense in ordinary remarks. The following is an example of unconscious insight (as Richet would say): the subconscious person one day noticed that the conscious person, Léonie, was tearing up paper that was left within her reach, and which she had just written during a period of distraction. How could they be preserved safely? Taking advantage of a longer period of distraction, she began her letter again, and put it in a photography album. This album, in fact, formerly contained a photograph of Gibert, who, by association of ideas, was connected with putting Léonie into a state of catalepsy. I had previously taken the precaution of having this photograph removed when Léonie was in the house, but the album nevertheless retained a sort of terrifying influence on her. The secondary person-age was therefore sure that her letters, if placed in the album, would not be dis-covered by Léonie. I must emphasize that all this reasoning was not done in a state of somnambulism, but in the waking state and subconsciously. Distracted, Léonie sang or daydreamed, while her limbs, obeying, in some form, a foreign will, thus took precautions against herself. In this way, the second personage thus benefits from all of her periods of distraction. Léonie walks alone in the streets and reck-lessly abandons herself to her reveries; when she looks around, she is very sur-prised to find herself in a completely different part of the city. *The other* thought it a good idea to bring her to my door. If we inform her by letter that she can return to Le Havre, she finds herself there without knowing how it came about. The other, being eager to arrive, made her leave as quickly as possible and without the benefit of luggage. Finally, let us add, as a final remark, that these subconscious and spontaneous acts have yet another trait which resembles intended acts: they introduce into normal consciousness a particular void, a systematic anesthesia. Since Léonie often came to my house, I assumed that she knew my address. I was very surprised, when, one day, while chatting with her during the waking state, I discovered that she was completely ignorant of it; furthermore, she did not know the neighborhood at all. The second personage having taken all these notions to herself, the first seemed no longer able to possess them.

We cannot finish this study on the development of the subconscious personal-ity without recalling a fact already pointed out which should need no emphasis: subconscious acts and latent sensations can exist during somnambulism, as well as during the waking state and can at any time develop in the form of a personal-ity. Sometimes it will present the same characteristics as during the previous day, as happens with Lucie, and sometimes it will be quite different, as happens with Léonie. These possible complications should not be overlooked.

We have called attention to these productions of a new psychological exist-ence, one no longer alternating with the normal existence of the subject, but absolutely simultaneous with it. Knowledge of this kind is indeed essential in understanding the behavior of neuropaths and that of the mentally deranged. In this chapter, we have only studied typical or generalized cases of this duplication, in order to see it in the simplest context and to be able to recognize it later, when the cases become more complex. We believe that this notion is important in the study of pathological psychology, and it is not lacking in significance from a philosophical point of view. We have grown accustomed to acknowledging quite easily the successive variations of personality. The memories and the character which form the personality can change without altering the idea of the self, which endures through every moment of existence. We believe it is necessary to reveal even more of the true nature of the metaphysical person and to consider the very idea of personal unity as a manifestation which can undergo modifications. Philosophical systems will certainly be able to accommodate these new facts, because they seek to express the reality of things, and one expression of the truth cannot contradict another.

2.8 Simultaneous psychological existences compared to successive psychological existences

By studying, in certain subjects, this second personality, below normal consciousness, which has revealed itself to us, we cannot help feeling a certain astonishment. We do not know how to explain the rapid and sometimes sudden development of this second consciousness. If it results, as we have supposed, from the grouping of images that have remained outside normal perception, how could this systematization have been achieved so quickly? The second person has a character, preferences, whims, and performs spontaneous actions. How, in a few moments, did it acquire all this? Our astonishment will cease once we realize that this form of consciousness and personality has not come into existence at this moment for the first time. We have observed it before and should have no trouble recognizing an old acquaintance: it is quite simply the personage of somnambulism which manifests itself in this new way during the waking state.

It is memory which establishes the continuity of the psychological life. Memory is what allowed us to form the notion of various somnambulic states; it is also what will make more accessible the subconscious existence which manifests during the waking state of the subject, and the alternating existence which characterizes somnambulism. In fact, we can demonstrate (1) that subconscious phenomena occurring during the waking state contain the memories acquired during somnambulism, and (2) that during somnambulism we discover the memory of all these actions and all these subconscious sensations.

(1) This point should already be considered as demonstrated by the study we made of posthypnotic suggestions. The subject sometimes performs all suggestions without knowing it, as we saw Lucie do, but in other cases, she makes, as needed, all the calculations and all the distinctions necessary to correctly execute what has been ordered. When the suggestion is linked to a reference point, it is the unconscious person who keeps the memory of the signal: "You told me to do such a thing when the clock strikes," Lucie automatically

wrote after waking from somnambulism. It is also what recognizes the signal, which the normal person does not take note of. "There is a stain on the top left corner of this paper," writes Adrienne about the portrait experiment. It is what combines the processes in these unconscious deceptions, something so peculiar that Bergson wrote about it.[44] When there is a calculation to do, it is still this same personage who does it, who counts the noises that I make with my hands, or completes the additions I ordered. Lucie's automatic writing affirms this over and over. Gurney[45] recounts that he had ordered a subject to perform an act in ten days and that he followed it up the next day by means of the spiritist planchette (a process which is, in my opinion, useless, but which the English almost always use to evoke automatic writing). This subject, who consciously did not remember the suggestion, wrote, without knowing it, that it was still necessary to wait nine days. The next day he wrote that he would perform the action in eight days. I repeated the experiment and got a different result – but one just as demonstrative. I suggested to Rose, during somnambulism, that she write me a letter in forty-two days, and then I woke her up. The next day, without going back to sleep, I asked her (using the procedure already described for distraction) when she would write to me. I thought she would write, as Gurney's subject had, "in forty-one days", but she simply wrote: "October 2". And, in fact, she was right; that date would occur in forty-two days, and the subconscious personage had done the math. My suggestion had become a simple suggestion with an unconscious reference point, which, moreover, was executed very correctly.

When it is necessary to suppress the sight of an object from the conscious personage (in the experiments of negative hallucination or systemized anesthesia), it is still our second personage who takes care of it. It takes for itself the awareness of this object, of which it holds the memory, and, consequently, prevents the primary personage from gathering these sensations in her ordinary perception. Here is an example which summarizes all these phenomena. I ordered Lucie one evening, during the somnambulistic state, to come the next day at three o'clock to Doctor Powilewicz's house. She arrived in fact the next day around half past three. But as she spoke to me upon entering, she seemed to experience a singular hallucination; she thought she was at home, took the office furniture for hers, and maintained that she had not left the house that day. Adrienne, when I questioned her, answered quite sensibly in writing that, following my order, she had dressed at three o'clock, that she had gone out and that she knew very well where she was. The memory of the suggestion, the recognition of the signal, the controlled act, the systematic anesthesia – everything depended on the second personage, who fulfilled my orders during the waking state (below the conscious person), as she would have done during somnambulism. In a word, posthypnotic suggestions establish a clear link between the first somnambulism and the second simultaneous existence.

However, suggestions form only a small part of the memories of somnambulism, and subconscious writing recalls the memory of all other incidents. Here is an easy-to-repeat experiment that Gurney[46] describes. During the somnambulistic state, he talks with a subject and tells her a story; then he wakes her up completely. At this moment, the subject has completely lost the memory of what was said, but if she puts her hand on the "planchette" and lets it write – seemingly at random – we will find the complete story on paper which the subject claims to have no knowledge of and which she cannot recall, even if she is offered a gold piece to do so. Here are some similar events. During various experiments, I had asked N, while she was in somnambulism, to make some small drawings in pencil, and she had sketched a house, a small boat with a sail, and a figure in profile, with a long nose. When she woke up, she had no memory of it at all and talked about something else entirely; but her hand, which held the pencil, began to draw on the paper without her knowledge. N ends up noticing the drawing and, picking up the paper, says to me: "Here, look at what I have drawn: a house, a boat, and a head with a long nose; what made me draw this?" While V was somnambulistic, I made her see a small dog sitting on her lap, and she had stroked it with great joy. When she was awakened, I noticed that she performed a strange movement with her right hand, which seemed to caress something on her lap. She had to go back to sleep to remove the idea of the little dog, which persisted in the second consciousness. We made a mistake to speak of spiritism in Léonie's presence while she was in somnambulism. When she awoke, she carried over various subconscious movements, trembling of the hand, as if she wanted to write, and singular movements of the head and eyes that seemed to be looking for something under the furniture. The second person was still thinking of the spirits. There is no need to cite other examples; it suffices to recall that with a subject presenting a high degree of automatic writing, like Lucie, one can continue by this means, during the waking state, all the conversations started during somnambulism.

We have already found that during somnambulism itself, the subject can sometimes recover the memory of certain states that have been forgotten during waking, and yet remain distinct from the hypnotic state: the memory of certain dreams, some delusions and sometimes hysterical crises. Furthermore, we are not surprised that subconscious writing also holds these memories. While Léonie has forgotten her natural somnambulism, her nightmares, and her crises when she is awake, Adrienne, through automatic writing, will tell us about all these incidents. This is a completely natural fact following, very simply, from the preceding phenomenon that I have been making a point of.

Another consequence of this kind of memory is that the subconscious person fully possesses the character and mannerisms which characterize the somnambulism itself. The subjects, when they write unconsciously, use the same names which they have taken in previous hypnotic states: Adrienne, Léontine, Nichette, etc. If the unconscious acts or the partial catalepsy can only be provoked by me with Lucie or Léonie, it is because, being asleep in a second state, they also obey only me. Finally, the nature of the intelligence during somnambulism has a most powerful influence on the nature of the unconscious act. Lem has no memory during somnambulism, so she cannot execute post-hypnotic suggestions when they are supposed to happen. The unconscious acts of N are childish, as is the very character of N or Nichette. However, since she has a great deal of memory, these unconscious acts can be obtained at any time and are very clear and accurate. Here is another curious observation, one made by chance. In the first studies I had done on N, I had found a very great capacity for suggestions by distraction in the waking state. I had finished these experiments and did not see this person for several months. When I saw her again, I wanted to try these same suggestions without somnambulism, but they did not have the same result as before. The subject, who was talking to another person, did not turn around when I ordered something and seemed not to hear me: there was, therefore, the full systematic anesthesia necessary for the subconscious act, yet the act was not executed. I then had to put the subject to sleep, but even in somnambulism, the behaviour of N remained so singular that I no longer recognized the characters I had studied some time before. The subject heard me poorly or did not understand what I said: "What is happening to you today?" I finally said to her. "I can't hear you, I'm too far away," she replied. "And where are you?" I asked. "I'm in Algiers, in a large square; you have to bring me back." The return was not difficult; we are familiar with these somnambulist journeys by hallucination. When she returned, she sighed in relief, straightened up and began to speak as before. "Will you explain to me now," I said, "what you were doing in Algiers?" "It is not my fault; it was Mr. X who sent me there a month ago; he forgot to bring me back; he left me there ... Earlier you tried to order me, to make me raise my arm," (it was the suggestion I had tried to make the day before). "I was too far away, I could not obey." I verified this singular story. It was true, another person had put this subject to sleep in the interval between my experiments and had caused various hallucinations (among others, that of a trip to Algiers). Not attaching enough importance to these phenomena, the subject had been awakened without removing the hallucination. N, the person awake, had remained apparently normal, but the subconscious personage preserved the more or less latent hallucination of being in Algiers. When therefore, without previous somnambulism, I wanted to give her commands, she heard but did not think she should obey. Once the hallucination was suppressed, everything occurred as it had done before. A change in intelligence during that somnambulism showed itself, even two months later, with a corresponding change in subconscious acts, just as Lucie 2's anger during somnambulism was displayed, upon awakening, by a bad mood manifested through automatic writing.

(2) Another consideration, to which we will now turn, brings these two states even closer. *Subconscious acts have some kind of hypnotic effect and themselves contribute to bringing about somnambulism.* I had already noted that two subjects in particular, Lucie and Léonie, in spite of my efforts, frequently fell asleep in the middle of experiments on unconscious acts in the waking

state; but I had related this sleep to my mere presence and their habit of somnambulism. The following circumstances helped me correct my mistake.
Binet had been kind enough to show me one of the subjects with whom he
studied subconscious acts by anesthesia, and I had asked his permission to
reproduce the suggestions by distraction on this subject. The experiment went
exactly according to my expectation: the subject, Hab, fully awake, chatted
with Binet. I stood behind her, moved her hand without her knowledge, had
her write a few words, answer my questions by signs, etc. Suddenly, Hab
stopped talking to Binet and, turning to me, eyes closed, continued by *conscious speech* the conversation that she had started with me through *subconscious signs*. On the other hand, she no longer spoke to Binet at all, she no
longer heard him, in a word, she had fallen into elective somnambulism. We
had to wake up the subject who naturally forgot everything when she woke
up. Now Hab did not know me at all, so it was not my presence that had put
her to sleep. Sleep in this instance was therefore the result of the development of subconscious phenomena, which had invaded and then erased normal
consciousness. Moreover, this fact is easily verified. Léonie stays awake in
my presence as long as I do not provoke phenomena of this kind; but when
these become too numerous and too complicated, she falls asleep. This rather
important observation explains to us a detail (which we had previously noted,
without understanding it), in the execution of the posthypnotic suggestions.
As long as they are simple, Léonie executes them without her knowledge,
while talking about something else. When they are long and complicated, the
subject speaks less and less while performing them, ends up falling asleep
and performs them quickly in full somnambulism. The posthypnotic suggestion is sometimes executed in a second somnambulism, not because one has
suggested to the subject to go back to sleep, but because the memory of this
suggestion and the execution itself form a subconscious life so analogous to
somnambulism that, in some cases, it produces it completely.

The subject is once again in a state of somnambulism: now we will show yet
another method which demonstrates an analogy between the states we are comparing. Most authors have noted that the subject *performs posthypnotic suggestions* upon waking, without knowing who made the suggestion and that, *in a new
somnambulism, this memory returns*.[47] It would be very easy to believe that the
subject only remembers an order received during a preceding somnambulism and
that there is only one memory transferring from one somnambulism to the other,
suggestions which are executed unconsciously, but whose execution has been
characterized by a small unforeseen detail. We see that the subject, when again
put to sleep, has a complete memory of these acts which have not been known to
normal consciousness. There is no need to cite examples: one has only to remember the posthypnotic suggestions we have spoken of, which were characterized by
unconsciousness during the waking state. When I put them to sleep again, all the
subjects repeat what they did to obey me and the various incidents which characterized the execution of my commands.

All that I have just stated applies entirely *to spontaneous subconscious acts*, in particular to those of Léonie. *In somnambulism, in the state of Léonie 2, she maintains a perfect memory.* In the letter which I referred to, there was a section that the waking subject had no knowledge of which was signed with the name Léontine. We now understand what this name meant: this is how she designates herself during the somnambulistic state. She could indeed tell me in this state that she had wanted to write to me to warn me of the illness of *the other*, and recited the contents of the letter to me. Besides, excellent proof that the acts of this type are indeed the actions of Léonie 2 is that (as we have said) the subject can fall asleep during their accomplishment: the same acts are then continued during the somnambulism without modification. I once surprised Léonie, writing a letter unconsciously (in the way I have described) and I was able to put her to sleep without interrupting her; Léonie 2 then continued her letter with much more vigor.

It is pointless to describe this phenomenon of memory in other subjects, because it remains absolutely identical. But I will now move on to a very important point. Certain subjects, like N, have, from the beginning of somnambulism, the memory of all the subconscious acts of the day before, whatever they are, even those which were obtained by anesthesia or by distraction. The subject Gurney often talks about was of this type, "Once she has written a phrase automatically with the planchette, she has no knowledge of it in the waking state, but, asleep, she almost always recalls it without error."[48] It should not be assumed that all subjects do this, because we would soon encounter a number of exceptions to the rule. Lucie does not find in the first somnambulism any memory of her subconscious acts. Léonie, Rose and Marie find in this same state only the memory of a certain number of acts of this kind.

When this occurs during somnambulism, a subject does not find the memory of subconscious acts from the day before. We should point out that these acts still exist in the same way and that consciousness continues to present the same duplication. Partial catalepsy on the left side and unconscious acts by distraction still exist in Léonie during the first somnambulism. In addition, these acts seem to remain associated with the acts that occurred the day before and which were not remembered. With Lucie, the subconscious personage, writing in the waking state, signed her letters with the name of Adrienne. She still signs them with the same name during somnambulism, and she continues to show, in these letters, the same knowledge and the same memories. If I order Léonie in the waking state to carry out an action during a distraction and without her knowledge, she is still unaware of it during somnambulism. But if, during this very state, I take advantage of a distraction to order her to perform "the same act as earlier," without specifying further, this act is very exactly reproduced, but still unbeknownst to Léonie 2, as it was a short time ago with Léonie 1. When I make this unconscious state, which seems to still exist, communicate either by signs or by automatic writing, it can very accurately relate all the other unconscious acts which are still unknown. It therefore seems that, in this subject, the subconscious acts and the images on which they depend make, below somnambulism, a new synthesis of phenomena, a new psychic existence, just as somnambulic life itself existed below the waking state.

When this is the case, the subject must be put to sleep more deeply, because the persistence of subconscious acts as well as anesthesia indicates that there are deeper somnambulisms. We know these various somnambulistic states, which one obtains sometimes by imperceptible gradations, sometimes by sudden jumps through lethargic or cataleptic states. *Each new state of somnambulism brings with it the memory of a number of these subconscious acts.* Léonie 3 is the first to remember and attribute certain acts to herself. "While the *other* was speaking," she says about an unconscious act in the waking state, "you told her to take out her watch. I pulled it out for her, but she didn't want to check the time ." "While she was chatting with M," she said about an unconscious act of somnambulism, "you told me to make bouquets. I made two. I did this and that …" and she repeats all the gestures that I had described and which had been completely ignored during the previous states. Léonie 3 also remembers actions which were carried out during a complete catalepsy which, in this subject, precedes the second somnambulism. It is to this memory that we alluded to at the beginning of this work[49], which shows that the actions taken in this state were not absolutely devoid of consciousness. In the first somnambulism, Lucie, who had absolutely no recollection of subconscious acts, nor of the personage of Adrienne, takes up these memories in the most complete way in her second somnambulism. We must therefore not deny the relationship between successive existences and simultaneous existences because the subject in the first somnambulism does not immediately find the memory of certain subconscious acts. It is often enough to be put to sleep more deeply for memory to be complete.

Moreover, these facts are easily understood, if we reflect on the conditions already studied for the return of memory. The memory of an act is linked to the sensitivity which enabled its execution; it disappears with it and remains subconscious as long as it is not linked to normal perception. It reappears when this sensitivity itself is restored. Here is an example. While Léonie is awake, I put a pair of scissors in her left hand, which is anesthetic; the fingers enter the rings, and open and close the scissors alternately. This act obviously depends on the tactile sensation of the scissors, and it is unconscious because this sensation is disaggregated, it exists apart and is not synthesized in the normal perception of Léonie at this time. I put the subject to sleep and I see that, in this new state, she is still anesthetic in the left arm. It is therefore natural that the memory of the previous act did not reappear and remains outside of personal consciousness. I put the subject in another state, she has regained the sensitivity of the left arm and now remembers the action she just did with the scissors. This is a new application, but one which is easy to predict, based on the studies we have done on memory. In this case, several simultaneous subconscious personalities are formed, just as several successive somnambulisms have previously formed.

I will add to this remark a well-known fact: when a suggestion has been given to a subject in a particular somnambulism, it can only be removed if the subject is brought back to exactly the same somnambulism. If I made a command to Léonie 3, I would not remove it by speaking to Léonie 2, or to Léonie 1. Why is that? Because my command is part of a certain group, of a certain system of psychological phenomena which has its own life apart from the other psychological systems which exist in the mind of this individual. To modify my command, we must begin by reaching the group of phenomena of which it is a part, because we do not change an order given to A by speaking to B. Sometimes these subconscious psychological systems, formed apart from personal perception, are few in number, two with Lucie or Léonie, one with Marie, three or four with Rose. Sometimes they are (I believe) very numerous. The somnambulisms of a subject are almost never the same. They change, especially when they are produced by different experimenters. I would explain in this way the misadventures of a somnambulist described by Pitres.[50] A witless joker had put her to sleep and had suggested to her that she desired to embrace the chaplain of the hospital, then woke her up and left. The suggestion tormented this unhappy woman in the most abominable way, but no one could manage to remove it from her, even when she was put into hypnotic sleep. The problem was that no one else could reproduce the same hypnotic sleep. The group of psychic phenomena which had received the suggestion always remained outside the state of consciousness which could be provoked and continued to act in the direction it had taken. This remark, *which shows us different subconscious existences as different somnambulisms*, does not have much theoretical importance, but is often very useful in practice.

These relations between subconscious and simultaneous existences on the one hand, and the various successive somnambulisms on the other, are obviously complicated and perhaps, despite all my efforts, difficult to understand. So I had tried in the past[51] to represent these facts by a schematic figure which unfortunately did not seem very clear, perhaps because I had tried to bring in too many elements. Let us now try to represent the result of these observations in a different and, I hope, simpler way. The conscious life of one of these subjects, of Lucie for example, seems to consist of three parallel currents, one under the other. When the subject is awake, the three currents exist: the first is the normal consciousness of the subject who is speaking to us, the other two are groups of sensations and acts more or less associated with each other, but absolutely unknown by the person who speaks to us. When the subject is asleep in first somnambulism, the first current is interrupted and the second comes to light, it shows itself in broad daylight and lets us see the memories it has acquired during its underground life. If we pass on to the second somnambulism, the second current is interrupted in its turn, to leave the third which then forms the whole conscious life of the individual, in which we see neither anesthesia nor subconscious acts. Upon awakening, the higher currents reappear in reverse order. It would unnecessarily complicate the figure to represent other subjects who have more numerous somnambulic states, natural somnambulisms, crises of hysteria, etc., but the general arrangement would, I believe, remain the same (Figure 2.7).

| *Waking* | *Somnabulism* | *Waking* | *Somnabulism* | *Waking* |

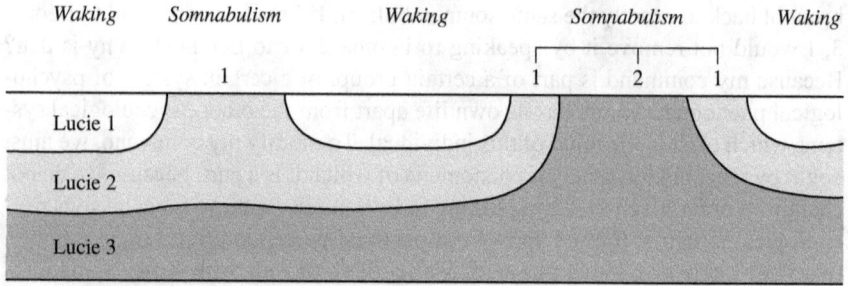

Figure 2.7 Relationships among Lucie's three personalities.

2.9 Relative importance of various simultaneous existences

A truth should never be exaggerated; otherwise it will turn into an error. That subconscious life resembles somnambulistic life – this much is obvious. That it is absolutely identical to somnambulism and can be assimilated to it – this is what we cannot admit. Léonie 2, the somnambulistic, talkative, petulant, child-like character, cannot exist with active influence below Léonie 1, this elderly woman who is calm and silent. This mixture would lead to perpetual delirium. In addition, the somnambulistic personage who possesses the absent sensibili-ties would supplement the normal personage and would leave it without any visible paralysis. Here is an example that my brother shared with me on the subject. A hysteric with anesthetic legs, Witt, presses her feet on a hot water bottle and, feeling nothing, does not realize that the water is too hot and burns her feet. This subject, however, contained a second personality which mani-fested itself perfectly through subconscious signs or in deep somnambulism and which possessed tactile sensitivity. When questioned, this second personage claimed to have felt the pain quite well. "Well, then, why didn't you pull your legs away?" She answered "I do not know."[52] It is obvious that the second per-sonage, who possesses the tactile sensitivity of the legs, could not have existed during the waking state in the same way as in profound somnambulism. In a word, the second personality does not always exist in the same way, and the connections or the proportions between the different psychological existences must be extremely variable.

To examine these variations, we can begin with an initial definite point: *The state of perfect psychological health: here, the power of synthesis being very great, all psychological phenomena, whatever their origin, are united in the same personal perception*, and therefore the second personality does not exist. In such a state, there would be no distraction, no anesthesia (systematic or general), no suggestibility and no possibility of producing somnambulism, since one cannot develop subconscious phenomena which do not exist. Most normal people are far from regularly being in such a state of mental health, and, as for our subjects, they very seldom are so.

However, for more than eighteen months, Lucie has remained without anesthesia, without suggestibility, and unreceptive to being hypnotized. Marie is now in a similar period, I do not know for how long. It is a relative state of health.

When this perfect health does not exist, *the power of psychic synthesis is weakened and lets escape, outside personal perception, quite a considerable number of psychological phenomena: it is the state of disaggregation.* I do not call this the hysterical state, although this state exists constantly during hysteria, because I believe that the state of disaggregation is something more general than hysteria and that it can still exist in many other circumstances. Disaggregation can be the moment of distractions, of systematized anesthesias, of general anesthesias, and of suggestions consciously executed by the subject. But these disaggregated phenomena remain incoherent, so isolated that, except for a few which still carry very simple reflexes, they have, for the most part, no influence on the behaviour of the individual. It is as if they did not exist. When Witt burned her feet, there were phenomena of pain somewhere within her, but so elementary, isolated, and incoherent that they could at most cause some convulsive contractions here and there, but could not direct an overall coordinated movement, like pulling away the legs. It is in this state that our subjects most often remain, when we do not take care of them and especially when they have not been put to sleep for a long time.

The only changes that occur naturally in this state are the various distributions of anesthesia. Thus, for example, Marie for several months oscillated between three forms of anesthesia. (1) She was most often hemi-anesthetic on the left. The body is divided into two parts by a vertical line passing through the middle. On the right, all the general or special sensitivities are preserved. On the left, the sensations of all the senses have disappeared. (2) After remaining fifteen days or three weeks in this first state, she often passes, for no apparent reason, into a second. The body is still hemi-anesthetic, but in another way: the body is divided into two parts by a horizontal line passing a little above the breasts, at the level of the shoulders. The entire lower part is absolutely anesthetic; the entire upper part including the head and the special sensitivities (except for particular reasons, the left eye and temple) regain a complete sensitivity. (3) Often the anesthesia changes its state again and is felt for a while all over the body, but in an extremely crude manner; as if the same amount of sensitivity was distributed by halving on a double surface. Other subjects will be able to distribute their sensitivity by other means, by choosing within each sense to perceive certain distinct impressions and by abandoning the others. We have seen that electivity and distraction are forms of the narrowing of the field of consciousness and of psychic disaggregation, like anesthesia itself. These are some of the variations which the state of disaggregation left to itself will naturally present.

If the person who puts the subjects to sleep approaches them, they experience a very particular emotion which causes them to feel a change within their consciousness. This is because the subconscious and disaggregated phenomena have grouped under this excitement, have gained strength, and have even robbed normal consciousness of some phenomena of which it had hitherto retained ownership. The anesthesia has increased: Lucie, who previously heard everyone, can no longer hear me. "I see your lips moving," she says, "but I cannot hear what you are saying." Here the subconscious personage who has formed took my words at that time for itself. Suggestibility also increased, but it was exercised in two ways: sometimes provoking the conscious acts of the first personage, sometimes the acts of the second (ignored by the first). It is a moment of partial catalepsy, suggestions by distraction, and automatic writing. It is the state in which spiritists are so delighted to see their mediums, so that they can evoke spirits through disaggregated phenomena. This state corresponds fairly well, it seems to me, to that which has already been described under the name of *somno-vigil* or *somnambulistic waking*.[53] We criticized the name, saying it was not a waking state. It is obvious that, if we understand by the word waking an absolutely normal psychological state, the subject is not in a normal waking state. When we are awake, we are not in the habit of walking or writing without being aware of it, but it should not be concluded that the subject is in a state of complete hypnotic sleep. Beaunis[54] presents very good proof; it is that there is continuity of memory between the normal waking state and what is spoken by the subject in this state. The subject will remember imperfectly a part of what was done and so has been at least partially in a waking state. But the other part of her being, the existence and characteristics of which we have superabundantly shown and which is now manifest, is indeed in somnambulism, as evidenced by another continuity of memories that we have just studied. But here again the somnambulistic state is not complete. The second personage has a little hearing which it has taken from the first, it feels the touch and the movements; but it does not see, at least not ordinarily, it does not move very easily, and above all it does not speak, or does so with great difficulty – all things that were possible during complete somnambulism. It is therefore a half-somnambulism, like a half-waking, and Richet had obviously found the right word, which we will adopt to designate this state. He called it a *hemi-somnambulism*.[55]

The above state is a transient and, so to speak, fragile state which oscillates between a more perfect wakefulness and a complete somnambulism.

If we stimulate these systems of subconscious ideas a little more, or make the first faltering personality disappear by means of some kind of fatigue, we come to true somnambulism. The first personality no longer exists, but the second has enriched itself with its spoils. It has now taken, in addition to the phenomena which were its own, those which belonged to the other synthesis. She sees, she moves, she speaks when she wants to. She remembers her previous humble existence: "It was I who did this, who felt this," but she does not understand how she could neither move nor act just now, because she is not aware of the change that has happened. After somnambulism, the first personality reappears and the second retreats without disappearing completely. It persists for a while, depending on its strength and the posthypnotic suggestions which have been made to it. It rises from time to time to accomplish them, then it retreats still more to occupy the small space that the anesthesia leaves for it during the state of disaggregation, which is now restored. If the return to health were complete, it would disappear entirely and there would be a new restoration of the psychic unity, which would undoubtedly take place around another center, but which would be analogous, in the extent of the field of consciousness and independence, to complete somnambulism. Let us try, in a new figure a little less systemized than the previous one, to represent these relative ranges of the various personalities, supposing for simplicity that there are only two (Figure 2.8).

The problem with the relationship between the successive secondary personality during somnambulism and the simultaneous secondary personality during the waking state can present itself in a more precise manner and take a particular form. We know that, during complete somnambulism, the second person has memory not only from her own actions during previous somnambulisms, or from acts she did during hemi-somnambulism below the primary consciousness, but even from actions consciously accomplished during the waking state by the first person, by "the other," as the somnambulists say. Since this somnambulistic personality already exists during hemi-somnambulism beneath the awareness of the waking state, is it not natural that it already has, at this moment, the knowledge of the acts performed above it by the ordinary personality? I had been struck by this reasoning, and, in my first articles on this subject, I had admitted, as a kind of law, that the first personality was completely unaware of the second, acting beneath it, but that the latter knew the first very well. I even used this law to explain the memory of the waking state during somnambulism. Gurney, who soon after this published studies on the same problem, recognized this law, but began to express some reservations.[56] "In many cases," he said, "it is not at all clear that the second personality has an exact knowledge of the first when it acts above it." Not only do I now recognize the accuracy of Gurney's exceptions, but I am prepared to add to them.

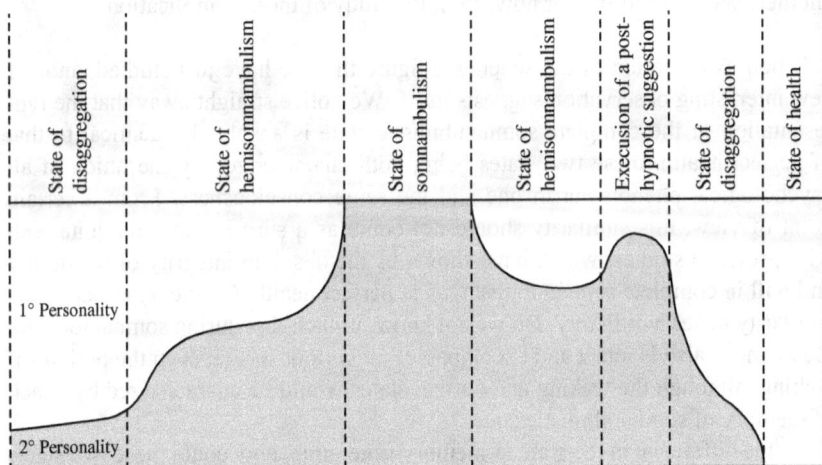

Figure 2.8 Extended relationships among different existences.

We must not give in to the illusion which leads us to identify the second personality during somnambulism with the second subconscious personality during hemisomnambulism. It has, in the first state, when it is complete, knowledge and memories as a consequence of the sensitivities which it has recovered. It has the memory of acts during the waking state because it has taken up the sensitivities of the waking state in addition to its own. But when it was rudimentary or imperfect alongside normal consciousness, it did not have these sensitivities and must not have had complete knowledge of what the first personage was doing. When Lucie 1 or Lucie 2, for example, exist simultaneously, they generally act each in their own way, and they are unaware of each other. If one knew the other, if the images of the tactile sense were associated with the images of the visual sense, a common consciousness for the benefit of one of the two persons would be reconstituted, which does not seem to take place.

When we want to verify these things, one of the great challenges to observation is that it is not possible to question the second personality on any fact, without thereby giving it knowledge and taking away from the primary personality. "The subconscious personage, however," said Gurney,[57] "now hears the signals and describes objects from the outside world that we ask it to talk about." No doubt, but it is easy to verify, for at that moment, the first personality is unaware of these signals and no longer sees these objects. When the normal self continues to actually see something, it is not at all certain that the abnormal self also sees it at the same time. We no longer dare to conclude, as Gurney has, that there is a difference between the two personalities and that one knows the other without being known by it. The situation must be the same for both.

It should not be forgotten, moreover, that in this chapter, we are discussing only the simplest sort of disaggregation, the most theoretical kind, one might say. It is easy enough to observe a very large number of variations and complications in which the two personages can more or less know each other and react to one another. We will refrain, for now, from the study of these complications.

Upon examination of the schematic figure that we have just studied, another new interesting observation suggests itself. We notice straight away that the representation of the complete somnambulistic state is absolutely identical to that of perfect health, these two states being both characterized by the union of all psychological phenomena in one and the same consciousness. From a certain point of view, this similarity should not come as a surprise and fits quite well with previous studies, which have shown us the absolute integrity of sensitivity and will in complete somnambulism, as in perfect health. On the other hand, this similarity raises a difficulty. Do we not know, in fact, that during somnambulism, the memory also is intact and encompasses all periods of life, even the periods of waking, although the waking and normal states would be characterized by a lack of memory of somnambulistic states?

If this difference in the state of memory is genuine, how could these two states of complete somnambulism and perfect health be identical? When two psychological states are absolutely alike, memory must be reciprocal.

Well, maybe it really is; maybe the state of perfect health, when it exists, brings about the complete memory of somnambulism itself. If our subjects, after awakening, do not keep the memory of their somnambulism, it is because they do not return to a state of perfect health and they maintain anesthesia and more or less visible distractions. If they recovered radically, if they widened their field of consciousness to the point of definitively embracing in their personal perception all the images, they should find all the memories which depend on them and remember completely even their periods of crisis or somnambulism. I must say that I have never observed this return of memory. This remark is based on the examination of a schematic figure and on reasoning more than on experience. Perhaps something like this could have been seen during the periods when Lucie *seemed* completely healed; but this idea had not occurred to me at the time, nor had I researched the subject. I also believe that it would have had a negative result. I never saw these hysterical people regain the memory of their second existence after their apparent healing. Perhaps these women, who are still young and in whom slight signs of hysteria reappear from time to time, are never sufficiently healed for this phenomenon to manifest.

If observation does not inform us on this point, history may provide us with some indications. We know of the misadventures of a subject who was famous during the greatest debates provoked by the study of animal magnetism. For several years, a woman named Pétronille, who was a patient at the Salpêtrière, had presented all the phenomena of somnambulism (clearly and well observed), as well as forgetfulness on waking. Much later, in her old age, this woman, released from the hospital, pretended to make a confession and claimed to have all along simulated all the phenomena of somnambulism. To prove her claim, she recounted all that she had been made to do during the alleged sleeps and regained all the memories. This fact caused quite a stir and was the occasion of many triumphant taunts against the magnetizers. Even today, some rather superficial authors, who see in all nervous phenomena – somnambulism, hysteria, and perhaps even epilepsy – as pure comedies, repeat from time to time, like a "delenda Carthago", this solemn warning to hypnotists: "Cave Pétronille."

Similar facts are also found in the history of spiritism, which we will speak of soon. The Fox sisters, who were, in 1848, the occasion for the development of all American spiritism, now grown old, mock, it seems,[58] their old exploits and claim to have always faked their unconscious movements and their conversations with the spirits. In reality, whether Pétronille was sincere or not, whether the Fox sisters in 1848 had real hysterical symptoms and real automatic movements, or whether they exploited a lucrative hoax, is quite indifferent to us. We might even point out that one can hardly accept the testimony of a sixty-year-old woman when she claims to explain the feelings she had at eighteen. She is no longer the same person and is no longer able to understand her own youth. She can very well now accuse herself of a deception which was never committed to explain things for which the memory has returned and which she cannot interpret otherwise.

Might these phenomena, in fact, be understood from another perspective? Is it not possible that at sixty, hysteria and the mental disaggregation that existed at twenty has completely disappeared and that the fully reconstituted mind has recovered all the images, as during a complete somnambulism? Phenomena of this kind would justify the theoretical comparison that we have been led to, between the state of health and the state of somnambulism. But it is useless to discuss further on facts so ancient and so little known. Perhaps those who have been able to follow hysterics for a very long time have been able to make similar observations on this complete return of memories after the disappearance of the disease. It would be interesting to bring them together. They would provide a curious insight into the complete healing of hysteria and confirm the hypotheses that we have made on distinct psychological existences in the same individual.

Leaving aside these problems, the solution of which is still doubtful, we can conclude with this remark. Psychological disaggregation leads to unequal groupings of thought whose relative importance is constantly changing. The state of perfect wakefulness and the state of complete somnambulism are two extremes: between them are many degrees in which the various existences coexist in shifting proportions.

The study of nervous diseases made great progress when it was proven that a woman is not only sick when she has her hysterical attacks, but is always hysterical, even in the intervals between her seizures. It is necessary to make similar progress in the study of somnambulism. It must be admitted that an individual does not choose to become a somnambulist when she wants, for a few moments, then, after waking, it is all over. Rather a subject is hypnotizable because she was in some way already a somnambulist and continues to be so after waking, sometimes for quite a long time. *The simultaneous psychological existences, which we were obliged to admit in order to understand these anesthesias, are due to this more or less constant persistence of the somnambulic state during the waking state.*

2.10 Anesthesia and paralysis

A hypothesis must be defended in two ways, by showing (1) that it is useful, that is to say that it brings together and clearly summarizes certain facts; and (2) that it is fecund, that is to say that it makes it possible to interpret other new phenomena for which it had not been imagined. The hypothesis of the disaggregation of psychological phenomena and their meeting in two or more distinct but simultaneous groups seemed to us to easily represent the various anesthesias and their singular characteristics. Let us see if there are any other new phenomena whose interpretation can be linked to this supposition.

The study of amnesia would raise an extremely interesting psychological problem. When a memory seems forgotten and no longer thought about, has it completely disappeared from the consciousness? Can we not say that, like sensations ignored by anesthetics, it is preserved in some obscure region that consciousness is unaware of? It is a very attractive theory and in some respects very likely. It is admirably expressed in Saint Augustine and has been defended with great skill by contemporary philosophers, such as Bouillier and Colsenet.[59] It is certain that this hypothesis seems to be related to the theses that we have supported so far. However, we will not discuss it. In composing this work, we had the pretension, justified or not, to create a work of experimental psychology and to deviate as little as possible from the facts that we were able, more or less, to observe ourselves. We have not, however, observed any facts which are directly linked to this somewhat transcendent hypothesis. The principal difference between an experimental study and a philosophical theory is that the former does not need to push ideas to their furthest consequences and stops at the point where the solid basis of observations and experience seems to diminish.

The only amnesia that we have studied is far simpler; it is the loss of a memory when it should normally present itself to consciousness. A subject who, during somnambulism, was suggested to forget a certain memory can no longer find it upon waking, any more than she can have the sensation of an object that she was forbidden to see. But the memory, like the sensation, persists in a second consciousness and can be found using the same procedures. We will not insist on this fact either, for we have studied the conditions of memory enough to admit, without further examination, that the various amnesias of this kind are explained in the same manner as the various anesthesias. To understand this amnesia, we need only recall a statement which has already been made. In all the figures which have been examined in section 2.6 of this chapter to explain perception (the simple phenomena T, T', M, etc.), anterior to the synthesis which forms perception, can be memories or images as well as sensations, and all the studies on the coming together or the disaggregation of these images would remain identical.

In pathological psychology studies, however, we often meet two new and very important phenomena: *paralysis and contractures*. If these facts can be linked to the theory of psychological disaggregation that we have outlined, they will provide a very important verification. Therefore, we will have to devote a special study to them.

As a rule, all anesthesia and all amnesia are followed by a paralysis. If I have forgotten the name or the location of an object, I cannot pronounce its name, nor make the movement to take the object from its location. A hysteric who completely loses the memory of all kinds of verbal images, or who loses all sensitivity of a limb, can no longer speak or can no longer move that limb. On the other hand, paralysis and contractures are almost always, except in quite exceptional cases, accompanied by anesthesia. "Tactile and muscular anesthesia always accompanies hysterical paralysis," said Charcot.[60] "The patient," says another author, "is only aware of his limb as a foreign body whose weight is bothersome, but can feel it in the part of the thorax that remained sensitive."[61] Likewise, contractures are generally painless and accompanied by a deep anesthesia of the muscle and almost always also of the skin which covers it.[62] These anesthesias, as one might expect, involve amnesias, and a hysteric, paralyzed like V, for example, can no longer manage to represent the visual or muscular image of the moving leg. In general, it is hysterics with numerous anesthesia and amnesias who have these characteristics, and they experience them on the side which is particularly anesthetic. Conversely, when the anesthesia disappears, we see the contractures give way, and the paralyzed limbs recover their movements. After all that we have said about the motor function of sensations and images, this connection between the suppression of an image and the suppression of a movement seems so natural that it is not necessary to emphasize the typical and regular cases; it is better to examine the exceptions which are numerous and important, and to investigate how they can be brought back to the rule.

A theory, formerly quite widespread and which today is hardly supported, seems to oppose the comparison that we want to make; for it absolutely separates paralysis and anesthesia, as two different and independent phenomena. Joly, in a recently published article, set out in detail all the facts which, according to him, demonstrate the separation of these two disorders. We can summarize under two titles all the arguments he puts forth: (1) *there exist anesthesias without paralysis*, and (2) *there are paralyses without anesthesia*. Can we explain such facts?

(1) "A hawk whose claws' sensory nerves are cut, no longer feels this limb, neither touch, nor the sting of a needle," said Claude Bernard, "but it preserves the ability to sit on its perch and to walk."[63] In a more general way, one can, according to the grouping of sensory nerves, suppress sensitivity and allow motility to persist; this is the old experiment of Bell and Magendie. "Therefore," says Joly, "movement exists without sensitivity." Not at all. Surgical lesions are, in my opinion, a poor method of psychological experimentation, because until now they have not been delicate enough and do not attain the precision necessary to produce specific results. The section of a sensitive nerve simply suppresses the material communication between the external impressions and the faculty of sensitivity of the animal. It absolutely does not destroy this faculty. Claude Bernard's hawk is still capable of feeling the sensations relating to its claw and, consequently, it retains the memory of all the images of the old sensations which were transmitted to it by this once intact nerve. No one has ever claimed that movement is always produced by a current sensation. We can write at this moment without having examples of writing before us; but that does not prove that writing is not a movement produced by images of old visual or muscular sensations. This is the case for most of the examples cited by the author: the anesthesia of which he speaks is produced only by anatomical lesions, hemorrhages, tumors, etc., which interrupt conduction, but do not suppress the psycho-physiology of sensation and image. No doubt there is no paralysis, but this is because there is no amnesia, because the anesthesia is not complete.

It is only in neuroses that the psychologist can successfully study disorders of sensitivity and movement. Now Joly does not seem to make much of this, for he says, "the disorders of the sensitivity in neurotics only reach the peripheral region of the nervous system."[64] This proposition seems to me unsustainable, because it is precisely in these disorders that the lesion is truly central and psychological. Let us therefore see if, in neurotics, there are disturbances of sensitivity without disturbances of movement. This much is certain: all observers have noticed that there are hysterics who are absolutely anesthetic and yet move very well. Deneaux's famous observation describes it best: "She put her muscles into play under the influence of the will, but she was not aware of the movements she was performing. She did not know what the position of her arm was, it was impossible for her to say whether it was extended or flexed. If the patient was told to put her hand to her ear, she immediately executed the movement; but when my hand was interposed between hers and her ear she was not aware of it. If I stopped her arm in the middle of the movement, she did not notice it; if I held her arm on the bed, without her notice and then told her to put her hand to her head, there was a moment of effort, then she remained still, believing that she had executed the movement. If I told her to try again, she would, but with more force and immediately the muscles on the opposite side of her body came into play (she was only hemi-anesthetic), and she recognized that her movement was being hindered."[65] This is a fine example of complete tactile and muscular anesthesia without paralysis. Many of the subjects I have studied, especially Marie, would evoke an absolutely identical reaction. How do these movements occur?

Like most observers, I answer without hesitation *that these movements are executed by means of other images and in this case by means of visual images.* "The loss of the motor images of language," Charcot has said, "does not always lead to the loss of language, because there are people who speak with auditory images and lose the muscular images without realizing it, for they do not feel their mouth speaking, but they speak all the same."[66] Hysterics likewise do not feel their arms move, but they move them nevertheless, because they have a visual representation of the movement of their arms and this visual image, as we have seen in all experiments relating to imitation, is sufficient to produce effective movement. The role of visual images can be demonstrated, I believe, by at least two observations. I have noticed, on two separate occasions, that when a hysteric completely loses the tactile and muscular sense, she is more likely to become paralyzed in the legs than in the arms. As soon as Rose becomes anesthetic, she is paraplegic. V likewise cannot lose muscular sensitivity without losing the use of her legs, but both still conserve the movement of the arms. Now, the movement of the arms is, especially for women, much more visible than the movement of the legs and leaves much clearer visual images in the memory. It is for this reason that they know how to move their arms yet cannot, like Lucie, move their legs with the aid of the sense of sight; they are less accustomed in this instance to the constant use of visual memory.[67] This second observation is commonplace: Duchenne (de Boulogne), Bell, Lasègue, etc. have long observed that these women, so restless when they have their eyes open, cannot move when they have their eyes closed, or when they are not looking at their limbs. "A mother feeding her child is paralyzed. She loses muscle control on one side and simultaneously loses sensitivity on the other. Given this strange and truly alarming circumstance, the woman can only hold her child to her breast with the arm which has retained muscular control and only if she is looking at her infant. If the surrounding objects distract her attention from the position of her arm, her flexor muscles gradually relax and the child is in danger of falling."[68] In a word, when she is distracted, other visual images fill her constricted field of consciousness, and the visual images of the movement of her arm fades away. It was, therefore, the visual images that replaced the absent muscular images and masked, by movement, the paralysis that this anesthesia should have produced.

However, this last observation is not completely convincing. If some anesthetic hysterics similar to Lucie become totally paralyzed when they close their eyes, most of them still retain movements, or at least, according to Pitres' observation, can continue the movement that was started with the eyes open (yet cannot start another with their eyes closed). This is easily explained because the visual images remain even after the eyes are closed and can, like the visual sensations themselves, determine a movement. Why, then, in some cases do they lose movement when their eyes are closed and, in other cases, keep it? I believe that there is an important concept which must be taken into account: *it is the notion of the position of the arm when starting a movement.* If Marie can raise her arm with her eyes closed despite being insensitive, it is because, when I ask her for a movement, she imagines her hand which was visible on her lap before her eyes were closed. She begins this representation to initiate the movement or to continue the movement whose beginning has been seen. But now I stop her movement without letting her see where her hand lands, or else I move her arm without warning and put it on her head. She has not felt it, and believes her arm is on her lap, or, more significantly, she no longer knows where it is, and says that she has lost it. I ask her to reach out to me, and her arm does not move or has only incoherent tremors. It is because, unaware of the initial position of her arm, she no longer knows what to visually represent in order to reach out to me. Much more significantly, without touching her arm, I make her believe that I am moving it. That is enough so that she no longer knows where it is and says to me in an apologetic tone, "Let me look for it and then I will give you my hand." It is not even necessary to have her look. It suffices, as we learned from a very nice observation of Lasègue reproduced by Pitres, to place her hand on a part of the body which has remained sensitive, the right cheek, for example, so that she learns the position of her arm, and then can imagine the movement and therefore accomplish it. These reflections on the importance of the visual impression of the position of the arm allow me to understand one of my former observations which I could not at that time explain. To study a well-known sign of hysterical anesthesia, I would take subjects' arms and put them behind their backs; then they could no longer manage to return them to their former position. If, on the contrary, I asked them to put their arms behind their backs themselves, most of them could then easily return them. This is because in the first case, they did not see where I had put their arms; and, in the second, they maintained the visual representation of the position of the arm they had themselves moved. Exceptions, therefore, fall fairly easily into the rule: if there are muscular anesthesias that are not accompanied by paralysis, it is because all sensitivity relating to movement has not been suppressed, and sensations and visual images have intervened to replace those which were lost. It follows from these experiences that one cannot conclude that movement exists independently of sensory images.

(2) Let us now consider the second form that this discussion can take. It is said that there are *paralyses without anesthesia*. Let us first of all rule out, as before, paralysis due to anatomical lesions, the type of paralysis produced by a section of the motor nerve, leaving the posterior nerve intact.[69] In my opinion, we could experiment in a much simpler way. Firmly tie the legs of a dog so that it cannot move, and then say: "You can see that there is paralysis without anesthesia, since this animal feels and does not move." This would be just as demonstrative. Here again, for a psychological perspective, we must look for paralyses without injury and see how they can occur despite the preservation of sensitivity. Some authors, like Huchard, Prégel, and Lober cite psychic paralyses of this kind which are not accompanied by anesthesia.[70] How can we understand this irregularity?

Take, for example, an experimental suggestion. I chalk a line on the floor and declare to a hysterical woman that she will not be able to cross this line. She shrugs, pretends I am kidding, and does not pay attention to what I have said. A few minutes later, she gets up to leave and quickly walks straight ahead. At the edge of the line both of her legs stop, completely stiffen and the body remains, leaning forward without being able to advance. She is furious. Backing away to gain momentum, she runs, but again she is stopped suddenly in front of the line. It is a kind of paralysis, because she is unable to lift her legs to cross the white line. But it is easy to see that her sensitivity has not changed; her legs are as before, one sensitive, the other insensitive (she was a hemi-anesthetic). We can conduct many such experiments. Tell a subject that her arm is glued to the table, that she cannot pick up a particular object, etc. Bernheim notes that, if it has been said during somnambulism that such an object paralyzes her, this effect will continue after awakening without the subject knowing why.[71]

In all these cases, the suppression of movement does not seem to me to be a true paralysis. It is an action which results in apparent immobility, but which is nonetheless at work. The suggestion, given either during somnambulism or during distraction, has given rise to a subconscious fixed idea. This idea stops the movement at the moment when the subject wants to produce it, and does so by means of the sensory images which the subject has completely preserved. The subject is no more literally paralyzed than a man in prison throwing himself against the walls would be. Natural pseudo-paralysis without anesthesia must be of this nature: "I get dressed to go out," said a patient of Descourtis, "and at the same time I remain motionless; I must be pushed outside. I am unable to enter a store, or, if I enter, I am inert ... I feel that there are two people in me, two wills and these two successive wills counterbalance each other, and keep me in place."[72] Charcot analyzed very important and very curious cases of this kind, for which he provides a likely explanation.[73] Emotion caused by an unexpected event, a "nervous shock," provokes a mental state analogous to hypnotism (or at least, different from the normal psychological state) during which the idea of injury or of paralysis has entered the mind. Once consciousness has returned to the normal state, this idea nevertheless persists underneath and stops, or "inhibits" all the movements that the patient wants to make. From a psychological point of view, as from a physiological point of view, the apparent suppression of movements can sometimes come from "a real abolition of the activity of the motor apparatus, sometimes from an increase in the activity of the apparatus used to stop."[74] Only the first is a true paralysis. However, previous studies do not seem to have succeeded in separating it from anesthesia.

2.11 Paralyses and contractures explained by psychological disaggregation

Far from being able to develop independently of anesthesia, these two phenomena of paralysis and contracture: (1) present the same variables and can be arranged with the same classifications; (2) are initiated within the same conditions; and (3) can be interpreted in exactly the same way as the phenomena of insensitivity.

(1) Just as there can be general anesthesia suppressing absolutely all the sensations of a sense, so too can there can be *total* paralysis, suppressing absolutely all the movements of a limb, and total contractures, stiffening at the highest possible degree all the muscles of an arm or a leg. These two forms of paralysis and contracture are the simplest and, if you like, the most frequent; they are recognized by consistent signs. In complete paralysis, a limb always falls down inert, obeying the laws of gravity; in general contracture, a limb, and sometimes the whole body, takes a fixed, invariable position, determined by the position and the relative strength of the different muscles. This attitude of the limbs in general contracture has often been described in connection with tetanus attacks or certain epileptic fits: the leg, for example, will be in forced extension, because the extensor muscles predominate over the flexors; the fist will be closed, turned slightly inwards, the body bent back slightly in an arc, etc. Just as anesthesia can be partial, affecting only part of the eye or a portion of the skin's surface, so paralysis or contracture can be *partial* and reach only one muscle or a group of muscles near the nerve, but only them. It is under this classification that the cubital, median, and radial branches (which have so often been described) should be classified. Finally, there is a third group of anesthesias which are very similar to the previous: it contains those which we have described under the name of systematized anesthesia. It is quite evident that there are paralyses and contractures which correspond to them exactly.

The old magnetizers had already observed that one can forbid a subject to make a certain movement, to pronounce a certain word, or to write a particular letter. "An individual cannot manage to write the letter A; he omits it when he writes his name."[75] "Systematic paralyses consists in the loss of special movements, or adapted movements. Subjects who are affected do not completely lose the use of their limbs; they are only incapable of using them to carry out a specific act and this act alone."[76] It is easy to understand how a subject, who can control their arm to make all possible movements except those which are necessary to write an A, resembles the subject who can see with their eye all objects except one designated person. Although this is a lesser known fact, there are systematized contractures; that is to say, contractures in which not all the muscles of the arm or of the hand are contracted to the highest degree, but in which only some are contracted (some more, others less), so as to give the limb an attitude that is rigid, but expressive. The arms, for example, may remain contracted in a threatening posture or that of prayer. *Paralyses and contractures can therefore present all the modifications that anesthesias present and can, therefore, be classified in the same way.*

(2) From another point of view, if we study the phenomena obtained by suggestion, we will see that paralyses and contractures occur under the same circumstances in which anesthesia occurs, and give rise to the same experiences. Posthypnotic suggestion brings about partial insensitivities and systematic anesthesias, and it will produce paralyses and contractures of the same kind.

During somnambulism, I command N to say her prayers, then wake her up before she has started. Once awake, her hands come together, without her notice, and assume the position of prayer, while she is talking about something else. This is an example of a subconscious act accompanied by systematic anesthesia, of which we are already aware. After a moment, needing to make another movement, she spontaneously moves her hands, and nothing seems to remain of the suggestion. At this point, N is asked to put her hands in the prayer position; at first, she refuses, finding the request ridiculous, finally she tries, jokingly, but closes her fists instead of extending her hands. "Here," she says annoyed, "I can no longer put my hands in prayer … ah! like this." And she crosses her fingers. "No," I tell her, "hold your hands against each other, like the statues in churches." "I know," she interrupts, "but I no longer know how to make my hands do it." This description naturally recalls that of agraphics, who lose the ability to write, but in the latter the faculty is destroyed; in the hysteric it is only disaggregated. Indeed, N no longer wants to think of prayer and begins talking about something else, but while she is speaking, the hands raise, without her knowledge and put themselves palm to palm. N no longer knows how to pray, unless it is done unconsciously. Is this not exactly what we observed in anesthesia, when automatic writing showed us the knowledge of an object which the subject could no longer see. Another day, I suggested to the same subject that when she wakes, she tie knots in a string which I have given her. Upon awakening, her hands quickly tied knots, without N being aware of it. I then ask her to tie knots in another string which I give her; she agrees with a laugh. Yet here her frustration begins again, because it becomes surprisingly tangled; she makes circles and loops with the string, but cannot tie a knot. She gives up and drops the string; the hands pick up the string (which lies on her lap) and subconsciously begin to make very good knots. Here is a similar experiment conducted with another subject. "When you wake," I said to Lucie 2 during somnambulism, "you are going to recite the numbers to me and write them on a piece of paper." After waking, she writes the numbers automatically, as we have often observed with her. Another person questions Lucie, and asks her to count to 10. She thinks that we are making fun of her and tries to count, but, to her great amazement, she no longer knows a single number and yet, simultaneously, the hand continues to write them. I use the same process with the alphabet, Lucie no longer knows any letters. I ask the subconscious personage the spelling of a word, "hat, house, etc.", she writes it correctly; but if we ask Lucie at the same time, she searches and pretends to have forgotten it. Even better, if, with a few precautions, we stop this automatic writing, without destroying the state of hemi-somnambulism which then remains, we see that Lucie has, at this moment, completely lost the faculty of writing consciously and that she can only express herself through speech.

Under these same circumstances, it sometimes occurs (more rarely it is true) that instead of paralysis, contracture occurs. I want to repeat a previous experiment with N and I suggest again that she pray when she wakes up. Things seemed to be going as they had before, but it takes longer for the hands to lower. Finding that the experiment has lasted long enough, I want to move the hands out of their singular position and I am quite surprised to meet with great resistance; the arm and hand muscles are fully contracted and hold in this position indefinitely. The subject now noticed her contracture and began to be frightened. She had to go back to sleep and the contracture then dissipated easily. Léonie also presented a similar phenomenon, but only once. I had suggested to her to take a flower from a bouquet when she woke up. She did so unconsciously; but after a moment she glanced at her hands and uttered a cry. The hand was contracted in an elegant, but awkward position, the thumb and index finger close together as if clutching a rose, the other fingers slightly curved, but also rigid. With her, it was easy for me to reach the subconscious personage even in the waking state. I allowed the subject to distract herself and forget about me, I then quietly asked her to give me the hand. Although Léonie could not consciously relax her hand, she extended it very easily and gave it to me without being aware of it. Without citing further examples, we see that *contractures, like paralyses, can present themselves in a systematized manner following a posthypnotic suggestion,* exactly like anesthesia. We further note that these *phenomena are no more real and definitive than the anesthesias themselves, that they exist only for the normal consciousness of the subject and disappear completely if one addresses another consciousness or another personality.*

However, the examples we have just cited present a significant drawback: these experiments have been carried out with subjects accustomed to hypnotic experiences, and they have been produced artificially. Do paralyses and contractures have similar characteristics when they are reproduced naturally? I think so, although it is sometimes quite difficult to verify. The greatest difference between the hysterics who have already been studied and hypnotized and the hysterics who have not been is that, in the former, the group of disaggregated phenomena separated from normal consciousness has been more or less reorganized into a personality, who knows and obeys the operator, while in the latter, this group of phenomena (which exist as well, as evidenced by their anesthesia and paralysis), is incoherent. Most often they are unable to understand and obey. Despite these difficulties, we can sometimes observe the same phenomena.

Several authors, including Dr. Lober,[77] have already noted that movements of a painful limb can sometimes be possible by diverting the patient's attention. I have had the opportunity to make a more general observation on this subject, which seems to me interesting and which I will summarize.

Dr. Piasecki (from Le Havre), knowing that I wished to examine a case of natural hysterical paralysis (of which there was no example at the time in the hospital), was kind enough to introduce me to one of his patients. It was a young woman of 30, whom we have already mentioned occasionally under the name of V.[78] She had been suffering for six weeks from a complete paraplegia, obviously of hysterical origin. In order to not interrupt our current study, I am only writing about the characteristics of this patient which interest us at the moment. The legs were absolutely flaccid and fell under their own weight; they had lost all tactile and muscular sensitivity up to the hips. The trunk had retained normal sensitivity and even had numerous points of hyperesthesia, especially along the spine. The upper limbs had only an extremely dull tactile and muscular sensitivity. The face and special senses remained more or less normal, except for the left eye, which was fairly strongly dyschromatopsic. Leg movements were completely impossible, even when the patient was looking at them. The arms, on the contrary, appeared to move easily and gestured incessantly. It did not take me long to realize that they moved well under one condition: V had to have her eyes open and look at them continuously. When her eyes were closed or were not looking at her hands, she lost the movement of the arms as well as that of the legs. If I raised her arm without her knowledge, while she was looking the other way, the arm stayed in the air and took all the cataleptic positions that I created. If I asked V to move it, and she was not looking at the arm that I had extended, her efforts were in vain. This would result in convulsive tremors of the whole body, she would complain that she was suffering a great deal and would have gone into a crisis, if I had not lowered the arm which had not moved.

After having quickly made these few remarks on the state of consciousness of the subject, I signaled to Dr. Piasecki to begin what had been agreed between us: he began to speak seriously with the patient so as to completely divert her attention. For my part, I moved away from her under the pretext of writing down a few words. When I saw that, following the habit of hysterics, she had completely forgotten my presence, I commanded her softly to raise an arm or to make this or that gesture.

Although previously she could not make any movement without looking at her arm and went into a crisis if she tried, she was now moving her arm, without knowing it, even bringing it behind her back. Emboldened by this result, I ordered her to lift the right leg, then the left leg, to bend them, etc. All of this was accomplished very accurately and with the greatest of ease. In this way, her legs, which had been paralyzed for six weeks, could move perfectly, as soon as they were ordered to move. Only this movement took place subconsciously, apart from the actual personality of the subject, who had lost the movement of both legs. I do not claim to have definitively cured this paraplegia; however, at the end of this session, I was able, without touching the subject and with only a few words, to remove this paraplegia, which has not reappeared for a year. In this way my visit and my psychological experiments were as advantageous for the subject as they were for me.

Hysterical contractures are much more common than paralyses, because the anesthetic muscles have a curious tendency to contract continuously under the slightest influence: massage, circular pressure, an approaching magnet, etc. We have been able to make several observations which bring natural contractures closer to those which have occurred in our experiments.

A twenty-six-year-old woman, obviously hysterical, had a quarrel with her husband and raised her fist to strike him. As if by a heavenly punishment, the right arm remained contracted in the position of a punch. After three days she came to ask for help, because the contracture had not subsided. Dr. Gibert was kind enough to include me. I first tried experiments with the magnet, which, I must say, had no influence on this peasant, who was very ignorant of the theories of magnetic transfer. She was very emotional; she cried and did not understand anything that was said to her. I took advantage of this emotion to make suggestions to her in the waking state. With a word, I made the contracture pass from right to left, from left to right, and finally I made it disappear.

Another similar example. A young sailor of nineteen, suffering from hystero-epilepsy and almost entirely anesthetic, received a rather violent shock at the bottom of the chest. Although he was not really hurt, he remained completely bent forward in a most painful position for a month, when Dr. Pillet, chief doctor of the hospital, obligingly offered to examine him. All the anterior muscles of the chest and abdomen were contracted and it was impossible to straighten him. This time it was by means of hypnotism that I sought to reach the fixed idea which obviously maintained this systematic contracture. I put him to sleep very easily and, without ordering anything, I simply asked him if he could straighten up. "Why not?" he replied in the dull tone that somnambulists have when they go to sleep. "Well then stand up, my boy." He did so immediately, and it was found that healing continued very well after he was woken up. There is no need to cite other examples, which are now well known. Those which I have quoted suffice to show that *these natural occurrences have the same characteristics as suggested paralyses and contractures,* just as natural anesthesias are identical to artificial anesthesias.

(3) Since it emerges from these discussions that paralyses and contractures are so close to anesthesia, it makes sense to see if they can be explained using the same hypotheses.

The eighteenth-century medical psychologist, Rey Regis (of whom we have already spoken), had observed that paralytics who have lost the movement of a limb can regain it. When the limb is moved and the patient is shown its movements, they are taught anew to use what they seemed to have forgotten.[79] Paralysis must be, in fact, an amnesia. As we have seen, the movement of the limbs being determined by the succession of certain images in consciousness, the loss of these motor images is sufficient to bring about the loss of the movement. In reality, these two things, forgetfulness and paralysis, are one and the same phenomenon considered from two perspectives, similar to image and movement. This assimilation is today generally accepted. But we must add, we believe, that this amnesia is of the same kind as all the others: that it is a disaggregation much more than a destruction of memories. To understand how the movement of the paralyzed limbs is preserved and takes place, when desired, without the knowledge of the subject itself, it is enough to admit that these images still exist and are simply part of another more or less coordinated group of psychological phenomena.

The simple disaggregation of psychological phenomena produces paralysis at the same time as anesthesia and amnesia, but we must suppose the genuine activity of the second group of images (which is separated from consciousness) in order to explain paralyses by arrest (which we have spoken about) and contractures. Certain paraplegic subjects, like Rose, cannot try to move their limbs without immediately producing small incoherent contractions in the muscles. In others, the limb whose movement they have lost shakes convulsively or stiffens entirely. Can we not assume that these movements and permanent contractions are due to the indefinite persistence of certain motor images, outside of the consciousness of the subject, who is unaware of them and cannot oppose their action? This is why it is sometimes enough to enter into rapport with the second personage, either by distraction or by somnambulism, to stop this unpleasantness. We can also distract this second group of phenomena with some type of work which causes it to forget to maintain the contracture during this time. "When the unconscious is occupied in automatic writing, we have noticed that the processes which ordinarily contract or paralyze the arm no longer have any effect, and the hand continues to write."[80] When Rose's contractures reappeared too often, I could make them disappear by suggesting that the leg sweat or by applying an imaginary mustard plaster. It seems that the unconscious, busy causing the leg to sweat or reddening the location of my star-shaped mustard plaster, no longer thought of contracting the muscles, for the contracture disappeared, while direct suggestions (commanding a movement of the leg) had been unsuccessful. Lucie's jaw muscles contracted and no suggestion could open her mouth, but it was enough to suggest to her to stick out her tongue to cause the contracture to disappear. It seems, therefore, that contractures are linked to psychological disaggregation like the paralyzes themselves.

2.12 Conclusion

We believe that the studies contained in this chapter have advanced the theory of automatism to the point that it will now be useful to summarize, in a general manner and without laying out the sequence of discovery and demonstration, the findings that have been obtained. While in the previous analyses we always considered positive phenomena, sensations, hallucinations, and movements, here we have examined the inverse, negative phenomena: anesthesias, amnesias, and paralyses. Indeed, this new way of looking at things has completely confirmed the previous approach. Just as there was never a sensation or hallucination without a corresponding movement, so also there was never an anesthesia or amnesia without a suppression or a modification of the corresponding movement. Here again the external and visible aspect of human activity is only a shadow of its internal psychological activity.

Let us look deeply into these negative phenomena, anesthesia and amnesia, and attempt to understand their nature. We find ourselves in the presence of an enormous quantity of strange, curious, and contradictory facts, which have been observed for a very long time and which had rendered this anesthesia virtually incomprehensible. The general impression following from this study was that, on the one hand, the subjects were sincere and absolutely did not feel any sensations produced in their anesthetic limbs, and, on the other, that they should feel very well and that their conduct was inexplicable (if one were to take their anesthesia at face value). In the presence of this problem, I do not pretend to say how things are in their absolute reality. Scientific hypotheses are not so ambitious. They have no other purpose than to bring together under one concept a very large number of phenomena which, when isolated, could neither be retained nor understood. From this point of view, it seems to me that an effective and useful supposition, which gathers and represents the facts well, would be: *things occur as if the basic psychological phenomena were as real and as numerous as in most normal individuals; but they cannot be, because of a particular weakness of the faculty of synthesis which brings things together into a single perception and into a single personal consciousness.* Or to put it another way: things happen as if the system of psychological phenomena, which forms personal perception in all people, were, in these individuals, disaggregated and gave birth to two or more groups of conscious phenomena, simultaneous but incomplete, groups which rob each other of those sensations, images and, consequently, the movements which would normally be united in the same consciousness and the same power.

The examination of this hypothesis made us aware of a very curious and hitherto little known alteration of human consciousness: the simultaneous doubling of the personality. The systems of psychological phenomena which formed the successive personalities of somnambulism do not disappear after awakening, but remain more or less complete below normal consciousness, and can alter and disturb in a most singular way.

From a more general point of view, the examination of this hypothesis has again revealed to us something very closely related to automatism, which forms the main object of our studies, by which I mean the activity which is antagonistic to automatic activity. On the one hand, we had already shown that the power of automatism is dependent on the narrowing of the field of consciousness. The series of thoughts and acts was more regular and more identical to what had already occurred in the past, while the phenomena united in current consciousness were fewer and less varied. But this aggregation of phenomena in current consciousness, in the personal perception of each moment, depends precisely on the power of synthesis, whose anesthesias we have become aware of in all their variety. On the other hand, what prevents us from saying that this has been nothing but an automatic succession of images and acts? Only this: that it is the result, or better yet, the continuation, of a synthesis executed in the past, and which, when it begins today, tends to replenish itself. The synthesis which forms personal perception at each moment of life therefore reveals to us the original activity which was once the source of what we now call automatism; for the perceptions which it now forms will later become the origin of habits and suggestions analogous to those which we have studied. Through this research, therefore, we have learned about the activity which is both the obstacle and the source of automatism. It only remains for us to focus on a few more details and to better identify the relationships that these two activities (that of the past and that of the present) can have between them.

Notes

1 Deleuze, *Instruction Pratique*, 4th edit., 1853, 119.
2 Bertrand, *Traité du Somnambulisme*, 1823, 256.
3 Teste, *Magnétisme Expliqué*, 1845, 415
4 Charpignon, *Physiologie du Magnétisme*, 1848, 81.
5 Braid, *Neurypnologie*, 1883, 247.
6 Philips, *Cours de Braidisme*, 1860, 120.
7 Liébault, *Du Sommeil et les États Analogues*, 279.
8 Bernheim, *De la Suggestion*, 1884, 27.
9 Binet and Féré, *Revue Philosophique*, 1885, I, 23.
10 Bernheim, *De la Suggestion*, 2nd edit., 1886, 45.
11 Richet, *La Grande Hystérie*, 1885, 724.
12 Binet and Féré, *Magnétisme Animal*, 1887, 236.
13 Beaunis, *Somnambulisme Provoqué*, 1886, 179.
14 Charpignon, *Op. cit.*, 282.
15 De Lausanne, *Principes et Procédés du Magnétisme*, 1819, II, 160.
16 Charpignon, *Op. cit.*, 79. – See also, Baréty, *Magnétisme*, 1887, 398. – Myers, *Proceed.*, 1882, 255. *Ibid.*, 1887, 538. – Ochorowicz, *Suggestion Mentale*, 1889, 404.
17 Baréty, *Op. cit.* 284.
18 Demarquay and Girauld-Teulon, *Hypnotisme*, 1860, 32.
19 Ochorowicz, *Op. cit.*, 337.
20 *Les Phases Intermédiaires de l'Hypnotisme*, *Revue scientifique*, 1886, I, 581.
21 Richer, *Études Cliniques sur la Grande Hystérie ou Hystéro-Épilepsie*, 1885, 318.

22 Cf. de la Tourette, *L'Hypnotisme et les États Analogues*, 1887, 179.

23 Mesnet, *Automatisme*, 1874, 19.

24 *Ibid.*, 22.

25 Liébault, *Op. cit.*, 68.

26 Ochorowicz, *Op. cit.*, 227.

27 Hysterical anesthesia was so thoroughly studied in the last work of Dr. Pitres, *Des Anesthésies Hystériques* (Bordeaux, 1887), that I will only emphasize the specific facts which justify my interpretation.

28 Pitres, *Op. cit.*, 41, 96, etc.

29 *Ibid.*, 54.

30 Charcot, *Maladies du Système Nerveux*, 1877, III, 348.

31 Wundt, *Psychologie Physiologique*, Trans., 1886, I, 415.

32 Binet, *Psychologie du Raisonnement*, 1886, 99.

33 Bernheim, *De l'Amaurose Hystérique et de l'Amaurose Suggestive*, Revue de *l'Hypnotisme*, 1887, 65.

34 Pitres, *Op. cit.*, 58 et sq.

35 An article by Binet, *Recherches sur les Altérations de la Conscience chez les Hystériques*, Revue Philosophique, 1889, I, 135, unfortunately too recent for us to be able to profit from the work, completely confirms, by means of some new experiments, the conclusions reached in this study on hysterical anesthesia. We are very happy to see this accord, which is important when it comes to research done under very different conditions on such delicate phenomena. We will take note, in the next chapter, at which particular point the studies of Binet complement ours. Other works, which we were unable to use, have also appeared since January 1889. We will simply note with pleasure that they completely agree with the observations on hysterical anesthesia that we had ourselves published in 1886 and in 1887 in the *Revue Philosophique*.

36 Pitres, *Op. cit.*, 156.

37 *Ibid.*, 137.

38 *Ibid.*, 63.

39 Bernheim, *De l'Amaurose Hystérique et l'Amaurose Suggestive, Revue de l'Hypnotisme*, 1887, 71.

40 *Ibid.*, 68.

41 *Ibid.*, 63.

42 There was a little difficulty about the name of this personality. She changed her name twice. I will not make much of this insignificant detail, which I have spoken about elsewhere, *Revue philosophique*, 1886, II, 589.

43 See exceptions in the next chapter.

44 Bergson, *La Simulation Inconsciente*, Revue Philosophique, 1886, II, 525.

45 Gurney, *Proceed.*, S. P. R., 1887, 294.

46 *Loc. cit.*

47 Gilles de la Tourette, *Op. cit.*, 153.

48 Gurney, *Proceed.*, S. P. R., 1887, 296.

49 Cf. Volume 1, Chapter 1.

50 According to Gilles de la Tourette, *Op. cit*, 127.

51 *Les Actes Inconscients et la Mémoire pendant le Somnambulisme, Revue philosophique*, 1888, I, 279.

52 See Binet's very interesting experiments in the article I mentioned above, on the phenomena of subconscious pain, *Revue Philosophique*, 1889, I, 143. The author notes, as do I, that these phenomena of simple pain produce less movement than precise sensations; and his reasoning, which seems to me very just, is that it is due to the simplicity and lack of coordination of these phenomena. We have already alluded to phenomena of the same kind in the first chapter of this work, pg. 61, which discusses Bain's theories.

53 Beaunis, *Op. cit.*, 166.

54 *Ibid.*, 166.
55 Richet, *Les Mouvements Inconscients*, in the homage to Chevreul, 93.
56 *Proceed.*, S. P. R., 1887, 320.
57 Gurney, *Proceed.*, 1887, 317.
58 Cf. Lewis et al., *Account of some so-called 'spiritualistic' seances*, *Journal of the Society Physical Research*, 1888, 360., 1888, 360.
59 Colsenet, *La Vie Inconsciente de l'Esprit*, 1880, 227 and Bouillier, *Ce que deviennent les Idées*, *Revue Philosophique*, 1887, I, 150.
60 Charcot, *Op. cit.*, III, 302.
61 Berber, *Hystérie et Traumatisme*, 1887, 19.
62 Cf. *Proceed.*, S. P. R. 1881, 228.
63 Joly, *Sensibilité et Mouvement*, *Revue philosophique*, 1886, II, 125.
64 *Ibid.*, 117.
65 *Ibid.*, 129.
66 Ballet, *Langage Intérieur*, 123.
67 Subjects of this kind will be able to preserve the visual images of the movement of their legs and remain paralyzed, however, because it is the muscular images alone for them which put the legs in motion. Rose could have the hallucination of seeing her legs move and still remain paraplegic. Lucie could not have had such a hallucination without moving her legs, or, conversely, can only be paraplegic if she loses both visual and muscular images.
68 Observation by Bell., Joly, *Op. cit.*, 129.
69 In all this discussion, moreover, we make no allusion to paralysis and contractures with an organic cause, which can present quite different characteristics.
70 Lober, *Paralysies, Contractures, Affections Douloureuses de Cause Psychique*, 1886, 17.
71 Bernheim, *De la Suggestion*, 163.
72 According to Langle, *De l'Action d'Arrêt ou de l'Inhibition dans les Phénomènes Psychiques*, Thèse, 1886.
73 Charcot, *Op. cit.*, III, 355.
74 Beaunis, *Recherches Expérimentales sur les Conditions de l'Action Cérébrale*, 1884, I, 145.
75 Philips, *Cours de Braidisme*, 120.
76 Binet and Féré, *Magnétisme Animal*, 253.
77 Lober, *Op. cit.*, 45.
78 For further biographical details, see the Appendix.
79 Paul Janet, *Un Précurseur de Maine de Biran*, *Philosophical Review*, 1882, II, 379.
80 Binet and Féré, *Archives de Physiologie*, 1887, 351.

Chapter 3

Various forms of psychological disaggregation

To study and understand a phenomenon, the observer is obliged to isolate it. One must choose the cases where this phenomenon occurs at the most basic level, or try, through experimental precautions, to eliminate the circumstances which could complicate and obscure it. To analyze the phenomenon of disaggregation, we chose subjects who presented it to the highest degree and, sometimes by closing their eyes, sometimes by working to distract them, we eliminated as much as possible the variables which modify or complicate it. We must now face reality, and consider the same fact as it presents itself in different, more or less unhealthy states, in all its diversity and detail. This will also be a new way of demonstrating more strongly the existence of this psychological modification, which seems at first sight in opposition to all our beliefs.

The essential characteristic of psychological disaggregation is the formation within the mind of two groups of phenomena: one constituting the ordinary personality, and the other (likely, moreover to be subdivided) forming an abnormal personality, different from the first and completely unknown by it. Without going into too many complicated and obscure details, we can say that psychological disaggregation takes many forms, depending on the relationships that exist between these two personalities and according to the degree of their mutual independence. (1) We will focus first on a case in which the separation is incomplete: the second personality is not absolutely independent of the first, but depends on it and only repeats or develops its thoughts or its actions. (2) The two personalities are as independent as possible and develop in different directions. It is the basic and uncomplicated form of disaggregation, and, after having studied it in an experimental way, it will be interesting to observe natural and spontaneous examples. (3) The two personalities are again brought together and dependent, but in an opposing manner: it is the second personality (that which is abnormal and subconscious) which dominates and determines the ideas and acts of the first personality. Perhaps, by studying these three cases, we will have the opportunity to describe and clarify to some extent these little-known and interesting psychological phenomena.

DOI: 10.4324/9781003198727-3

3.1 The divining rod. The exploratory pendulum. Thought reading

Popular beliefs and superstitions, anticipating philosophical speculation, have always attached great importance to the subconscious movements of our limbs. We are so convinced that our arms and legs are made to blindly obey all the peculiarities of our personal will that we are absolutely amazed when we see them temporarily emancipated. Who has not been surprised by a cramp, a tremor, an involuntary movement of their limbs? But this astonishment increases and soon becomes a superstitious terror when these movements, acting independently, take on a meaning and give expression to an idea, advice, or a threat. It is an intelligence that is communicating, so it must be a spirit alien to humanity, good or bad, that must be implored or that must be feared.

One of the oldest and simplest practices for these mysterious revelations is the use of the *divining rod*. It is a stick, usually taken from a hazelnut tree, which is fork-shaped and which was formerly used in the countryside to discover water, hidden metals, and even the traces of criminals. The diviner (because it is only a privileged person who can use this instrument) takes in both hands the two branches of the fork and advances on the ground which they must explore, taking care not to voluntarily move their arms. If, along the course, the rod oscillates or bows until twisting the wrists of the diviner (who cannot resist), it is there that it is necessary to excavate to find water or treasures. The famous Jacques Aymar even led the magistrates on the trail of two criminals from Lyon to Toulon.[1] It is likely that, in some countries, belief in the revelations of the divining rod still remains.

Just as village diviners use the hazelnut stick, there are fortune-tellers in the cities who use a more elegant process. A ring hung at the end of a string suspended into a glass: the diviner holds the end of this *exploratory pendulum* and asks it questions which it must answer by the movements or the hitting of the ring against the glass. This little game deserves some celebrity, because it provoked the first research of Chevreul and it was the starting point for experimental studies on the subconscious phenomena of the human mind.

However, another parlour game has today gained popularity once given to the pendulum. This exercise in England (where it is very widespread) is called the *willing game*, and in France *thought reading* or *cumberlandism*, named after the one who introduced it a few years ago. I borrow the description of cumberlandism from authors who have studied it carefully and who make use of the typical terminology used to describe it. The "willing game" usually takes place as follows: a member of the group who must play the role of "thought reader," or "percipient" (diviner), leaves the room; the rest of the group choose some simple action that that person will need to perform or hide something they must find. The diviner is then brought back and one or more "willers" lightly touch their hand or shoulder. Under these conditions, the chosen action is often quickly accomplished or the object is found. The "willer" guarantees in good faith that he gave no directing impulse.[2] I once had the opportunity to attend a session of this kind given by the Russian, Osip Feldmann, who had, a few years ago, a fairly large reputation as an emulator of Cumberland. Although sessions of this kind, especially when they are public, always leave some doubt and cannot be reported with as much confidence as personal experience, I believe that, in this case, the precautionary measures against possible deceptions were pretty well taken. In this session of "mentevism," as he called it, Osip Feldmann succeeded, not always, but quite often, in performing the act of which we were thinking while we tightly clutched his wrist. He was more successful with the complicated experiments rather than the simpler ones, those that involved a lot of movement rather than those that had to be done in place. He also succeeded better with certain people than with others. I tried in vain to direct him, but he did not read any of my thoughts, while he read several of my friends very well. He even managed to read a person who did not touch him, but who was content to follow him everywhere, staying a meter away. This experience has been reported in England.[3] But here is a tour de force which I have not seen reported anywhere. Instead of being held directly by the person who had chosen the action to perform and who played the role of "willer," he interposed between her and himself a third person, completely ignorant of the action that was to be done and whose role consisted only of holding, on one side, the wrist of the diviner and on the other the hand of the willer without thinking of anything specific. I saw this curious experiment succeed once with great precision.

In order to witness experiences of this kind, it is not necessary to attend the somewhat suspicious sessions given by professional diviners. Many people can, without any preparation, execute them very well. I have seen young girls play this diviner role in a remarkable way and, simply led by a person who held their hand and tried to remain motionless, who not only performed the movements, but also wrote, as under dictation, the words that the person was thinking.

We have compared these three facts, the divining rod, the exploratory pendulum, and thought reading, which are certainly similar. It is obvious that these phenomena of movement cannot be explained by the action of external physical objects, sources, metals, evidence of criminals, or hidden objects on the rod or on the diviner, as many believed in the past.[4] "Why", Gasparin has said, "are the corpuscles of water not felt when we are chasing gold? Why did Aymar's rod turn towards the footsteps of the assassins and yet remained insensitive to the corpuscles of a large river like the Rhone?"[5] In England, where one finds an active and intelligent curiosity about all these questions, several observers have undertaken a series of long and costly experiments to study the divining rod – something that we would never have thought of doing in France. The accounts of these experiments can be found in the articles by Sollas[6] and Edward Pease,[7] which also provide comprehensive bibliographies of the issue.

The conclusion of this research was what one would expect: "Everything depends on the ordinary insight of the diviner and the rod has nothing to do with it. The action of the hidden object does not relate to the rod, but to the mind of the diviner." Chevreul came to the same conclusion when he showed that physical objects do not influence the pendulum, but that the thought or the sight of a movement determines its oscillations: "When I held the pendulum in my hand," he writes, "a muscular movement of my arm, although insensitive to me, brought the pendulum out of the state of rest and the oscillations, once started were soon increased by the influence that the sight exerted, to put me in this particular state of disposition or tendency to movement."[8]

If we imagine that the pendulum must oscillate in one direction, it undertakes this movement; if we imagine that it stops, it remains motionless.[9] Finally, it is obvious that it is the willer's thought that plays the main role in mind reading experiments. During the session of which I have spoken, the diviner at one point seemed to be mistaken and to do an entirely different act from that which had been chosen. To an inquiry, the diviner replied, "But I'm the one who's wrong. I forgot the chosen act and was thinking of something else." "I have noticed," writes an English observer, "that if an object was first hidden in one place, then moved to another, the person who leads me does not fail to lead me to the first place, and then take me to the actual one."[10] In a word, in all these experiences, the role of thought is indisputable.

But we must not forget that in all these cases, the subject who held the rod, the pendulum, or who directed the diviner, asserts (and we often have sufficient reasons to believe in his sincerity) that there has been no voluntary movement made and they are the first to be surprised at seeing the phenomena taking place. Several people whom I had hold the pendulum of Chevreul were amazed and frightened to see the ring obey me and oscillate in the direction that I indicated. The movement is however real; "The patients," says an experimenter, "pretend that they did not move, when in reality they moved my hand like a feather."[11] It must be concluded that they moved it (1) *unintentionally* and (2) *without realizing it*.

(1) The unintentionally produced movement should no longer surprise us; we already know that the will is not required to produce the most complicated acts, and that perceptions, or even sensations, are always accompanied or expressed by movements when they are isolated. Here, the subject is asked to think of only one thing and the images therefore remain as isolated as possible. Also, sometimes the words (as in my experiments with the pendulum) or even the sight of a movement are enough to provoke it. Bertrand, taking up Chevreul's experiment, has even shown that imagining a movement produces the same effects as real perception. "The circle that I imagine," he says, "gives an impulse just as clear, although perhaps weaker, than the circle that I perceive."[12] To be able to reproduce this experiment, one must belong to the visual type and usually have movements determined by visual images. This is why many people, who usually act otherwise, cannot set the pendulum in motion by this means. From previous studies we already know and can without hesitation conclude, as Chevreul did, "There is therefore an intimate connection between the execution of certain movements and the act of thought which is relative to it, even though this thought is not yet the will which commands the muscular organs."[13]

(2) But there is a second question that seems to me at least as interesting and is one which we do not usually take enough into account. Why do these individuals make these movements *without knowing it*? An automatic movement determined by an image is not necessarily an ignored movement. When we yawn seeing someone else yawn, we know what we are doing. The movement is caused by the visual or auditory image; very well then, but why does it not bring with it the muscular sensation which ordinarily follows any movement. There is obviously here a beginning of anesthesia, at least momentary and systematic. From my observation, individuals who belong to the motor or muscular type are not, as one might think, the best subjects for this kind of experiment. Accustomed to using and paying attention to their muscular sensations, they do not let these involuntary movements of their hand go unnoticed and they stop them right away. It is, on the contrary, the auditory and especially the visuals which are most successful, because they never pay much attention to their muscular sensations. In this case in particular, absorbed by the image to which they are forced to pay attention, they entirely neglect the muscular sensations. This is exactly the mechanism that we encountered in the formation of subconscious acts, and we can say that, in all the experiences that we have recalled, there is at least a beginning of psychological disaggregation of sensations and subconscious movements.

To verify this, we will note that these exploratory pendulum experiments, for example, are that much more successful when one chooses a subject in whom this psychological disaggregation is sharper and more advanced. Between the fingers of a hysterical anesthetic, the pendulum works wonders and performs all possible movements, because the muscular anesthesia is already complete and these sensations do not interfere with the movement produced by the visual or auditory images. So far these are only very slight movements, "perhaps less a contraction than a relaxation of muscular tension at the moment when the pendulum or the diviner advances in the right direction."[14] The group of subconscious phenomena does not intervene in an active way; it is content to retain muscular sensations outside of normal consciousness. But sometimes things are not so simple, and the movements produced cannot be explained only by the action of conscious images. The movement, barely initiated by their influence, is increased, clarified, and interpreted completely without the knowledge of the subject. To explain the particular experience with Osip Feldmann that I have reported, it must be assumed that the intermediary between the willer and the diviner repeated, without knowing it, with the left hand the impressions she had received, without feeling them, on his right hand. The diviner who lets himself be guided does not always consciously interpret the small impulses he receives. He is himself quite surprised by the act he performs and which he was not aware of when he did it.[15] He asserts that he did not feel how he was being led and that he does not know why he did one thing instead of another. Far better, we have seen people play this role of diviner, without seeming to understand the small impulses which were communicated to them, and accomplish nothing, and yet to be able to say exactly what we had thought, what we had wanted to make them do, if they were hypnotized some time after the experiment.[16] The sensation had belonged so completely to the second consciousness that it only manifested itself in the second existence brought to light through somnambulism. There is in certain cases, therefore, more than an automatic act, involuntary manifestation of a visual or auditory image; there is a real subconscious action, a real collaboration of the second personality with the first.

Such collaboration, so evident in some cases, is not always easy to understand. Did we not admit (while having reservations) that the two groups of phenomena were unaware of each other and that consequently, they could not collaborate on the same work. Undoubtedly, the two personalities (we name them by convention, because, in the present case, the second is far from being complete) do not know each other directly and do not combine the different thoughts into the same consciousness. But they can know each other indirectly, as we can know the ideas of others. One of the subjects of which I have spoken, N, sometimes mixed into her automatic writing words which had no meaning, but which were the reproduction of those which she pronounced by mouth. If I had her, using unconscious writing, do an arithmetic operation, and if another person asked her to recite numbers consciously, we noticed in writing the confusion between the two sets of numbers. This confusion also took place, but very rarely, with Léonie. I do not remember ever having seen it with Lucie, but that is easily explained. It is enough that I pronounce a word for the subject's hand to write it automatically; why should she not also write the words spoken by the subject's own mouth as under dictation? Communication between the two personalities here is by the sound of speech, as between normal people. But let us go further. We know that the second personality has tactile and muscular sensitivity in the anesthetic limbs and that despite this the first person can move them by means of visual images. Is it not natural that the unconscious feels these movements which it did not produce, but which it observes? I suggested to Léonie that if she touches my paper, her arm will become contracted. She has completely forgotten this command and wants to make a joke by tearing up my notes, following her deplorable habit. Barely had she touched the paper than her arm stiffened. The contracture was produced by the second person, who moreover boasts of it in writing. She therefore felt, by the kinesthetic sense, the movement that Léonie herself made, by means of visual images, and the contact with the paper. One of the observations which seemed to me to be the most original, in the article by Binet and Féré, on the unconscious acts of hysterics, relates to what they very happily call a stammering of writing.[17] A hysteric, anesthetic in the right hand, could not write, even spontaneously, without repeating the same letter two or three times, without her knowledge. Collaboration in all these examples is evident. The act is started by normal consciousness, thanks to the images at its disposal. This act causes a muscular or other sensation in the second personage and this weak, unintelligent one repeats it or develops it automatically.

However, in some cases, this explanation of the collaboration is not enough. It is very likely that by association of ideas, conscious thought brings about other thoughts which are subconscious and which then develop in their own way, without the person who has felt the first phenomenon feeling what follows. This supposition seems bizarre, because it must be admitted that the phenomena are, on the one hand, united by the association of ideas and, on the other, disaggregated into two personal perceptions. But this does not seem impossible to us. However, since the explanation of this fact is more problematic and actually plays a rather weak role in the experiments which we have just reported, we postpone this discussion until the end of this chapter, where we will encounter phenomena of this kind that are more numerous and more precise.

It suffices to note here that, one way or another, the collaboration of the two groups of phenomena is necessary. Chevreul pushes the explanation of the facts as far as possible, citing the tendency to movement created by conscious images. But when the facts go beyond this theory, he falls back onto the more banal explanations of deception and simulation. We must also see how Mirville effortlessly succeeds in showing that the recording pendulum can be very spiritual without the person who holds it recognizing anything of the kind. He then reverts to his old refrain: it is a demon or his subordinate agents who speak through the pendulum. We must go further than Chevreul and, after admitting the existence of acts without will, we must discuss thoughts without consciousness or outside of our consciousness, if we want to get rid of the countless little devils of Mirville.

3.2 Historical summary of spiritism

The facts that we have just observed concerning certain society games are very basic and very simple, if we compare them to those which gave rise to one of the most curious superstitions of our time: I mean *the utterances of the talking tables and the messages of the writing mediums*. We have been shown to be as unfair to spiritists as to magnetizers; we have made fun of them too often and we have scorned them too much. They too had absurd theories to explain facts which were important and well observed. The leaders of spiritism have been aware of the facts of psychological disaggregation which we have described for years. It seems that all science must go through a period of bizarre superstition: astronomy and chemistry started out as astrology and alchemy. Experimental psychology started out as animal magnetism and spiritism: let us not forget this and not mock our ancestors.

The works of spiritists, like those of magnetizers, can be divided into two groups. Some expose a quantity of more or less banal or fantastic theories to explain a small number of poorly described facts: these are in general completely unreadable. The others, although still talking too much about the spirits and their hierarchy, put more emphasis on the facts observed and the descriptions of the sessions. They are interesting and more pleasant to read than you would think.

After having begun reading, not without dread, the large volumes of Mirville, and studying the *Revue Spirite* and the theories of Gasparin or Chevillard on spiritism, I eventually ended up finding some enjoyment. You can find everything in these works, which are sometimes written with palpable verve and enthusiasm. Sometimes they are delicious stories, like that of the good Bénézet and his pedestal table which interrupts his conversation to run after butterflies. Or the story of evil and unseemly spirits who hide themselves on chairs and bite people when they sit down. And above all the story of the misadventures of poor Mr. X who flees before the revolt of his furniture and hides behind a sofa that has remained faithful. Sometimes it is scholarly research absolutely devoid of criticism, it is true, but sometimes it is very intriguing. Oftentimes there are very interesting and very fine psychological observations, which are far from useless for observers today. It is unfortunate that the dimensions of this work do not allow me to say enough about these different authors. We can only seek the facts most frequently observed by opposing writers, and therefore the most likely reliable, and separate them out from all these reflections, these discussions, these theories that suffocate them. Emerging science gives systems more room than facts; it is precisely the opposite that takes place in a slightly more advanced science.

We know, in its broad outlines, the history of spiritism, and I cannot enter here into details, which would take up a whole volume. We know that, around 1848, two young American girls, the Fox sisters,[18] had the singular honour of hearing the first of the mysterious knocks which nothing could explain. They quite naturally attributed them to the soul of an individual who had died in the house, and, with courage above all measure, engaged in conversation with this personage. According to a convention established by these young ladies, one knock meant "yes" and two knocks meant "no." Mirville appears to claim merit for this invention as one of the witnesses in the Gideville[19] presbytery case. This is a question of priority to be discussed between France and America. I do not believe, however, that the question is of great importance, because a passage from Ammien Marcellin ensures that in the fourth century AD, the leaders of a conspiracy against the emperor Valencia interrogated magic tables in roughly the same way.[20] The process would therefore be very old. In any case, it was in America, Mirville himself agreed, that, thanks to the Fox sisters and Judge Edmonds, the spiritist epidemic made its initial progress. The latter was especially amazed at the knowledge that the spirits he interrogated had of his own thoughts. "My most secret thoughts," he said,[21] "were known to the intelligence that corresponded with me." Thanks to the knocking on the walls and the movement of objects, "the spirits began to preach spiritual truths in America, and their visible arguments led to a conviction that a less sensitive kind of preaching could not have produced."[22] Their influence quickly spread through all American society.

These strange facts which occurred in the new world were first announced by the newspapers in several cities in Germany: Bremen, Bonn, Stettin, etc. They were announced in France by a small brochure by Guillard titled "Table qui danse, et table qui répond." "It gives a detailed account of the many questions which a table and a huge chest of drawers answered in the most relevant way."[23] But soon, a letter from a New York merchant, addressed to a resident in the city of Bremen, came to describe the procedures to follow in order to reproduce the same wonders. It was immediately tested. Several people sat around a table in the cabalistic position, so that the little finger of each person touched the little finger of their neighbour, and they waited. The ladies soon cried out, as the table trembled under their hands and began to turn.[24] Other furniture, armchairs, chairs, then hats also turned – even people, by forming a chain with their hips.[25] They commanded the table to "dance," and it danced, "stand still," and it obeyed. Broomsticks jumped up and down, as if they had become witches' brooms,[26] and many other wonderful things were done.

The epidemic was not long in passing to France. Although certain authors claim that there were attempts of this kind as of 1842, it is really only in 1853 that one finds very authentic experiences in Bourges,[27] in Strasbourg, and in Paris. Success was complete and soon exceeded even that of the Germans. The table, under the pressure of the hands placed on it, was no longer content to turn and dance. It imitated the various rhythms of the drum, the little war with line or platoon fires, the cannonade, then the creaking saw, hammer blows, and the rhythm of different tunes;[28] it was, as we understood it, a vast field open to experiment. But in Europe, as in America, people soon tired of these insignificant games and learned more intelligent exercises. The tables were asked to answer questions with a number of conventional knocks which meant "yes" or "no," or which corresponded to the different letters of the alphabet. It was now easy to ask questions and have conversations with them.

However, these procedures were still very primitive and very complicated; they were perfected in two ways. On the one hand, the signs which the tables were to use were simplified, in successive steps (which I cannot review).[29] Signs were tried which were faster, and more familiar in writing. First a pencil was attached to the foot of a lightweight table, then small pedestal tables were used, simple baskets, hats, and finally small boards specially built for this use and which write under the slightest impulse. On the other hand, great progress was made with the discovery of *mediums*. It did not take long to notice, in fact, that the ten or twelve people gathered around the table did not all play an equal role. Most could withdraw without inconvenience, without the table movements being stopped or modified. Others, on the contrary, seemed essential, because if they withdrew, all the phenomena were suppressed and the table did not move. These people, whose presence, whose intermediary was necessary to obtain the movements and responses of the talking tables, were designated by the name of *mediums*.

Thanks to these advances, operations became simpler and more regular. Instead of a dozen people standing around a table, listening and counting the number of noises it produces in its movement, there is only the medium, hand resting on a small movable planchette, or even directly holding a pencil. Her hand, drawn by a movement of which she is not aware, writes, *without the help of her will or her thought*, things that she herself does not know and that she is quite surprised to read later.

Mediums, these essential and privileged individuals, do not all have the same powers and fall into so many categories that we cannot list them all. Physical mediums or typtologic mediums, like the Fox sisters in America, provoke, by

their mere presence, noises in the walls or under the tables. Mechanical mediums use a planchette, a spinning top, a beaker basket, etc.[30] Gesturing mediums
answer questions with involuntary movements of the head, body, hand, or by
running their fingers over the letters of an alphabet with extreme speed.[31] Writing
mediums hold the pencil themselves, and write upside down or backwards, or use
specular writing,[32] or obtain other kinds of variously transformed writings. The
drawing mediums let their hand wander at random and are quite surprised to see
"the house inhabited by Mozart on the planet Jupiter made up of musical notes."[33]
It is the work of one of these drawing mediums that the *Revue Spirite* offered as a
bonus to its subscribers, "a superb head of Christ composed and drawn medianim-
ically by the medium J. Fabre, photographic reproduction, 3 fr 50".[34] Some among
these draw only the background of their painting, and then the figures stand out as
clearly as on the photographer's negatives. There are pantomime mediums, "who
imitate, without being aware of it, the expression, the voice, the posture of people
they have never seen, and play scenes from the life of these people in such a way
that one cannot help recognizing the individual they represent."[35] The speaking
mediums cannot prevent their mouths from speaking words of which they do not
suspect the meaning and which they are quite surprised to hear. The same power
"acts on their organ of speech, as it acts on the hand of writing mediums ... The
medium expresses himself without being aware of what he says, although he is
perfectly awake and in his normal state ... He rarely retains the memory of what
he has said."[36] The auditory or visual mediums hear words despite themselves or
see scenes which they then readily report.[37] Finally the intuitive or impressionable
mediums "are affected mentally and they then translate their impressions through
writing or speech."[38] All these varieties, the last especially, are very interesting
and sometimes seem to be quite similar to many known facts.

"What distinguishes the so-called American spiritist school," writes the *Revue
Spirite*, "is the predominance on the part of the phenomenal. In the European
school we notice, on the contrary, a predominance of the philosophical part."[39]
This remark seems fairly accurate. French observers seem to care very little about
the physical phenomena that had first attracted attention, knocking on the walls or
dancing tables. They hardly concern themselves either with the conditions under
which the medium writes, nor with the external circumstances of the phenomenon. They only deal with what they call the philosophical part, that is to say, the
content of the message they seek to interpret. This choice was perhaps not very
constructive, because it leads them to many strange assumptions.

All agree on one point: that the words and ideas contained in this message must
come from an intelligence foreign to that of the medium themself. But they are far
from agreeing on the nature of this intelligence. Some claim that this intelligence
is certainly that of an evil and diabolical spirit and see in these mysterious writings
only manifestations of the devil. This is the thesis of Chevalier Gouguenot des
Mousseaux, Mirville, and Richemond, the latter concluding his inquiry of dancing
tables in this way: "Instead of watching and making tables dance, faithful priests

and laymen will shudder when they think of the danger that threatened them, and their faith, and rejuvenated by the vision of the marvels that brings to mind the time of the primitive Church, they will be able to raise mountains. Thus, seizing their pastoral staff in defense of their dear flock, NN. SS. the bishops, and, if necessary, N.S.P. the pope himself, will cry out in the name of the one to whom all power has been given in heaven, on earth and in hell: '*Vade retro*, satanas,' words which will never receive a fairer application."[40]

But most of the people who innocently turned the tables could not accept such a terrible assumption and did not understand this solemn warning. To explain the messages of their mediums, they presumed causes that were always intelligent, and far more harmless. They were simply the souls of the great men of antiquity, of our parents or our friends who preceded us into the other world and who, by this process, are willing to maintain friendly relations with us. It was easy to build on this information a small system of elementary philosophy which somehow explained most of the facts observed and at the same time gave satisfaction to the deepest feelings of the human heart and nourished a love of the wonderful. It was the work of a certain Rival, a former countermark seller, it seems,[41] who, under the name of Allan Kardec, wrote the code and the gospel of spiritism. His *Book of Spirits*,[42] so named because it is "dictated, reviewed and corrected by spirits," was a great success. All the other authors, the newspapers, and the magazines which were more and more numerous[43] and, curiously enough, the mediums themselves in their automatic writing, did little more than comment on it. "This book," said the *Revue Spirite* (which was also founded by Allan Kardec), "is today the focal point at which the majority of minds converge."[44]

It is absolutely useless to summarize here this philosophical system which provides, moreover, no real interest. This work was done in Tissandier's little book, which examines the theories more than the facts of spiritism.[45] It suffices to know that this doctrine is a mixture of current religious ideas and an ordinary spiritualism that naturally supports the doctrine of the immortality of souls and completes it with a vague theory of reincarnation, analogous to the transmigration and metempsychosis of the ancients. The only somewhat original idea, although already known, is the perispirit theory. The perispirit is a material but impalpable envelope that the spirit drags with it, and which, like Cudworth's plastic mediator, establishes an intermediary between the soul and the body. It is thanks to the perispirit that the spirit, incarnated in a body, sets its limbs in motion and that, disembodied after death, comes into contact with tables or with the hand of mediums.

Under the influence of this doctrine, the experiments made at first somewhat at random became regularized and took an agreed and solemn form. Countless societies were formed in which one conversed easily with the soul of his great-grandfather or with the spirit of Socrates. The magazines publish a quantity of small letters signed with illustrious names associated with the name of the medium who acts as intermediary. Here, for example, is how some messages are signed: Mesmer, Albert medium; Eraste, Ambel medium; Jacquard, Leymarie medium; Paul the Apostle, Albert medium; Jacques de Molé, Miss Béguet medium; John the

Evangelist, Mrs. Costel medium, etc.[46] Those involved have the best possible relationship with all of these characters: Gutenberg improvised, by Leymarie's hand,
a short speech in good French – on the printing press, naturally. The chairman of
the meeting publicly thanked the spirit of Gutenberg, asking him to take part in
the interviews of the company when he deemed it appropriate. Gutenberg immediately replied by the hand of another medium: "Mr. President, thank you for your
kind invitation; it is the first time that communications like mine have been read
to the spiritist society of Paris, and I hope it will not be the last."[47] Nothing could
be more appropriate. At the same time, young people in love with metaphysics let
their hand wander on paper and then read with delight endless dissertations on the
reincarnation of souls, on the origin of the terrestrial globe, on the theory of fluids,
etc. Their fearlessness is equal only to their imaginativeness.

Unfortunately, people tend to tire of everything, and when all the great men
had written variants on the book by Allan Kardec, they realized that the game
was little varied and engaged in even more adventurous experiments. Since 1868,
the spiritists of the continent have tended more and more to join their American
brothers to deal with the physical phenomena, which they had neglected. France
had had enough of the spirits speaking (by the hand or the mouth of the mediums), it wanted to see them a little and even take their photographs. It was quite
natural, and it was now a question of materialization phenomena. Thanks to the
necessary intermediary of the medium, (which played a role here quite difficult to
specify) people made objects move that nobody touched, they made pencils write
which rose and moved all alone, they made writings appear on slates enclosed
in sealed boxes, and finally they showed the amazed faithful, arms, heads, and
bodies that appeared out of nowhere in dark rooms. The Eddy brothers, Daniel
Dunglas Home, Miss Florence Cook, the medium made famous by Crookes, and
others acquired in these exercises a just celebrity.

Sometimes people photographed these appearances, sometimes they molded
them, which was far more authentic. "Reymers," said the *Revue Spirite*, "graciously sent us a case of spirits' hands and feet molded with paraffin."[48] The spirits
had been kind enough to put their hands or feet in the molds. Attempts led, on the
one hand, to the famous photographs of Katie King and, on the other, to the sensa-
tional trial of photographer Buguet, which Bersot recounted in such a funny way.
This trial ended nothing. One of the most compromised characters, the medium
Leymarie, received, after her conviction, an abundance of letters of condolence.
Judge Carter of the United States of America attached to his own letter a remarkable photograph, "The representative," he wrote, "surrounded by twenty-three
spirits, obtained by spiritist photography."[49] The photography of spirits may still
be going on.

But spiritism was transforming more and more and became little by little the
industry that Gilles de la Tourette exposed, and which has little aim other than to
exploit the naive. I do not think that this spiritism of today should be completely
confused with that which existed in the past and which aroused the enthusiasm of
Allan Kardec and the religious terrors of Mirville. These are two very different

things. The few sincere believers who still exist painfully defend the doctrines of the master against new sects and religions, occultism or theosophy, which are far more ambitious and complicated than modest conversations with the souls of the dead.

3.3 Hypotheses relating to spiritism

The phenomena which gave rise to the doctrines which we have just summarized deserve careful study and discussion. Disdainful skepticism, which consists of denying all that one does not understand and always falling back on explanations of deception and mystification, is no more appropriate here than with regard to the phenomena of animal magnetism. This movement, which has led to the founding of approximately fifty different newspapers in Europe and has inspired the beliefs of a considerable number of people, is far from insignificant. It is too widespread and too persistent to be caused by a simple farce, provincial and transitory.

However, if one examines the phenomena alleged by the writers of spiritism, it is absolutely necessary to make some distinctions. The exaggerated gullibility which would be required to take seriously all the nonsense which clutters magazines of this kind would be even more ridiculous than skepticism: the doctrine of all or nothing is not scientific criticism. Moreover, it could be said that choosing this approach is absurd and arbitrary, because we eliminate precisely that which we cannot explain. No, the choice is not arbitrary: it is determined, as in any historical study, by the criticism of testimonies. An intelligent author, who shows common sense and a standard of criticism in other works, deserves to be believed over the one who is inexperienced and famous only for their naivety. When Bénézet (whom we remember with amusement) tells us that he saw soft candies, still wet, fall from the ceiling, because the devil had sucked them, I should be permitted to take a pass on that. Now, the annals of spiritism are filled with facts of this kind[50] told by similarly candid authors. If, after having read some of their letters, no one would believe these people, even if they reported more likely things to us, such as a storm or the fall of a meteor, why should we take them seriously when they discuss their dealings with the other world? Furthermore, elimination is very easy, and even less known authors consistently speak of a small number of phenomena, the only ones which we will take into account.

Even among these latter facts, which are frequently and seriously reported, I think it necessary to make a further distinction. Spiritists designate under the name of physical phenomena those which occur outside the medium and apparently without her intervention: knocking in the walls, the famous direct writing which takes place far from the medium by means of a pencil moving independently,[51] and especially the contactless table risings, as well as the displacements of untouched objects, so well-studied by Gasparin and Crookes. These things, at least the latter, should not be taken lightly. They are perhaps the elements of a future science, which we will talk about later. In any case, they do not have to interrupt our current study. Whether the medium acts by means of their arm and writes like everyone else, or whether they manifest their thoughts by the movement of the pencil placed far from them – from a physical point of view, these experiences are very different from each other. But from a psychological point of view, this does not change the nature of the thought which manifests itself and the challenges which interest us remain exactly the same. I hasten to add that these restricted phenomena are exceedingly rare and that I would be very embarrassed to speak of them, because, in spite of all my curiosity, I have never seen anything like them. At least nine-tenths of those who have dealt with spiritism will admit, if they are sincere, that it is not these phenomena of direct writing or contactless rising that determined their convictions, because they also know of them only by reputation. Let us content ourselves with studying the psychological problem of writing mediums and not mention the physical phenomenon whose existence is at least still problematic.

A first attempt to explain the movement of turning tables was made at the onset of their success by certain physicists. Abbé Moigno[52] strove to prove, in the *Cosmos* of July 8th, 1854 that the tables only turn because they are pushed. He cites several ingenious experiments imagined by Strombo, professor of physics at the University of Athens, which highlight this kind of impetus. If, for example, the surface of the table is covered with a very mobile layer of talc, the fingers of the experimenters slide on the surface of the table and fail to communicate any movement to it. Experimentations with Babinet and Faraday's devices, the successive layers of paper which turned under pressure in the direction of movement of the table, where the indicator needle warned the assistants of their least movements, are too well known for me to say more. These procedures put in evidence the movement of experimenters and mediums. We are in agreement with Mirville, that it is not necessary to invent so many devices to prove that the hand of the medium moves; we already had our suspicions. The best mediums are those who do not need tables and who hold the pencil themselves, and everyone can see the movements of their hand. What we have to explain is *how this movement can be involuntary and unconscious, while remaining intelligent.*

The first two characteristics of this involuntary and unconscious movement seemed to the physiologists to be fairly common and fairly simple things. "Many movements," said Carpenter, "take place in us without our knowing it, not only organic movements, but also a great number of acts of the relational life, which habit or distraction momentarily make involuntary and unconscious. We laugh, we scratch, we blow our nose without knowing it and without interrupting our conversation." Carpenter writes, "I saw John Stuart Mill pass along Cheapside in the afternoon, when the street is full of people, and move easily along the narrow sidewalk without elbowing anyone or bumping into lamp posts, and he himself assured me that his mind was occupied with his system of logic, on which he had meditated every day while walking from Kensington to the offices of the East India company. He had so little awareness of what was going on around him that he did not even recognize his closest friends."[53] We can cite a great number of more or less curious facts of this kind. Consider Gasparin, who explains in an analogous way the movement of tables, or Bersot, who finds a little too easily that things are simple, or several others who likewise compare the facts of spiritism with these automatic acts which one accomplishes by distraction. It seems to me that what we see here corresponds to a supposition already pointed out in regard to suggestion. We yawn, they say, when we see yawning, we blush when we see blushing; so it is quite understandable that a subject picks up flowers when ordered to do so and that an imaginary flame burns the skin. No doubt there is a slight similarity between the involuntary march of the distracted logician and the automatic writing of mediums; but what a difference, what a distance between the two phenomena. The involuntary acts that are alleged are usual, simple repetitions, without originality and without intelligence. Automatic writing on the contrary (it should not be forgotten), is very intelligent. "Some are willing to accord to the tables only a sort of Boeotian fluid," said Des Mousseaux, "but lo and behold, the tables speak, converse, and conduct dialogues with us; and they sometimes soliloquize."[54]

It is quite simple to demonstrate this intelligence in spiritist phenomena; the simple primitive table which strikes the floor in accordance with the letters of the alphabet shows a sometimes surprising memory of these conventional signs. "We note that in Belgium, to communicate more quickly, the table will speak using all three feet. The alphabet is divided into three groups of letters: 1. from A–H, 2. from I–P, 3. from Q–Z. Within each group the letters are assigned a number, A is designated by one tap, B by two, etc. In the second group, I again by one tap, J by two, etc. Each foot corresponds to one of these groups exclusively. So if the first foot taps three, it's a C, the third letter in the first group, if the second foot taps once, it's I, the first letter in the second group, and so on." With a basic system of this kind, one quickly obtains a long communication which, on top of it all, is written in reverse.[55] How can we compare a calculation of this kind to the automatic act of scratching or blinking eyes?

Communications written in this way are far from being works of genius, as we will see; however, they are incomparably more than a simple mechanical reflex. We know the experiences of Mme de Girardin's turning tables. She questioned the table and asked it the definition of love; the table replied, "suffering."[56] The word is not new, but for a table, it is nonetheless curious. There are planchettes which compose Latin verses, write fables, tell of the creation of the world,[57] or allow themselves puns. The hand of the medium who writes without awareness, discusses, reasons or jokes; she stops suddenly when she has had enough and ends by saying, "see you tomorrow, goodbye, enough for today." Then it is no longer possible to obtain anything further.[58] In the presence of such innumerable facts, one cannot help finding that the physiologists, with the theory of unconscious cerebration, stopped at the threshold of the question. Allan Kardec's *Revue Spirite* takes this phrase as its epigraph: "Every effect has a cause, every intelligent effect has an intelligent cause." And Mirville is not wrong when he concludes, "There are in these tables phenomena of thought, intelligence, reason, will, freedom, even (when they refuse to answer), and phenomena like these have always been attributed by the philosophers to the work of spirits or souls."[59]

Another fairly famous explanation also takes into account two characteristics of automatic movement, but neglects a third: it demonstrates how this movement is intelligent and involuntary, but it does not explain how it can be unconscious. These are, as we understand them, the theories of Chevreul, which we have already described as they relate to the recording pendulum and which the author tried to later apply to all phenomena of spiritism. "Taking into consideration the ability, once acquired, to have one foot or the other of a table tap, as well as having faith in the intelligence of the table, I can understand how a question addressed to the table awakens in the person who acts on it (without any suspicion of having done so), a thought whose consequence is a muscular movement capable of causing one of the legs of the table to tap, in accordance with the sense of the answer which seems most likely to this person."[60] Put more concisely, thoughts cause, as we know, involuntary movements. It is the conscious thought of the medium which sets the table in motion without her knowledge; "The oracles promulgated by the planchettes are only the indications of what is in the minds of the people who direct the planchettes,"[61] and the spiritist's experiences are only a more complicated expression of the experience of the recording pendulum.

This simple explanation runs into a difficulty that we have already pointed out (in regard to the pendulum), which here becomes far more serious. These intelligent acts are not only involuntary, they are also unconscious: not only is the subject unaware of their movements, but they are unaware of the thought which directs this movement. They are not the subject's thoughts (the answers which seem likely to that individual) that are manifested by the movements of their hand. There are other thoughts and other answers which they did not anticipate and of which (when they read them) the subject is the first to be surprised. This phenomenon does not seem well known by the authors who discuss spiritism, because we know that they immediately suggest a trick and deception when it comes to this unconsciousness of the medium. Yet this is the essential point of all these phenomena, the one which gave rise to all superstitious beliefs.

The best proof of this unconsciousness would be that of which spiritists speak of constantly and which they never provide. "Experience has shown," says Des Mousseaux,[62] "that the table teaches me things that I cannot know and which exceed the measure of my faculties." This is a fact which would be decisive, but the complete demonstration of which would require meticulous precautions of which these enthusiasts are quite incapable. It may be said that an authentic fact of this kind has yet to be demonstrated. Besides, if I have completely avoided speaking of lucidity and other similar faculties in connection with somnambulists, I am not going to deal with the question incidentally in regard to mediums. Apart from lucidity proper, we cite other analogous facts which completely separate automatic writing from the normal consciousness of the subject. Some people, it seems, can automatically answer (by means of the planchette) questions asked mentally and not expressed by speech, and of which their normal consciousness has no knowledge. Facts reported by Myers and especially the case of Newnham[63] (if the author can guarantee the literal accuracy of the terms of this observation) are most extraordinary and indicate to psychology an absolutely new path. But these phenomena of mental suggestion in automatic writing, which ought to be noted, require a very special discussion which would divert us entirely from the present object of our studies. Let us simply say that, in certain cases, the hand automatically answers questions of which the consciousness of the subject has and indeed could have no knowledge. But that these cases are extremely rare and cannot provide general proof of the unconsciousness of spiritist movements.

Let us look for evidence that is less decisive, no doubt, but easier to verify. I will first point out an opposition, an antagonism which is easily seen between the character and current thoughts of the medium and the content of automatic writing. Let us not focus on the honest and chaste young girls who remain stupefied reading the gross obscenities which their hand wrote without warning: this example is overused and all those who have dealt with this problem have already pointed that out. Rather here is an individual who believes in the power of spirits and seriously invokes them during a meaningful circumstance of his life. He expects a serious response, and that is what he thinks about. He is therefore indignant at the jokes with which the *spirits* answer him and which are in opposition to his expectant focus. In spite of himself, the medium's hand only makes pleasantries of questionable taste, draws arabesques, signs "Pompon la Joie", etc. The medium, of a serious nature, protests that this nonsense is not of his doing: "My character," he says, "cannot change thus, whether I like it or not; it is impossible for me to understand these sudden and extreme mental variations that are repeated ten or fifteen times in an evening, under the influence of a cause as simple as touching or not touching the edge of a planchette."[64] Elsewhere we see that, instead of answering the questions seriously, the pencil makes small drawings and, when we object, it replies that it has the right to have fun.[65] In another example, instead of answering as the medium wishes, it writes, "It is time to go to sleep, go to bed".[66] This opposition of character between a medium and *their spirit* can extend to mutual reproaches and violent disputes. Father Almignana has great difficulty in responding to the foolishness addressed to him by his own hand[67] and cannot explain how he can find two beings so unfriendly towards one another within himself. Other *spirits* are not shy in attributing errors to the stupidity of their mediums, whom they blame for not being passive enough and disturbing their writing.[68] This dissatisfaction, more or less legitimate, can become exasperation and go as far as anger. Not only is the spirit then distinct from the medium, but it persecutes and martyrs it in a thousand ways. We then find ourselves in the presence of these obsessions which Allan Kardec finds quite natural,[69] and which result in cases of madness unfortunately all too real.[70]

A second compilation of evidence, relating to the unconsciousness of medianimic phenomena, is provided to us by Myers' very interesting collection of observations. The medium knows so little of what his hand has written that he cannot read it himself and has to ask other people to interpret his message; or, what is even more curious, he is obliged to request the spirit to repeat and to write more legibly, which it does moreover with ample good will. Sometimes the medium is mistaken when reading the message. He reads for example J. Celen instead of Helen,[71] and the spirit is obliged to repeat and correct it. In other cases, writing on the planchette allows for bizarre jokes, interjected without warning, or a Greek word which no one understands. The word CHAIRETE is read with surprise and it takes quite a while to understand that it is the Greek word χαίρετε.[72] Or the planchette, instead of answering seriously, mixes its letters and makes anagrams. The story of the spirit which calls itself Clelia[73] truly forms a psychological document whose importance cannot be overstated. A person who tries automatic writing and who, according to the custom, asks the spirit questions, receives as an answer a series of juxtaposed letters apparently without meaning. "What is man?" they ask; "Tefi Hasl Esble Lies" was the response. "How shall I believe?" "neb 16 vbliy ev 86 e earf ee," and so on, whatever the question. However, when we persist and ask the spirit if these are anagrams, the planchette deigns to answer "Yes." It was only the next day, after much effort that the medium was able to arrange the letters in such a way as to give them an almost intelligible meaning "Life is the less able" "believe by fear even 1866," and the planchette declared itself somewhat satisfied, although, in certain interpretations, it indicated another layout of the same words. Is there anything more curious than an individual who presents problems to himself and yet does not always find the true solution? All these observations of Myers (which are very numerous) highlight perfectly the independence of the two series of conscious phenomena, those which form the ordinary mind of the medium, and those which are manifest through the writing of the planchette.

Finally, to acknowledge this unconsciousness of spiritist phenomena, I believe that we must refer to the testimony of the mediums themselves, which we cannot judge lightly. We should revisit here all that Richet has said about somnambulism, when he wanted to demonstrate its undeniable reality. I saw very honest people writing in the manner of spiritists, and they assured me that they did not know what their hand was writing. When one would have believed their word on more serious subjects, can one doubt it now? There are thousands of individuals who, for thirty years, repeat the same assertion. How can the same lie be prolonged for so long in America, Germany, France and England? We can take these words from Des Mousseaux as the sincere expression of all mediums: "When my spirit seems to speak to me from the heart of the table, I lose consciousness of its action. I have neither the feeling of what it feels in its substitute home, nor of what it thinks there, since I do not know at that moment, while I await the favours of its word, what it will tell me and if it will deign to speak to me or operate."[74] Indeed, it is easy to understand that it is precisely this character which made the fortune of the spiritist religion. An involuntary movement related to our own thoughts (as demonstrated in Cumberland's experiments) would not have been otherwise surprising; but what seemed inexplicable were these calculations, these reflections, these conversations, foreign to the consciousness of the medium. It was after having felt the impossibility of relating these intelligent manifestations in any way whatsoever to the normal intelligence of the medium, that it was thought necessary to appeal to a spirit different from one's own. We then understand why the explanations of Chevreul, like those of Faraday and Carpenter, were mocked by the true spiritists; it is that they also fell short of the main question.

Were, then, the assumption made by the spiritists, for their part, necessary? And if an intelligence other than that of the medium was needed to explain the messages, should we necessarily invoke the souls of those who are no longer with us? If a hypothesis should not fall short of the facts, neither should it take them too far, and this one goes far beyond the problem that we want to explain. How did the readers of these messages not realize that these rantings, while presenting some intelligent combinations, are fundamentally horribly stupid and that it is not necessary to have experienced mysteries from beyond the grave to write such nonsense. Corneille, when he speaks by the hand of the mediums, does no more than write simple verses, and Bossuet composes sermons which a village priest would not want to preach. Wundt, after having attended a session of spiritism, complains strongly about the portrayal of the depths of degeneration reached by the spirits of some of the greatest people after their death, because they seem to only talk like persons demented and decayed.[75] Allan Kardec (who doubts nothing) evokes time after time souls who live in various abodes and questions them about heaven, hell, and purgatory. He is right, after all, because this is a good way to be taught about interesting issues. But read the deposition[76] of Samson or Jobard, of poor Auguste Michel or Prince Ouran, and we will see that these brave spirits are no better informed than ourselves and that they themselves should read the descriptions of heaven and hell given by the poets to have some idea of what they are. The same author, always fearless, devotes a chapter to the evocation of suicides by love. One can read, out of curiosity, the grievances of Mlle Palmyre, as well as the lamentable story of "Louis and the bootstitcher."[77] However, after these cloying readings, it is necessary to recite the beautiful verses on the lugentes campi, "Hic quos durus amor crudeli tabe peredit," and to see once more Dido's great shadow, "Illa solo fixos oculos aversa tenebat ... ." These are far truer, even though the authors did not cite anyone at all. It would make complete sense to give up hope of a next life, if it had to be spent with individuals of this kind.

In their defence, the spiritists do not invoke names to sign their messages during automatic writing, or change their style of writing while maintaining the uniformity of their declarations of such and such opinion. The writing of the planchette is very docile and it does everything that is asked of it. It parallels the thinking of those present and repeats all of their ideologies. Among the Catholics, Abbé Bautain sees a basket writhing like a snake and fleeing before the book of the Gospels when presented to it, asking for prayers and indulgences.[78] With the Protestants, the tables no longer fear holy water, no longer show respect for scapulars, and announce that in less than ten years the papacy will fall. Des Mouseaux, who sees demons everywhere, asks: "Was it you who tempted the first woman?" "Yes," answers the planchette. "Was it in the form of a snake?" "Yes." "Are you one of the demons who enter the bodies of pigs?" "Yes." "Who tormented Madeleine?" "Yes." He should have asked, with the same air of conviction, "Are you Achilles?" or "Are you Don Quixote?" so that the table could have answered

"Yes," once again. For those who believe in the old black magic, spirits obey magic formulas and tremble in front of sacred triangles. It is true, as Morin demonstrated, that one can, instead of reciting the inevitable formulas, declaim verses from Horace and obtain the same success.

This intelligence, which certainly exists and which manifests itself in the writing of the planchette, becomes everything that one wants. Let us not give that too much importance and confuse a question of positive psychology with the most disturbing problems of metaphysics and religion.

3.4 Spiritism and psychological disaggregation

"Everything has already been said." This was already being written by the moralists of the seventeenth century, and naturally the remark is all the more true today. The hypotheses which seem the most original and the most unexpected have been previously expressed without anyone deigning to pay them any heed. The theories of psychological disaggregation, which have been studied very recently by Richet and Myers, and which I myself have recently formulated, seemed absolutely new to me. However, to my great surprise, I found them perfectly expressed in a small work which dates back to 1855. It is a short pamphlet of 93 pages, unsigned, that I picked up on the Left Bank, because of the singularity of the title, "Seconde lettre de Gros-Jean à son évêque au sujet des tables parlantes, des possessions et autres diableries. Paris, Ledoyen, 1855." I could not find the name of the author who chooses to hide behind such a designation: I think he is a philosopher who is associated with the eclectic school, with which he shares a clarity, ease, and pleasantness of style, and which doctrines he shares. He has the habit (as do the psychologists of this school) of personifying the faculties of the human spirit, yet by this means he manages to explain, in the most sensible and scientific way, phenomena very little studied and so misunderstood in his time.

Several quotes will allow us to summarize the psychological theory contained in this small pamphlet: "Incited by the outside world, or stimulated by materials already acquired, our intellectual faculties form in us ideas or thoughts. Consciousness or our inner wisdom gives us knowledge of them; our will, or faculty of reacting to ourselves, at the same time provides consciousness with the idea of our personality, the idea of the self. It remains to establish the connection. By the movement of the will toward the intelligence, which we call attention, the idea or thought is confirmed in its relation with the self, brought back and united to it. This is what happens in the ordinary normal state."[79] This thing called sleep "is the period during which the will, the intellectual faculties, and the organism collapse in on themselves, loosening the bonds which unite them, and silently repairs the forces exhausted by the work of the day. However, one might ask whether sleep is an absolute state and always the same? Far from it ... sleep and wakefulness constitute only one and the same hierarchy of states which, on the one hand, by successive modifications, descend towards perfect sleep, immobility, and almost complete disjunction from the will, the intelligence, and the organism, ... and, on the other, rise toward the perfect state of wakefulness, a supreme tension of the will, the intellectual faculties, and the physical apparatus, directed towards an ardently pursued goal, each modification resulting *from a different degree of activity* and the *close bonding of will, intelligence, and of the organism*, each endowed with a certain life of its own."[80]

"In certain individuals and for one cause or another, organic life, sensitivity and intelligence are overexcited or elevated, while the will remains in a state of weakness, malleability, or intermittency. What can be more natural, simpler, or easier to grasp than the *temporary and partial rupture* of the hierarchical link? The phenomenon that concerns us (the talking tables) is nothing else than this more or less complete, more or less prolonged, suspension of the action of the will on the organism, the sensibility, and the intelligence, which retain all their activity. The various degrees of this *disjunction*, as their different forms reveal themselves, succeed one another quite naturally."[81] In experiments with talking tables, "the young girl hears the question and forms the answer in her mind, where the knowledge of the agreed upon mode for translating it, by means of the movements of the table, including all possible ideas and thoughts have been previously deposited: these are the first elements of the phenomenon; but here several different states or degrees of the same state present themselves.

(1) First, not only is the young girl aware of the response formed in her mind, but she is also relating it to her own faculties: this is the ordinary psychological condition. But here is what the abnormality consists of: it is that the answer is expressed by the movements of a piece of furniture without the intervention of the free and reflective will ... The will, the self, is separated from the physical apparatus, which finds itself alone, in a position of independence [this is, as we know, the case with the recording pendulum]. (2) With the will beginning to split from intelligence, the young person has only a half-knowledge of the answer, which is more complete, more extensive, or is even expressed in other terms. The mind, in a word, is in a semi abnormal condition. The organism, on the contrary, operates under the same conditions as before, directed by intelligence without the intervention of the will [we observed some cases of this kind when studying the willing game]. (3) This degree coincides especially with involuntary writing and speech, but it should also be observable in the phenomenon of talking tables. The girl knows the answer that forms in her intelligence, but she knows it within her as if it did not come from her; attention collects it, but without establishing a link between this thought and the self [this degree seems to me to correspond to the possessions and impulsive madness which we will discuss later]. (4) The young girl has *no internal knowledge of the response which was formulated in her intelligence outside of the self.* She is only informed as the movements of the table express it: *the intellectual division is complete.* At the same time dissenting thought enlarges its domain. It is no longer a matter of questions addressed to the table, on the contrary, she spontaneously questions the people present, one after the other. She addresses this or that subject or throws herself into this or that

sequence of ideas. Distant memories are awakened without the girl being aware of it, romantic inventions, sentimental fantasies, ramblings, all that can be produced when intelligence and imagination are left to themselves, with this difference, that ordinary dreams are witnessed by the dreamer, whereas these, although equally formed within the dreamer, are only witnessed at the moment they are revealed to everyone else. This is an initial psychological outline of the phenomenon of the *talking table*."[82]

"What is required for the pen to be replaced by speech? That the impulse is communicated to other nerves … This is usually accompanied by a serious disorder of the innervation: there is nothing surprising in that."[83]"The man whose hand alone shies away from the action of the will is not taken away from himself in the way that someone whose language and speech, (this instrument so directly connected with thought and will), is freed from the authority of the self." In our peaceful writing medium, ordinary thought calmly persists, "but when the physical crisis takes on a violent nature, oh! then the internal division is complete, absolute, persistent. Far more, the elevated *second personality*, ardent, unrestrained, *stifles the other* for a moment, annihilates the first and, in the names of Jupiter or Apollo, alone possesses all the intelligence and the whole organism of the priestess in delirium … *Deus, ecce Deus…*"[84] "We have seen in the same individual *two simultaneous streams of thoughts, one which constituted the ordinary person, the other which took place outside of her.* We are now in the presence of the *second person alone* (in somnambulism), the other remaining annihilated in sleep, from which derives the impossibility for the ordinary person remembering anything of what has happened during her attack when she wakes up. Such is perfect somnambulism or sybillism."[85] "The talking table, involuntary writing, involuntary speech, rappings or medium knockings, somnambulism, these are the different forms of the phenomenon of intellectual split, which could perhaps be appropriately designated with the term sybillism. According to its highest mode of manifestation and because of the unquestionably important role which it played in the world, (being transformed into a public institution) sybillism was for centuries the basis and the sanction of religions."[86]

Due to its importance and the difficulty of obtaining the brochure, I hope I will be forgiven for this long quote. It must be recognized that, under its bizarre title, it very well summarized everything that a few contemporary authors and I thought we had discovered by studying automatic writing and somnambulism. Besides, this coincidence between the reflections inspired by simple common sense and the conclusions drawn from precise experiments is most gratifying and proves that, in one way as in the other, we have approached the truth.

The essential point of spiritism is, we acknowledge (with Gros Jean), the disaggregation of psychological phenomena and the formation, outside of personal perception, of a second series of thoughts unrelated to the first. As for the means that the second personality uses to manifest itself without the knowledge of the first (movement of the tables, automatic writing or speech, etc.,) this is a secondary matter. Where does the noise, heard in the tables or in the walls, and answering questions come from? Is it a movement of the toes, or a contraction of the peroneal tendon supposed by Jobert de Lamballe (which caused such a stir at the Academy)? Is it a contraction of the stomach and a true ventriloquism, as Gros-Jean supposed, or else another particular physical action as yet unknown? Are they produced by automatic movements of the medium herself, or else (as seems probable to me in certain cases) by the subconscious actions of one of the assistants, who in the midst of the darkness demanded by spiritists, deceives the others and deceives themself, and becomes an accomplice without knowing it? It doesn't matter now. This action, whatever it is, is always an involuntary and unconscious action of one kind or another, and "the involuntary speech of the intestines is no more miraculous than the involuntary speech of the mouth."[87] It is the psychological side of the phenomenon which is the most interesting and which should be studied further.

Although the work which we have just analyzed was written in 1855, it was not understood nor did it have any influence, either on spiritists, which is natural, or on psychologists, which is more astonishing. Some continued to admire, others to mock the talking tables, without otherwise advancing the study. However, we must point out some short, but fairly clear, passages from Liébault, which express a similar opinion:

"This doubling of the action of attention in intellectual operations also takes place during the waking state, and then these operations, on two oppo-sites planes, do not always both present themselves to consciousness; there is often one which is unconscious."[88] Littré, in his *Philosophie Positive,* 1878, and Dagonet in the *Medico-psychological Annals,* 1881, allude to theories of the same kind to explain the speeches of the Cévennes convulsants.[89] Taine (as we have already mentioned) in his preface draws attention to a fairly ordinary case of automatic writing; he notices that the fact is curious, but does not go further than that.

It is necessary to go back a few years, to find in an article by Charles Richet, the precise expression of a theory of spiritism, comparable to that which we have just read: "Suppose," he said, "that in some individuals there is a state of *hemi-somnambulism* such that part of the encephalon produces thoughts, and receives perceptions, without the self being aware of it.

The consciousness of this individual persists in its apparent integrity. However, very complicated operations will carry on outside of consciousness, without the voluntary and conscious self appearing to feel any modification whatsoever. Another person will be in the person, who will act, will think, and will want without consciousness, that is to say without the reflective, conscious self having the slightest idea."[90] And in another passage: "These unconscious movements are not delivered at random. They follow, at least when operat-ing with certain mediums, a true logical direction, which makes it possible to demonstrate alongside the conscious, normal, regular thought of the medium, the simultaneous existence of another parallel thought which follows its own cycles, and which would not appear to consciousness if it were not revealed by this bizarre recording device."[91] We find, it seems, similar ideas and a more complete study of this interpretation of spiritism in two German works that I have not had the opportunity to read, the *Philosophy of Mysticism* by Baron du Prel[92] and the book by Hellenbach, entitled *Birth and Death*.[93] But the author who, to my knowledge, has contributed the most to developing the scientific study of spiritist phenomena is certainly Frederic Myers. This author, in fact, in several important articles published by the *Society for Psychical Research*[94] has exposed a very ingenious theory of mental disaggregation which is both psychological and physiological. We will not present here Myers' theories on spiritism, although they are more developed than the previous theories and go into more detail about the phenomena. We prefer initially to proceed, in a more general way and demonstrate how we relate these facts to the studies we have recently discussed on this subject, and then to return to the points of detail that separate our interpretation from that of Myers.

Previously, in fact, without knowing any of the works of which we have just written and without thinking of studying spiritism, we examined, from a psychological point of view, the somnambulism of hysterics and the acts they perform by suggestion. This study led us to the observation of subconscious acts, partial anesthesia, automatic writing – in a word, all the characteristics of spiritist phenomena. While these authors began, with the study of spiritism. to arrive at the theory of multiple personalities and the study of hypnotism, we found ourselves joining them, despite having started from the other side. This encounter leads us to believe (something easily demonstrated), that the phenomena observed by spiritists are precisely identical to those of natural or artificial somnambulism and that we have the right to apply the theories and the conclusions we reached in the previous chapter to this new question.

3.5 Comparison of mediums and somnambulists

The first observation which will bring spiritism closer to our previous studies is that most of the mediums whose descriptions we read exhibit behaviours and present unhealthy symptoms which are not unknown to us. Almost always (I do not say always so as not to prejudge an important question), they are neuropaths, when they are not simply hysterical. We are told that the movement of tables begins only when women or children, that is to say people predisposed to nervous symptoms, come to put their hands on them;[95] making a chain around a table operates very well in some circumstances, although in one case, the group is unfortunately obliged to interrupt things, because two ladies fall backwards in convulsions.[96] We also learn that a man who had had good results with the talking table was unfortunately afflicted with a tremor and a continuous oscillation of the arms to such a degree that they prevented him from eating.[97] There is also a description of a young girl, an excellent medium, who entered into a violent attack of nerves when she was shown a blessed rosary while she was engaged in these spiritual operations.[98] "It is undoubtedly because of the horror that demons have for the rosary," they say. Perhaps, but that is not the only possibility. "When the spirits get angry, the mediums are suddenly plunged into a state of nervous disturbance or tetanic stiffness."[99] We often read in American descriptions that speaking mediums were "vigorously exercised,"[100] violently tormented, by the spirits, which means in good French that in the midst of their operations they had a violent attack of nerves. In English descriptions, one obtains, on the contrary, very scanty information on this point. At most, one notices from time to time that the medium presents some choreic movements,[101] or that the experiences of automatic writing may be very tiring and must be interrupted because of the delicate health of the medium.[102] I admit that I would have been curious to have some additional information on this delicate health. However, this discretion of English authors about the symptoms of their mediums is linked to a general opinion concerning mental disaggregation, which we will discuss separately. It should not be said that all mediums have nervous attacks – that would be an exaggeration – but rather that they very often have nervous attacks and that their activities predispose them to nervous symptoms.

Nothing is more decisive, from this point of view, than Charcot's observation of several young people of the same family who all become hysterical as a result of the practices of spiritism.[103] This coincidence between the crisis of nerves and the act of writing unconsciously is found in our subjects. Sometimes a hysterical crisis that has begun can be transformed by suggestion into unconscious movements and automatic acts; sometimes attempts to cause partial catalepsy and subconscious writing lead to a crisis of hysteria. G could easily and safely be put into complete somnambulism, but she did not tolerate hemi-somnambulism. I had to give up studying suggestions by distraction in the waking state with her. They inevitably brought on a nervous breakdown, which had to be stopped with complete somnambulism.

If the mediums do not present with nervous attacks when they evoke the spirits, they do not always remain unscathed, and they often end their brilliant career in an unfortunate way. Sooner or later many of them fall into "subjugation," as Allan Kardec expresses it with a kind euphemism; that is to say, they end up quite simply insane.[104] Unfortunately, there are many examples of this. Must it be said that it was spiritism that drove them mad? I believe that would be an exaggeration. The faculty of mediumship depends on a particular morbid state analogous to that from which hysteria or alienation can later emerge, so that mediumship is a symptom and not a cause.

Never have these relationships between mediumship and nervous attacks been so evident as when spiritists try to heal a true hysteric who has seizures. Here, in abridged form, are two observations which are very instructive. A young girl had violent attacks of hysteria. Those assisting her put it in her head that she was possessed by a wicked spirit named Frédégonde. In subsequent attacks she sees Frédégonde and speaks of him. "I see," she says, "luminous spirits that Frédégonde dare not look at ... etc." While in crisis, she is asked to pray for her enemy in order to appease it. "Oh! I will do that then," she declared, "I forgive

Frédégonde," and from that moment the crises calmed down.[105] Another hysteric who was having convulsive attacks was declared to be under the fatal influence of an evil spirit named Jules. After the spirits were consulted with the intermediary of a medium, Jules was challenged, cautiously, for his evocation tired the medium. He was spoken to gently and in a pleasant tone so as not to anger him. After many talks and epic adventures, and especially thanks to the intervention of a good little spirit named Carita, a promise that he would leave his victim alone was obtained from this villainous Jules. After hearing the first news of these negotiations, the hysteric changed the nature of her crises and kept shouting during her attacks: "Go away, go away." Once she was made aware of the conclusion of this peace treaty, she calmed down and achieved relative healing.[106] Although I do not have such authority over the spirits of the invisible world, I obtained an almost identical result, to which I have already made reference. A woman, during her crises, was constantly talking about a sorcerer who had cast a spell on her. I revealed the soul of the sorcerer, who asked that we pray ten Hail Marys on the rosary to lift her curse. After having accomplished this formality, the patient was much better, or at least she changed the nature of her illness, as hysterics usually do. We see, by all these examples, that there are great analogies between the subjects whose doubling we have studied and these mediums which serve to evoke spirits.

But let us take this comparison further and point out even more precise analogies between mediumship and somnambulism proper. Spiritists may say that it is impossible to find somnambulists as obedient and as discreet as their table or their washstand;[107] the table does not work alone, it takes a medium to turn it and in this way the medium does not differ very much from a simple somnambulist. In order to offer proof, it could be demonstrated that many characteristics of spiritist writing resemble those of somnambulism: for example mediums are elective and do not operate in front of just anyone. A young English girl, S, whose very interesting story was published in England,[108] possesses, by a singular fortune, five or six familiar spirits: Johnson, Eudora, Moster, etc. I was anxious to witness their exploits, and S, who was then at Le Havre, was kind enough to lend herself to some experiments. Unfortunately, that day the spirits were in a very bad mood and the famous board on which the medium pressed her hand wrote only insignificant words: "Johnson must go … Eudora is writing", and in particular these endlessly repeated words, "Most of things, most of men." S attributed this failure to the absence of her brother, who ordinarily questioned and led the spirits. This explanation seems very likely to me. I could not make myself heard by spirits, nor give them orders, any more than an unknown person could make suggestions by distraction to Léonie or Lucie. Is it not curious to note this characteristic of somnambulistic electivity, even among the *spirits* of a natural medium?

But there are more decisive occurrences which spare us from emphasizing these. We read: "The people who are most successful in turning the tables are those who, under other circumstances, also have attacks of somnambulism."[109] "A good somnambulist is, in general, an excellent medium."[110] Finally, just as mediums sometimes fall into crisis during their work, they also very often fall into somnambulism. "I found myself one day," said a magnetizer, "in a spiritist group where the young lady of the house, who was a medium, had fallen asleep at the table by the flow of the magnetic fluids running through the chain. The spirits had withdrawn without releasing her, as they often did, leaving the group very embarrassed. I made myself known as a magnetizer and, volunteering to awaken the subject, cleared things up within three minutes, to everyone's general satisfaction."[111] Here, on the same subject, is an experience which was shared with me by the witnesses themselves and conveyed in such a way that it seems to me to present a great probability of truth. An assembly of spiritists was in a state of great excitement, for the spirit which deigned to respond to them was nothing less than the soul of Napoleon. The hand of the medium who served as an intermediary indeed wrote fairly interesting messages signed with the name, Bonaparte. Suddenly, the medium, who spoke freely while his hand was writing, stopped; face pale, eyes fixed, he stood up, crossed his hands on his chest, took a haughty and meditative expression and walked around the room in the traditional attitude that legend lends to the emperor. No one could make themselves heard, but the medium soon subsided of his own accord and fell into a deep sleep from which they could not wake him. He did not wake up until an hour later, complaining of a severe headache and having completely forgotten everything that had happened. Spiritists explain these facts in their own way. As for me, I can only see in it a natural development of hemi-somnambulism which became a catalepsy or a complete somnambulism.

These kinds of observations are made so frequently that magnetizers have noticed them and tried to compare them to the phenomena studied by the spiritists. "Mediums are incomplete somnambulists," writes Perrier.[112] Chevillard, the soul damned by spiritists and all the more hated as he comes closer to the truth, insists on this point several times. "It is the same phenomenon," he says, "that produces somnambulism and spiritism."[113] "The medium produces the knocks herself in the table, but does not have the muscular sensation of it and does not believe it of herself."[114] "The medium is a somnambulist or a partially hypnotized individual; the consultant becomes an unconscious magnetizer and the medium is indeed magnetized, yet partially, since she retains a certain initiative."[115] Lafontaine also writes, "The medium is in a mixed state which is neither somnambulism, nor the waking state … Under her unconscious direction, the pencil traces sentences of which she has never been aware."[116] Wonderful, but these authors do not explain how all this is possible, how the somnambulistic existence can continue in the waking state as a second personality. Spiritists do not understand what they are being told. "The medium is not a somnambulist," exclaims Allan Kardec, "since she is wide awake and causes things to happen."[117] "Is it not folly," Mirville says, "that this second soul of the magnetizers exists at the same time as the other."[118]

No doubt it may be strange, but it is true, and we can show by examples borrowed from the spiritists themselves that the somnambulistic state, that is to say, the second *successive and alternating* existence, occurs in mediums and is identical to this second *simultaneous* existence manifested by the subconscious writing during waking. "O stretches her hands out on the table and falls asleep … soon a foreign voice announces herself as the personality Luisa, a Portuguese woman who died a long time ago and who barely speaks French. We speak with her, who uses mouth of the medium … "[119] This is somnambulism and the second successive existence. Towards the end, Luisa says, "The little one is tired, I'm going to leave …" and O goes back to sleep peacefully, and then unexpectedly wakes up. Once awake, she continues subconscious writing, which is signed by Luisa. This is the disaggregation and the second simultaneous existence.

It is absolutely necessary to describe a remarkable observation (including some details) published by the *Revue Spirite* as it relates to this subject. Mrs. Hugo d'Alésy[120] is an excellent medium; she complacently lends her hand to all spirits who wish to enter into contact. Thanks to her, a large number of souls, Eliane, Philippe, Gustave, and many others, wrote messages about their occupations in the other world. But this lady possesses a far more remarkable quality: she can lend to the spirits not only her arm, but her mouth and her whole body; she can make herself disappear and give way to them and allow them to become *incarnate* in her brain. It is enough for a magnetizer to put her into a light sleep. After an initial period of ordinary somnambulism, during which she still speaks for herself, she stiffens for a moment, then everything is changed. It is not Mrs. Hugo d'Alésy who speaks to us, it is a spirit that has taken possession of her body. It is Eliane, a little girl with a slight, adorable lisp, a touch of whimsy, a little character who must be handled delicately.

A new contracture and the scene changes. It is Philippe, or Mr. Tétard who chews tobacco and is a heavy wine drinker, or else it is Father Gérard who wants to give sermons, but who finds his head heavy and his mouth bitter because of a previous incarnation, or it is Mr. Aster, a rude and obscene character who is quickly dismissed. Now it is a baby, a little girl of three: "What's your name, Sweetheart?" "Zeanne." "And what do you want?" "Go find Mommy … and my lil' brother and Daddy." She plays and doesn't want to leave. Another contracture and here is Gustave. Ah, Gustave deserves to be listened to. He is asked to paint, because he was an "art student" during his lifetime: "Listen carefully," he answers through the mouth of the poor medium, who continues sleeping, "It takes time to paint something charming; it would take too long; we could grow beards by then … I have already tried so many times to manifest myself, but for that fluids are required … to communicate on earth with one's friends, it is very difficult; up there we are like little birds, but on earth, it is not like that. Ah! It's annoying to be dead!" (The valiant Achilles had said the same thing when he came to drink the black blood of his victims. Clearly the spiritist mediums do not have an inventive spirit). Gustave continues, "Yet we no longer have a lot of tedious things to do; we do not have to go to the office, or get up in the morning. We do not have to wear boots with corns on our feet … But I did not remain long enough on earth; I left just as I was about to enjoy myself … If I return to earth, I want to be a painter … I will go to the school of fine arts to heckle the others and laugh with the cute models ... With this, I wish you a good evening."[121] Who will come after Gustave? Egad, it is the poet, Stop, to bring things to an end, "because Stop means stop." This one is melancholy, and he says in a lilting voice, "My soul needed love and I searched without finding it ... If I had been given a little more time, I would have put that in verse for you ... I know that it loses something in prose, ... but, considering the hour, I went with what was shortest." After this session, which must have been tiring, the medium is awakened, and finds herself to be Mrs. Hugo d'Alésy once more.

I would like to know what psychological difference spiritists can find between these incarnations, which are published in their *Revue*, and the personality changes or objectification of the types that Charles Richet described at about the same time in the *Revue Philosophique*. Laymen like myself cannot find any. But here is where this observation becomes quite interesting. The author of these articles, Camile Chaicneau, tries to prove to us that it is indeed the spirits who are thus embodied in the somnambulist. During the medium's waking state, without Mrs. Hugo d'Alésy's personality disappearing, it is possible to obtain written communications from these same minds; but they will then be subconscious, produced without the knowledge of the subject herself, who continues to speak of something else. In these messages, Eliane is still flirtatious, Father Gérard writes sermons, Gustave makes the same jokes and tries to draw the little picture he has promised: they have kept the same character, the same expressions, the same memories, although the medium now has no knowledge of all this.[122] This has all been perfectly observed and would prove, if necessary, that spiritism should not be scorned by psychologists. But I will now ask a second question: how do these subconscious and post-somnambulistic personalities differ from the personages of Adrienne, Léonore, etc., writing during the waking states of Lucie and Léonie, without their knowledge, and showing the same memories of previous somnambulisms? In one respect, perhaps, these observations are more complex than mine. While I noticed the persistence of simple somnambulism during the waking hours, the author notes the persistence of somnambulism modified by hallucinations and personality changes during waking hours.

In a word, it is a combination of Richet's experiences and my own. Well, let us try this ingenious combination. While Lucie is in somnambulism, I suggest that she is no longer herself, but that she is a little boy of seven named Joseph involved in a comedic scene that is well known and which I will skip over. Without ending the hallucination, I awaken her suddenly, she does not remember anything and seems to be in her normal state. Some time later, I put a pencil in her hand and distract her by talking to her about something else. The hand writes slowly and painstakingly without Lucie realizing it, and when I take the paper from her, here is the letter that I read, "Dear Grandpa, on New Year's Day, I wish you perfect health and I promise you to be very good. Your grandson, Joseph." It was not New Year's Day, and I do not know why she wrote this; perhaps because in her mind a letter from a seven-year-old child sparked the idea of New Year's wishes, but is it not obvious that the hallucination was preserved in the second personality. Another day, I put her into somnambulism again, in order to observe character transformation, and to take advantage of her literary knowledge, I transform her into Agnes, from Molière, who is both candid and naive. I ask her this time to write a letter on a subject that I indicate to her; but before she begins, I wake her up. The letter, which was written unconsciously during the waking state, accurately portrayed the character and was signed with the name Agnes. Here is another example: this time I suggest to her that she is Napoleon. Before I wake her up, the hand automatically wrote an order to a General ordering him to rally the troops for a great battle and was signed with a flourish "Napoleon". I ask you how the story of Mrs. Hugo d'Alésy differs from that of Lucie? Until proven otherwise, I am prepared to believe that the two phenomena are absolutely the same, and that, therefore, they must be explained in the same manner: the disaggregation of personal perception and the development of several personalities which sometimes develop successively and sometimes develop simultaneously.

3.6 Cerebral duality as an explanation of spiritism

The difficulties really begin only if we get into the details, if we try to realize the form and the particular laws of disaggregation in a particular case. It is in regard to these details that I would be disposed, albeit hesitantly, to put myself in opposition to Myers, who has studied all these curious phenomena so well. I am not talking about his tendency to consider the phenomena of disaggregation as compatible with normal health. That is a general question which relates to somnambulism as well as to spiritism and which we will discuss a little later. Rather he tries to explain the phenomena of spiritism and in general the development of two parallel consciousnesses by a well-known anatomical model of the nervous system, the division of the brain into two symmetrical parts and the existence in people of two brains.

This division of the brain into two parts has already given rise to many hypotheses, from La Mettrie, who says that Pascal had a mad brain and an intelligent brain, to Gaétan de Launay, who considers dreams made on the right side of the brain as absurd and those made on the left side as logical.[123] There have been many anatomists and physiologists who have related to this duality all the complicated and embarrassing phenomena of the human mind. If I have avoided talking about these hypotheses, it is because, on the one hand, I undertook not to enter into studies of cerebral physiology, and, on the other, because this supposition does not seem to me to explain very much. In fact, we all have two brains, and we are neither mad, nor somnambulists, nor mediums. Diminished hypnotic states and unilateral hallucinations of different characteristics for each side of the body are interesting psychological occurrences, which have in recent times been linked to cerebral duality.[124] They seem to me in general to depend on something else: they are hallucinations with reference points,[125] which natural disease or even suggestion have attached, some to the right and others to the left. These hallucinations and all such experiences seem to me hardly demonstrative. If I had to express an opinion on the theories of cerebral localization, I would gladly align myself with Bastian's,[126] which he expresses in these terms: "We are perhaps dealing less with areas topographically separated within brain tissue than with distinct mechanisms of cells and fibers existing in a more or less diffuse and intertwined form." It is for these reasons that I chose not to submit these hypotheses on cerebral duality to a separate discussion.

But Myers, when he returns to this theory concerning spiritism, presents it with arguments which are more clearly psychological and which, therefore, require further discussion.

To summarize his theory in a few words, Myers believes that there is a significant analogy between the phenomena of the unconsciousness of mediums and automatic writing, on the one hand, and on the other, the disorders of blindness or verbal deafness, and agraphia or aphasia which occur as a result of certain localized lesions in the left hemisphere. However, in these cases, the restoration of language and writing, when it occurs, happens thanks to a substitution of the right hemisphere. Automatic writing must therefore also relate to the functioning of the right hemisphere. "Automatic writing seems," he says, "to often depend on an obscure action of the less used hemisphere.... In Louis V's case, the alternate predominance of right or left hemisphere" produces motor and sensory variations.[127] Automatic writing comes from the same source as the writing of agraphics, "the employment in the act of writing of untrained centres in the right hemisphere of the brain."[128] Without commenting on the substance of the question which is physiological, I do not find that Myers' arguments are conclusive.

"The medium who writes in this way, says this author, does not feel his own hand writing, he is like an individual suffering from verbal blindness,[129] who cannot read writing." Not at all! The patient in question senses the letters, but does not understand them; the medium does not have the sensation of movement, and is simply anesthetic at this time and for this particular moment. If they have sensation, if they look at their paper to see the letters, they will read them perfectly. But there are cases where they hesitate and cannot read. It is the message which is badly written. I too occasionally cannot read my own writing, and I do not have verbal blindness. In this case, one might answer, the medium calls on the movements of their hand to start the message again; they are like Charcot's famous patient who could only read by following the letters with his finger. The analogy is a good one; Charcot's patient felt the movements of his hand following the letters, he used muscular sensations to read and not visual sensations; the medium does not feel muscular sensations anymore when the message is written for the second time, they call upon visual sensations this time to read a better written letter. There is nothing in all of this that resembles verbal blindness.

"But now consider the writing itself. It is sometimes awkward, embarrassed, reduced to a letter indefinitely repeated or simple scribbling. So, Myers claims that it is the product of the right brain, which has not been exercised enough." Bold conclusion: one can write badly without using only the right brain. Writing is more inexperienced when it takes place under new conditions, without the subject seeing the paper, without the use of images, etc. It depends on a new intelligence which only has muscular images, which are often rudimentary and sometimes not well known, like cataleptics repeating the same letter over and over.[130] This automatic writing, we are still told, frequently reveals a bad character, conceited, deceptive, immoral; it swears and uses obscenity; it resembles the curses that are only heard from aphasic patients. In one case as in the other, the blame lies with the right hemisphere of the brain which is uneducated and immoral. But how can swear words, obscenities, and nonsense only come from the right hemisphere? Should we therefore return to Gaétan de Launay's dream theory? The explanation of these improprieties in automatic writing seem to me much simpler: we find them, whatever has been said, in somnambulism, in hysteria, in childhood, wherever the personality is weak and unable to govern its words.

A more interesting argument is found in a curious characteristic of automatic writing; it often affects, it seems, the inverted form, in such a way that to read the message it is necessary to look at the sheet inside out by making it transparent or to read it in a mirror. This form of writing is found in children who are left-handed and sometimes in aphasics. I will not discuss this question, for I have not had occasion to observe this phenomenon; none of the subjects who presented automatic writing wrote this way. The phenomenon is therefore quite rare and could hardly serve to establish a general theory. Furthermore, we know that the group of subconscious phenomena which are manifested by mediums through writing is the same as what appears in somnambulism. If this writing is that of a left-handed person, why do all subjects not become left-handed in somnambulism? Well, among a fairly large number of subjects, I have not seen a single one which exhibited this characteristic, and Myers cites only one example, which he is quite right to consider himself, as doubtful. Finally, note that mirror writing is not as difficult as we generally believe. After two or three brief attempts, I learnt to write this way fairly quickly. This form of writing, which it would be interesting to study, seems to me to depend on certain very particular circumstances and not to be a general characteristic of automatic writing. Myers' arguments therefore do not seem to us sufficient to equate the automatic writing of mediums with agraphy disorders produced by a localized lesion of a hemisphere.

Let us consider the question from another point of view. Is it therefore quite certain that an individual who has lost language capacity because of a lesion of the left hemisphere, can only recover it through the substitution of the right lobe? Charcot himself, with his theory of the different sensory types of language, suggested to us another possible hypothesis. The patient can restore their language capacity by developing another faculty of representation, the faculty of audio representation, for example, to compensate for the erasure of visual images.[131] We will then witness a new education in language or writing that can present all the phases that Myers has pointed out, without the right brain having to intervene more particularly than usual. This demonstrates that it is possible to produce, in the same individual, several kinds of languages differing by the psychological images used, far more than by the cerebral hemisphere which produces them.

It is a difference of this kind, psychological rather than anatomical, which seems to exist between the various simultaneous languages of the medium, as between the various actions of subjects in hemi-somnambulism. Each of the personalities which develop in these situations is made up of a synthesis of images grouping around different centers. But the images constituting the new personalities are not produced by new organs and added to those which formed normal consciousness. No, the images always remain the same, as they are in all people, whether they are produced by the whole or by a part of the brain. It is their grouping and their distribution which are changed. They are aggregated into smaller groups than usual, which give rise to the formation of several incomplete personalities instead of one more perfect personality. These separations and these new groupings of psychological phenomena are sometimes done in a very regular way, according to the quality of the images coming from a particular sense. For example, one of the groups will include tactile images, another visual images. Things must happen this way in genuinely hysterical mediums, because their disaggregation, as we know, goes as far as complete anesthesia. But it may be that way in other people, in the mediums who *appear* to be relatively healthy. The division and the grouping of phenomena is much less simple, the images from the same sense being able to be distributed in different syntheses according to very complex laws of association. Among these people, in fact, the disaggregation does not go as far as anesthesia with fixed limits, but stops at anesthesia with variable limits, which is distraction. In either case, it is only a matter of grouping the images normally produced in the mind.

We believe this interpretation allows us to understand certain facts that would otherwise be difficult to explain with Myers' theory. How could certain mediums like S have several spirits of different character who function independently of one another? Myers, as he did with regard to the six existences of Louis V, arranges all the abnormal existences into one, in opposition to the normal existence, but this is quite artificial. The psychological existence that we call normal does not have such clear-cut characteristics which set it apart from others. Nor are the different abnormal groups different forms obtained by hallucination of the same personality. They are very distinct from each other, as somnambulism is distinct from the waking state. Léonie and Lucie have three personalities, not two, and Rose has at least four distinct personalities; should we assume that they have three or four brains? It is hardly likely. I prefer to believe that these are simple psychological groupings which can be numerous, because they do not correspond to the physical division of the nervous system. Undoubtedly, a certain physiological modification must accompany this psychological disaggregation. But it is absolutely unknown to us, and it must be abnormal and far more intricate than this regular division of the brain into two hemispheres.

Be that as it may, spiritism has shown us many useful examples of the mental disaggregation we had studied experimentally. Mediums, when they are perfect, are types of the most complete division in which the two personalities are unaware of each other and develop independently of one another.

3.7 Impulsive madness

It is not only in hypnotic sleep and in premeditated experiences that one encounters irresistible suggestions and impulses. Many unfortunate people are naturally, and through their whole lives, under the domination of a fixed idea of this kind. They feel compelled by an invincible power towards an act which horrifies them. It is this impulsive madness that these singular aberrations of humanity will encounter, which is so instructive for psychologists. This disease has been too thoroughly studied by alienists and by some psychologists, like Ribot, and too well known for me to need to describe it here. I only want to show how this particular form of psychological automatism relates to all those which have already been studied in this work.

Let us leave aside the sudden acts committed by certain epileptics during a momentary eclipse of consciousness.[132] As we have already shown, these actions are too similar to the acts of cataleptic individuals to merit a new study here. Accomplished abruptly, without reflection, without resistance, without leaving any trace in normal memory, they are the brutal, instantaneous expression of an image remaining alone in a consciousness which is almost entirely destroyed. Always reproduced in the same way with each attack,[133] they are part of a crisis. They belong to an automatic mechanism which starts up as soon as the personal consciousness is obscured. The impulses that interest us most are those that take place during the patient's waking state, while they are capable of perception and reflection. The subject is aware of them and feels that they let themselves be carried away by an outside force.

The simplest acts of this kind will be nervous movements, tics, jerky grimaces of the face, trunk, or extremities,[134] movements that the subject declares are carried out in spite of themselves, but of which they are aware and which, with effort, they could resist. Certain choreic movements are of this kind, but already present a greater complication; it is right, in fact, to distinguish vulgar or gesticulatory chorea, which is similar to simple tics, from great rhythmic chorea, which differs from it in that the irresistible movements are not made at random, but appear ordered and have a determined goal.[135] There are rotating, climbing, shouting varieties, in which the patients jump, run, make animal cries, etc. Although they are not usual, perhaps it is necessary to relate to these varieties, these grimaces or expressions of involuntary and persistent physiognomy. "Certain expressions," says Luys, "seem to freeze permanently on the physiognomy, features of terror persisting eight months after the accident which had caused them." All these choreic follies, said Maudsley,[136] are characterized by their automatic nature; each nervous center seems to act on its own account. These are indeed impulses during the waking state and during a period of normal consciousness, but the individual who feels them does not seem able to resist them.

But, in other more dramatic cases, the individual who is aware of his impulse may resist it for a time and succumb only after a desperate struggle. They are violent and sudden *desires* which cross their minds and which push them to perform an absurd or criminal action. They sense that their desire is ridiculous or odious; they resist it and try to think of something else. The *urge* to do this act becomes more specific, more relentless. They reject it and try to flee from it. They cannot and remain panting, sweating, in this insane struggle against themselves, which of necessity nearly always ends in defeat. Once the act is accomplished, they breathe, calm down, rejoice, not in the act they have done, which is still abhorrent to them, but in the relief they experience in no longer feeling this horrible torture and in regaining the free disposition of their mind. In all the works on alienation, one can find innumerable examples of this really cruel moral disease. In his latest book on "degenerates," Dr. Saury summarized the most typical and frequent forms that these impulses take. We cannot dwell on the childish impulses to actions like removing a stone from a wall or picking up bits of straw,[137] nor on the terrible impulses towards crimes of homicide or fire starting. The character of these desires, as all the patients describe them, is that they seem unreasonable to the very one who experiences them. They have no plausible motive nor interest;[138] they are in contradiction with the deepest and most intimate feelings of the individual. A woman feels an irresistible impulse to kill her children, whom she adores. An unhappy young man runs away to Africa, then commits himself to a hospital so as not to kill his own mother, for he feels that he can no longer resist the terrible impulse which drives him. This is why the patient resists with all their strength and a singular lucidity and requests help from all sides. While the truly insane abandon themselves to their delirium and delight in it, these impulses are repulsive, like something foreign. This is a remarkable characteristic which gives a very special importance to this mental disturbance.

In order to clarify this description, allow me to summarize in a few words an observation that I was able to make at the hospital in Le Havre. Not that the case in itself is of great interest, for it falls within a category of very well-known phenomena, but because the discussion is more easily made with a specific example. An unhappy young man of seventeen, D, is the son of a father and mother who were both deranged and both ended their lives by suicide. Until recently, he has had a relatively calm existence, although he is occasionally disturbed by nervous attacks. He has violent fits of melancholy during which he hides, isolates himself, and remains there crying, for no reason in particular, about his fate. He worries about how he will earn a living, how he is to learn his trade, etc., while at the same time he reasons with himself and finds that these worries are not based in reality, and then weeps once more. Other times, he has hot flashes in his face and choreic tremors in his left leg that last for nights at a time. At one point these convulsive tremors became generalized to all his limbs, to the degree that people believed (falsely, in my opinion) that he was having an epileptic attack. For the past few years he has had an almost constant fear of being alone. Yet he hates society. So he does not know what to do, and again is in tears. He has an intense agoraphobia, and, when it is necessary to cross an open place, he begs someone to accompany him, or else follows closely behind people, with a dreadful fear that he will never be seen again. The final and most tragic incident which brought him to the hospital is as follows. One evening he felt one of his anxiety attacks coming on. He could not eat or drink and spent the night awake, moaning. His left leg trembled and shook continuously. However, in the morning he made an effort to go to work and, as he is an apprentice hairdresser, began shaving a client. He barely had the razor in his hand, when his face began to sweat; his tremors increased and spread to his arms. A horrible thought crossed his mind: he desired, he wanted to cut the throat of the man he was shaving. Terrified by the idea of this act, he resisted with a sort of rage and clung to the chair so as not to fall. He tried again to lift his razor, but the impulse returned, even more terrible. He ran to his room with loud cries. The people in the shop ran after him and only just caught him before he cut his own throat. Transported to hospital, for two days he was in a state of complete bewilderment, refusing to eat, and was constantly agitated with choreic movements. Finally, he calmed down and told me all he had experienced. He is now feeling better, but he has a new melancholic idea which he did have before: he is convinced that sooner or later he will kill himself as his parents did, and this idea only increases his sadness.

At the beginning of this section we said that these impulses resemble the suggestions made to somnambulists. However, there is seemingly a great difference, which is quite obvious and makes this an important comparison. The subjects that we studied carried out the suggestions in two main ways: either with full awareness, in which they accepted the act, did it willingly and believed themselves free in their conduct; or without accepting the act, but then they were completely unaware of the act and performed it without knowing it. In both cases, they are different from the impulsively insane who do not act unconsciously, know very well what they are doing, and yet abhor it and resist with all their might. There is something new and original in this. Our somnambulists, however, presented analogous phenomena, which we have not reported so far because they are complicated exceptions and it was not necessary to hinder the exposure of relatively simple phenomena. We must now return to these irregular cases.

One day during somnambulism, Léonie told me that she had received an interesting letter. I asked her to bring it to me the next day, but I did not remind her after waking her up. The next day, wide awake, she brings me the letter, but says to me with a little concern, "I do not know what is happening to me with this letter. Three times I picked it up to take it with me. Every time I took it out of my pocket and held it tightly, I felt I did not need it. But I must have picked it up again, because here it is in my pocket." Another observation of the same kind: I tell Léonie, during her somnambulism, to bring me a specific bundle of papers that she had at home when she returned to Le Havre. A few months later while she was preparing to come to Le Havre, she experienced the following. She was about to close her suitcase when she saw a rather bulky bundle of papers inside. "Am I foolish and absent-minded enough," she said, "to have put these here? I will certainly not need them," and she removed the papers. A few moments later, she checked her luggage again and the papers were still there. "Ah, this is too much," she said, and she removed the papers, locked them up, and arrived in Le Havre without them. One day I arranged with a young man, who I knew was hypnotizable, that, after I woke him up, he would give me his genuine impressions of his experiences. During the hypnotic sleep, which was quite deep, I asked him to get my hat off the table and put it on my head, then I woke him up. I questioned him then, according to our conventions, but he said nothing interesting to me, because he had forgotten everything, and (a singular detail already reported) he was convinced that I had not succeeded in putting him to sleep, despite the fact that I had him experience several hallucinations in the last half hour. Nevertheless, after a while, he takes on an abnormal appearance, wanders around the room, and complains of a slight and sudden headache. While he is talking, he has moved decidedly closer to my hat; he picks it up and turns it over and over, then suddenly drops it, shouting, "Ah, what do I want with your hat? What am I doing? This is really too idiotic!" He sits down again and his frustration subsides. There is no need to cite other examples of the same kind.

Although the act seems to be known by the subject, who sometimes accepts it, as in the first case, and sometimes rejects it, I believe that this consciousness is entirely secondary and that the essence of the suggestions happened subconsciously. The memory of the suggestion and the notion of the moment when it had to be executed, all this belongs, as always, to the second layer of phenomena, to the somnambulistic person persisting beneath the waking state. The act was initiated and half executed by motor images belonging to this layer and therefore separated from normal consciousness. But the division was not complete, as in the simple experiments with Lucie, or at least it did not remain complete. The results of the act, or simply the movements of the limbs, were *seen* by the first personality. She did not feel the act in itself, because she did not know what it was, but she saw the external manifestations as she would have done with the action of another person.[139] She then accepted the act, which was initiated again, or else she suppressed it with a powerful resistance. This is the case in many of the suggestions which are said to be conscious; the subject continues, with goodwill, an act which they themselves have not started. They even take responsibility for it and invent reasons to explain it; but the act was nevertheless a subconscious phenomenon, subject to the laws of psychological disaggregation.

At times (by way of experiment), one can give or take away from the subject this *reflective consciousness* of the act which was started by the second psychic group. If we distract the subject while she is performing the act, she will not notice anything and things will proceed quite regularly. If we do not distract her, she will use what little force of perception she has to observe her own actions and thereby be able to accept or resist them.

Typically we talked to Lucie while she was carrying out a suggestion and we saw how remarkable the disaggregation was with her. One day, during somnambulism, I suggested to her a rather complicated act: to take an object from the pocket of the person who had accompanied me, and, once she was awake,

I avoided talking to her. She seemed surprised by my silence, and got up as if to walk around the room, but she would take a most singular roundabout route. She would take three steps towards the person I had indicated, then stop short and turn around. She advanced three steps again and stopped once more. She stamped her feet, gnashed her teeth, took up some work to distract herself, then got up to do it again. All these gestures can be translated as follows: during a moment of distraction, the legs walked to accomplish the act that the second personality wanted to perform. Lucie, who was not distracted enough, noticed this movement and said to herself, stamping her feet, "Ah, what am I doing?" and (voluntarily) was about to sit down again. This struggle between the two consciousnesses lasted for more than twenty minutes, before the act was performed, in its entirety, during a longer period of distraction. However, the suggestion would have been executed immediately, if I had taken some precautions to avoid this return of awareness to prevent Lucie's preoccupation with her subconscious acts.

It is the same for automatic writing. Ordinarily we take precautions to prevent the subject from noticing it: we choose people whose arms are anesthetic, we hide the arm by a screen, we distract the subject by talking to them about something else. But when these precautions are not taken, or when the subject has partially retained the muscular sense of the arm, the writing is perceived and read as it is written, or the movements of the arm are felt. S, whom I have spoken of, felt the movements of the board under her fingers and, by quite a long exercise, had managed to guess her automatic writing before reading it. She said to me, without looking at the planchette, "Ah, it is Johnson who wrote this," and indeed the *spirit* had signed "Johnson." Many spiritists have observed this phenomenon, but occasionally they have also noted an even more curious occurrence. It is that the medium, thus guessing the writing of their spirit, sometimes completes it consciously and collaborates with it during these singular essays. "If there is an absolute division at the onset, so that the ideas are known only as the words appear, the word which is already written often leads to guessing what will follow. The girl becomes, unintentionally at least, the collaborator of the second person formed within her … 'It is the Countess who writes,' said N, speaking of her spirit, 'but we think together.'"[140] The muscular sense thus becomes, as Richet said,[141] the way in which a large number of subconscious phenomena enter into consciousness after the execution of an act has already begun. Many events in our everyday life are of the same kind: "When you read a book or hear a speech that is not very engaging, you can remain indifferent for a while, but, if you feel an involuntary yawn, then you no longer doubt, you are authentically alerted to your boredom and the awareness that you have of it is increased."[142] These occurrences show us that there can be a kind of knowledge and awareness of the act which is unconscious, that is to say, which has its starting point outside of the personality of the subject.

How do subjects understand and express the psychological state that we have just described? What do they think of themselves when they see themselves acting in this strange way? It is always the same word that they use to describe their state.

"What is happening with you?" I said to Lucie in a situation similar to that which I have described. "It is so strange that *I want* to do this, and yet it is so foolish," she responded. I had suggested to Léonie to come to my house and since she had not arrived, I went out to meet her and found her on the street. "I have been to your door," she said, "and left, I cannot understand why *I wanted* to go to your house." "What do *I want* with your hat?" said the young man, whose suggestion I have described. In a word, they all interpret their state by saying that they want to do something, and they then give in to this desire, or else they resist it, as the case may be. This expression should not surprise us, because the consciousness of a desire is little else (if we want to analyze it), "than the sensation of nascent movements sketching out a function or an act."[143] This is precisely what our subjects are experiencing, an act in the making. And since they are unaware of its true origin, they interpret it as a want or a desire.

At this point we can return to our impulsive patients, whose psychological character now becomes more understandable. On the one hand, despite being aware of their impulses, they are very disaggregated individuals. "Such people have lost their unity," said Leuret. "They are still aware, but within them something different from their self, is also aware. They still have wants, but the something that is within them also has wants. They are dominated, they are like slaves, their body is a machine obeying a will that is not their own."[144] On the other hand, they are aware of the movements they are making, they feel the impulse, interpret it as a personal desire, accept it or resist it – actions that disaggregated individuals do not ordinarily do. "It is something that compels me," the patient D described to Georget. "I was terrified that I would cut the throat of the man I was shaving." "Why were you afraid that you would do this?" Georget asked him. "I could see my hand rising to strike, I had just enough time to run away." The patient does not understand that the idea and, consequently, the act of cutting the throat was suggested by connecting the razor to a group of phenomena which is within him, and of which he is completely unaware. He saw only the result of the suggestion, the movement of the arm, and that is why he interprets it by saying: "I had a terrible urge to cut his throat." These impulses, therefore, show us an interesting type of incomplete disaggregated acts, that is to say, half known by the subject, but originating in the second consciousness, rather than the first, as we have seen in our studies with the recording pendulum.

3.8 Fixed ideas. Hallucinations

Impulses sometimes exist in another form, which comes across a little differently; instead of presenting itself as an act, at least as a desire or a want, it is a simple idea equally fixed and obsessive, but which does not seem to have any tendency to provoke an act. Sometimes these ideas manifest themselves in the form of an auditory hallucination, a phrase that patients suddenly hear echoing in their ears without any logical explanation, "without having any relevance to their previous thoughts."[145] One hears a voice repeating, "Do not move, or you are lost," and he therefore remains motionless, in an apparent stupor.[146] Another hears a voice which commands him to throw ten francs into the Seine.[147] Sometimes these ideas seem to remain more abstract, without taking the form of an auditory hallucination.[148] For example, it will be a question that the patient continuously asks himself: "Why are the colours unevenly distributed? Why are trees green? Why is mourning in black?"[149] It can be a fear, an idea of persecution; "an individual constantly thinks that he will be poisoned by the grapes of a vine near which a fragment of silver nitrate fell,"[150] Or it can simply be an insignificant and absurd idea: "N constantly thinks that his servant loves wine and he cannot get rid of this unrelenting idea."[151] These unhappy people do not accept their fixed ideas as part of their own thoughts, (as we accept the most absurd ideas in our dreams). They resist these ideas and they are aware of the absurdity of their situation. "The fixed idea appears to them as a foreign body lodged within them which they cannot expel, but it does not manage to invade them completely."[152] "If I could think like you," said one, "I would be happy. But I am overwhelmed by sinister ideas which I cannot help believing. I would rather be completely mad than to have kept my intelligence in most matters."[153] Lastly, in others cases, the fixed idea appears to the conscious mind suddenly, in the form of a visual hallucination that arises without the patient being aware of its origin. Occurrences of this kind are so well known that it suffices to point them out and to inquire how these different kinds of fixed ideas relate to the laws of psychological automatism.

The problem is the same as with motor impulses. The abnormal phenomenon is not integrated into the personality; it is foreign to the self, which wants to reject it. It seems to belong to another psychic group, like disaggregated phenomena, and yet it is conscious, while those disaggregated phenomena were unconscious.

We find similarities in our hypnotic experiences which allow us to study the psychology of alienation. Léonie had a sort of incomplete hysterical crisis, she was agitated and screaming and it was impossible for me to calm her. Suddenly she stopped and said to me in terror, "Oh! who is speaking to me like this? It scares me." "No one is talking to you, we are alone." "But yes, there, to the left." She gets up and wants to open a cupboard to her left to see if someone is hiding inside. "What do you hear?" I asked her. "I hear a voice to my left repeating, 'enough, enough, keep quiet, you are bothering us.'" Certainly the voice that spoke had a purpose, but I hadn't suggested anything like it and had not even thought of causing a hallucination at the time. Another day, the same subject, during the first somnambulism, was very calm, but obstinately refused to answer anything I asked her. She heard the same voice to her left, saying, "Come on, behave, you have to answer." We know enough about this subject to guess that these words came from the lower personnage who existed below this layer of consciousness. It was very easy to verify it with automatic writing or by causing a deeper somnambulism, according to the theories of disaggregation that we have demonstrated. Is it possible that the ideas of the second subconscious personnage become auditory hallucinations for the first?

Let us reproduce the incident experimentally. During a deep somnambulistic state, I instruct Léonie 3 to say something to *the other*, for example to say "Hello," then I wake her up. The hallucination occurs in the same way and Léonie again asks, "Who said hello?" But this time, I also heard the word "hello," because the mouth pronounced it perfectly, although in a lower register. In this case, these hallucinations of subconscious origin were the result of hearing genuine automatic speech, similar to the writing of mediums. The subject heard her own subconscious speech, just as the medium reads her own automatic writing, and both attributed this speech or this writing to beings different or other than themselves.

These words of subconscious origin are no less rare than other impulses of the same genre and are presented with the same characteristics. "Often," said one of the young Cévennes prophets, "I do not know how the word that the spirit has begun within me will end. It has sometimes happened to me that, believing I was going to pronounce a particular word or phrase, it was instead a simple, inarticulate song which my voice produced ... While I speak, my mind pays attention to what my mouth pronounces, as if it were a speech made by another, but which leaves vivid impressions in my memory."[154] The famous Lisa Andersdocter, in 1841, sang and, in spite of herself, delivered more or less eloquent speeches.[155] X, aged fifty (an older hysteric), from time to time felt the need to go into a corner and complain loudly and voice her secrets.[156] Finally the disturbed subjects, of whom Saury speaks, very often have impulses to curse and utter obscenities despite themselves, similar to the medium's disposition to write them. But when the subject hears their own voice speaking in this way, or when they sense, through the muscular sense, the words beginning to form, they imagine that they hear a foreign voice and assign it a location using their own assumptions. "A patient speaks to himself out loud and then claims that it is a voice he hears; if his lips are held together, he still hears the voice, but we feel his lips move beneath our fingers."[157] "X hears voices, but it is easy to see that his tongue moves, in spite of himself as the interior voice speaks."[158] I had the opportunity quite recently to verify this phenomenon with a mentally disturbed patient. An excited and semimaniacal individual claimed to communicate from afar with Counts and Marquis living in Paris. I asked him to say hello on my behalf to the Marquis. He rubbed his head on one side (it was his cabalistic sign to transport himself to the Marquis) and said aloud, "Marquis, I bring you greetings." Then he tilted his head to the side, as if to listen with great attention; but his mouth spoke softly and murmured, "You will tell this gentleman that ..." I could not hear the rest, but the patient straightened up and said to me aloud, "The Marquis asked me to thank you ... I heard him perfectly." It was obviously his own words that suggested his auditory hallucination.

Is it not natural to interpret fixed ideas in the same manner, and should we not, as many alienists, like Moreau (de Tours), Max Simon,[159] and others do, consider these fixed ideas as impulses of the function of language? "'They are influencing my thoughts,' said an insane woman ... , 'I am made to speak in spite of myself.'"[160] She was perfectly right, because hearing yourself speak in spite of yourself is also thinking in spite of yourself. Repeating the same sentence over and over again, without having the will to do it, is to have a fixed idea.[161] The conscious mind develops its fixed idea as it chooses and increases its delirium, but the idea itself comes from automatic speech which does not depend on this conscious thought. Did not Moreau (de Tours) believe in a similar theory when he wrote: "In the mental conceptions of the insane, what is active or belonging to the state of wakefulness is the psychological consequences which the fixed idea entails, the deductions which the patient logically draws from this idea, the feelings and the passions which it raises. But the fixed idea, the morbid thought which summarizes in it all delirium, because it is the starting point of all aberrations, belongs entirely to the passive state of sleep; it arose under similar psycho-organic conditions."[162]

Whatever the simplicity and, in some cases, the truth of these hypotheses, I do not believe that they are sufficient to consistently explain these kinds of collaboration between the group of subconscious phenomena and the group of conscious phenomena. Often the intermediary between the two groups, that is to say the physical phenomenon produced by one and felt by the other, is not visible. There is not always a gesture or a word which presents itself in order to communicate to one of the people the thoughts and the modifications of the other. When a thought, an auditory hallucination and especially a visual hallucination suddenly appears in the consciousness of the insane, it must be recognized that the unconscious phenomena have suddenly and automatically brought about a conscious phenomenon without intermediary. This much is obvious; but as we already noted at the beginning of this chapter in regard to the divining rod, it is not easy to understand. Did we not say, in fact, that these two groups of phenomena were separate or disaggregated, and that it was precisely this characteristic which formed the two fields of consciousness? How can these phenomena both relate to one another by association and yet be disaggregated?

Let us first point out that this natural phenomenon, which is present in mental illnesses, is not unknown to us and that we have often encountered it in our experimental studies. When we described suggestions by distraction, we pointed out in passing a very curious fact: it is the conscious hallucination produced by a suggestion which remains subconscious. I command Léonie, while she is distracted and chatting with another person, by whispering quietly that this person has a beautiful green outfit. Léonie did not hear what I said (a disaggregated subconscious phenomenon belonging to the second field of consciousness), and yet she cried out, "Oh! how funny your coat is, it's all green. I hadn't noticed earlier." (A conscious phenomenon belonging to the first field of consciousness). So despite the disaggregation, a subconscious phenomenon produced a conscious phenomenon by means of a sort of association of ideas.

There are many similar examples. I whisper softly, "When I touch your thumb, you will see red, when I touch your little finger, you will see yellow." (It is a suggestion by distraction with a reference point.) I touch the left hand, which is *anesthetic*. Despite the fact that I touch the thumb *which she does not feel*, it brings about the conscious hallucination of red, and the touch of the little finger brings about yellow, and there is never an error. With another subject who was completely anesthetic at this time, I operate differently. I pinch the back of her hand; Marie feels nothing; but I ask her with an insistence that amounts to a suggestion for her: "Do you hear something?" "Yes," she says, "it sounds like bells." A few moments later, I pinch her arm and even though she does not feel anything I still ask: "Do you hear something *else*?" "But yes," she said, "it sounds like a whistle." Consequently, when I pinch her on the back of the hand, she hears bells and when I pinch her on the arm, she hears a whistle. Although when I repeat the experiment she feels absolutely nothing on her arm: it is a subconscious sensation which serves as a point of reference for a conscious hallucination.[163]

Is it necessary to look for new instances? Examples of this kind are found among the best known phenomena of hypnotism. The old portrait experiment is an excellent one. It has been suggested to the subject that they see a portrait on a card and consequently they always see the portrait on the designated card. They recognize it by certain signs no doubt, but the sensation of these signs was never conscious and it was only the second personage who told me by automatic writing that there was a stain at the top of the card. The point of reference was still subconscious, although the hallucination was conscious. What can be derived from these phenomena? Simply what I had foreseen. It is that the automatic association of ideas is one thing, and that the synthesis which forms personal perception at each moment of life and the idea of the self is another. One can be destroyed, while the other remains. This supposition, moreover, agrees quite well with all that we have said of these two behaviours. The association of ideas is the manifestation of an elementary synthesis which has already been carried out in the past and which has linked the phenomena to one another once and for all. Personal perception is formed by current synthetic activity, which, by a continued effort repeated at each moment, brings back to the unity of the self all the phenomena which occur, whatever their origin. This force of synthesis, perhaps weakened in the present, renders the subject incapable of perceiving a particular auditory sensation or tactile sensation, and yet, by means of an older automatism which has not been destroyed, this unperceived sensation can bring about other images that are part of those that the subject still perceives. Although these remarks undoubtedly do not remove all the difficulties, they permit us to understand how these new phenomena, fixed ideas and certain hallucinations, are simply more complicated applications of the older rules.

3.9 Possessions

The disaggregated element of thought has therefore already manifested itself in these complex phenomena, either by a phrase softly spoken and constantly repeated, or by hallucinations. It can manifest itself in many other ways and introduce the most diverse disorders into the physical and mental health of the conscious individual.

We already know that this can be the origin of crises, anesthesia, contractures, and paralysis, and we do not have to revisit this subject. But why would this thought not produce expressive attitudes in the body and physiognomy of the subject which would remain fixed in spite of them and as a result would keep them in a perpetual state of terror, or of sadness? To have one's body in the attitude of terror is to feel the emotion of terror, and if this attitude is determined by a subconscious idea, the patient will be affected during consciousness without knowing the reason. Before a crisis Lucie would sometimes say, "I'm afraid and I don't know why." At which time her eyes looked haggard and her gestures expressed terror. The unconscious has its own dream, it sees the men hiding behind the curtains and puts the body into an attitude of fear. If Lucie does not seem too concerned, it is because she is anesthetic. "I cry and I don't know why," said Léonie, "I feel sad for no reason and it is ridiculous." It is the second person who feels sad to have left Le Havre and who causes the tears. "I don't know why I feel sad," said a poor boy with melancholy madness. "I am always sighing." We must again assume that there is a subconscious idea which directly causes the sighs and indirectly causes the melancholy of the unfortunate person.

It would be necessary to review all the mental pathology and perhaps even an important part of the physical pathology to show all the psychological and bodily disorders that can produce a persistent thought apart from the personal consciousness. Allow me simply to give a final complex example of these disturbances, and to summarize one more of my observations. The facts themselves are always relevant, and there is no harm in giving many descriptions even if the interpretations are wrong.

One of my subjects, whom I have often cited as Marie, presented an illness and cure which were equally curious. This young girl was brought from the countryside to the hospital of Le Havre at the age of nineteen, because she was considered mad and there was little hope of her recovery. In reality, she had episodes of seizures and delirium that lasted for days at a time. After a period of observation, it was evident that the disease consisted of intermittent attacks recurring regularly at the time of her period with longer lasting, less serious attacks occurring irregularly in the intervals. Let us consider the former. As her period approached, Marie's character changed; it became dark and violent, which was unusual for her. She had pains and nervous twitching in all of her limbs. During the first day of her period, however, things progressed almost normally until, barely twenty hours after it had begun, it stopped suddenly and a great shiver shook her whole body, then a sharp pain slowly travelled up from her abdomen to her throat and the great crises of hysteria began. The convulsions, although very violent, did not last long and never had the appearance of epileptoid tremors, but they were replaced by the longest and most intense delirium. Sometimes she uttered cries of terror, speaking constantly of blood and fire and fleeing to escape the flames; sometimes she played like a child, talking to her mother, climbing on the stove or on the furniture, and disturbing everything in the room. This delirium and these convulsions alternated, with rather short moments of respite, for forty-eight hours. The scene ended with several bouts of vomiting blood, after which everything returned, for the most part, to normal. After a day or two of rest, Marie calmed down and remembered nothing. In the intervals between these major monthly attacks, she retained small contractures sometimes in the arms or in the intercostal muscles, varied and very changeable anesthesia and, above all, absolute and continual blindness in the left eye. (We have seen elsewhere the nature of this hysterical blindness.) From time to time Marie also had small crises without great delirium, but which were characterized above all by postural poses of terror. This disease, so obviously related to her menstrual cycle, appeared to be only physical in nature and not very interesting for a psychologist; for this reason I initially took very little interest in this person. At most I conducted several hypnotic experiments with her and made some studies on her anesthesia, but I avoided anything that might have disturbed her towards the time when the great attacks were approaching. She thus remained seven months at the hospital without the various medications and hydrotherapy bringing her the least bit of relief. Besides which any therapeutic suggestions, specifically suggestions relating to her period, had only negative effects and added to her delirium.

Towards the end of the eighth month she complained of her sad fate and said with a sort of despair that she knew well that everything was going to start all over again. One day, out of curiosity, I asked her, "explain to me once again what happens at the onset of the illness." "But you know very well … , everything stops, I have a great shiver and I no longer know what is happening." I wanted specific information on how her periods had begun and how they had been interrupted. She did not answer clearly, because she seemed to have forgotten most of the things I had asked her. It then occurred to me to put her into a deep somnambulism capable, as we have seen, of bringing back apparently forgotten memories. I was thus able to find the exact memory of a scene which up until then had not been known in its entirety. At the age of thirteen, she had experienced her first period, but as a result of a childish idea or of something heard and misunderstood, she got it into her head that there was shame in it and searched for a way to stop the flow as soon as possible. About twenty hours later, she sneaked out, found a large tub of cold water and submerged herself in it. It seemed to have been successful, her period stopped immediately and, despite a great chill which developed, she was able to return home. She was sick for quite a while and was delirious for several days. She eventually recovered and menstruation did not reappear; when it did reappear five years later, it brought with it the disturbances I have described. Therefore if we compare the sudden stop, the chill, the pain that she currently describes in the waking state with the story that she told in somnambulism (which, moreover, has been indirectly confirmed), we come to the following conclusion: every month, the scene of the cold bath repeats itself, bringing about the same stop to menstruation and with it a delirium (which is far more intense than it was initially), until an additional hemorrhage takes place via the stomach. In her normal consciousness, she has no knowledge of this and does not even understand that the chill is brought about by the hallucination of the cold; it is therefore likely that this scene takes place below this consciousness and leads to all the other disturbances.

Having developed this supposition, and after having taken the advice of Povilewicz, I tried to remove from the somnambulistic consciousness this fixed and absurd idea that menstruation is stopped by a cold bath. At first, I could not do it; the fixed idea persisted and the menstrual period which arrived two days later was very similar to the previous ones. Having more time to reflect, I began my attempt again: I could not succeed in erasing this idea except by a singular means. It was necessary to bring her back, by suggestion, to the age of thirteen and to put her back into the initial conditions of delirium, and then to convince her that the period had lasted three days and had not been interrupted by any untoward event. This done, the next period arrived on its date and continued for three days without causing any suffering, convulsions, or delirium.

After having observed this result, it was necessary to study the other incidents. I will not go into the details of the psychological research, which was sometimes difficult. The crises of terror were the repetition of an emotion that this girl had experienced when, at the age of sixteen, an old woman killed herself by falling down a staircase; the blood she always spoke of in her fits was a memory of this scene. As for the image of the fire, it probably occurred by association of ideas, because it did not relate to anything specific. Using the same procedure as earlier, I brought the subject, by suggestion, to the moment of the accident, and I managed, not without difficulty, to change the image, to show her that the old woman had stumbled and did not kill herself, and to erase the terrifying conviction. The crises of terror did not happen again.

Finally, I wanted to study the blindness in her left eye, but when she was awake Marie objected saying that she had had this blindness since birth. It was easy to verify by means of somnambulism that she was mistaken: if we change her into a five-year-old child according to known procedures, she regains the sensitivity she had at that age and we find that she then sees very well with both eyes. So it was at the age of six that the blindness started, but at what moment? When awake, Marie persists in saying that she does not know anything about it. During somnambulism, and thanks to successive transformations, during which I have her play out the main scenes of her life at that time, I note that blindness begins at a certain moment in connection with a trivial incident. Despite her screams, she had been forced to nap with a child her age who had *lesions all over the left side of the face.* Shortly after, Marie developed similar lesions which appeared almost identical and *in the same location* on her face. These lesions reappeared for several years around the same time, but until now no one had paid any particular attention to the fact that *she was anesthetic on the left side of her face and blind in her left eye.* Since then, she has continued to experience this anesthesia (at least as far as has been observed), to some later period, which she reached through suggestion. She always has this same anesthesia, although the rest of the body at certain times resumes its complete sensitivity. I use the same technique as before. I bring her back to the child who terrifies her so. I make her believe that the child is very nice and has no lesions, but she is only half convinced. After two rehearsals of the scene, I succeed and she hugs the imaginary child without fear. The sensitivity on the left side reappears without difficulty and, when I wake her up, Marie sees clearly with the left eye.

It has been five months since these experiments were made. Marie has not presented the slightest sign of hysteria, she is doing very well, and above all is gaining strength. Her physical appearance has absolutely changed. I do not attach more importance to this healing than it deserves, and I do not know how long it will last, but I found this story interesting as it illustrates the importance of sub-conscious fixed ideas and the role they play in certain physical illnesses as well as in mental illnesses.

Let us further add to and complicate these phenomena. Let us suppose that this subconscious life does not manifest itself only in the surprised mind of the patient with involuntary contractions, gestures, or words repeated over and over, but that it acts unceasingly in an intelligent and coordinated way. The patient finds that without their knowledge and despite themselves, their arms and legs are perform-ing complicated acts. They hear their own mouth order them or mock them; they resist, they argue, they fight against an individual who has been created within themself. How can this patient interpret their state; what should they think of themself? Is it not reasonable for them to say they are possessed by a spirit, per-secuted by a demon who dwells within them? Why would they doubt, when this second personality, borrowing its name from the dominant superstitions, declares itself Astaroth, Leviathan, or Beelzebub? The belief in possession is simply the popular interpretation of a psychological truth.

Sometimes the two personalities live in fairly good accord and do not mistreat each other. Some women are even quite proud of this breakdown of their personality and like to consult, on all the concerns of life, "that small part that they believe resides in their heart or in their stomach and which gives them good advice."[164] "They have friendly discussions with a revelatory superintelligence which speaks to them by their mouths."[165] Estelle, Despine's famous patient, does nothing without consulting "a good genie which she feels obliged to obey."[166] "A subject never answered questions," said Charpignon,[167] "without first saying: 'I will consult the other one … it is the genie responsible for guiding and enlightening me.'" Most often the secondary spirit is not so good natured. It torments its victims and gives them only bad advice. We know well Moreau (de Tours)'s patient, so curious in his arguments with "the Sovereign,"[168] the convulsants of Saint-Médard, whose spirits forced them to spin indefinitely on one foot or prevented them from eating,[169] and the nuns of Loudun, tormented by the evil spirits who embodied their passions.[170] Sometimes there are several spirits in the same person, some good, others bad, who quarrel with each other: "A child is possessed by two spirits, one bad, the other good; in his crises, his voice changes tone and speaks successively for one and then the other."[171]

These spirits are not only content to talk; they act. Here is a story from the Superior at Loudun that we were inclined to consider misleading: "One of the spir-its that was in her, Beelzebub, wanted her to burn. She did not consent. He threw her against the fireplace and she was found all drowsy, head almost touching the fire."[172] However, a similar incident happened almost before our eyes. A person, annoyed with the automatic writing that his hand wanted to do, took the papers and threw them away. This second personality was furious and, by means of a convulsion, put the subject's hand into the fire and it was seriously burned. It then boasted of it in its automatic communications. One of the best summaries of these phenomena can be found in a description written by a possessed person describing his own state: "I cannot explain to you what is happening in me during this time and how this spirit unites with mine without depriving it of knowledge and freedom, behaving like another self. It is as if I had two souls, one of which is dispossessed of its body and the use of its organs, and it is all it can do to restrain itself as it watches the one who writes. The two spirits fight in a single arena, which is the body, and the soul is divided. According to one part of oneself, it is the subject of diabolical impressions, and, according to the other, expresses the movements which are specific to it and which God gives it."[173] The various epidemics of possessions of Loudun, Saint-Médard, Morzine, Verzegnin, Plédran, etc.,[174] are well known. They show us all possible examples of these various destructions of the mental composite.

3.10 Conclusion

Mental disaggregation, the formation of successive and simultaneous personalities in the same individual, the automatic functioning of these various psychological groups isolated from each other – these are not artificial things, the bizarre result of experimental manipulation. These are perfectly real and natural things that experiment allows us to discover and study, but does not create. These things reveal themselves naturally in all manner of ways and degrees. Sometimes a very slight separation leaves only insignificant phenomena outside of the mind, incapable of acting by themselves and docile servants of conscious thought. They exaggerate, they modify the manifestations of normal thought, but they do not oppose them. Sometimes the second personality speaks of its own account, takes on the name of a spirit and brings to light its own thoughts, but only when the first personality allows it and leaves it free to act. Sometimes the abnormal group is substantial enough alone to impose itself on the subject's awareness, to disturb and take away its freedom. But, from the most insignificant subconscious act to the most terrible possessions, it is always the same psychological mechanism, which gradually brings about the complete dissolution of the mind.

In this chapter, we have not looked for new laws. We have simply found numerous and sometimes complex applications of old laws. Our hypotheses seemed to us to be sufficient to explain the various facts of the divining rod, of spiritism, of impulsive madness, and of hallucination. This is a confirmation which indeed has value. But, at the same time as our hypotheses were confirmed by applying them to these new experiences, they also became more defined in their most intricate aspects. In this chapter, far better than in the previous one, we have seen the difference and sometimes even the opposition which exists between pure and simple automatism, which is the result of simple past syntheses, and the current activity of the mind, which unites phenomena into new groups and units. The phenomena which are united and dependent in the first automation can very well be separated and independent in the second. The two activities of thought are distinguished and become more and more defined.

Notes

1 Cf. Gasparin, *Des tables tournantes*, 1855, II, 124. De Mirville, *Des Esprits et de leurs Manifestations Fluidiques*, 1863, I. – Appendice, 61, etc.
2 Myers, Gurney, Podmore, *Phantasms of the Living*, 1886, I, 14.
3 *Ibid.*, 15.
4 Charpignon, *Physiologie Magnétique*, 1852, 61. Rutter, *Journal du Magnétisme*, 1852, 64, etc.
5 Gasparin, *Op. cit.*, 140.
6 Sollas, The Divining Rod, *Proceed.*, S. P. R., II, 1884, 73.
7 Pease, The Divining Rod, *Proceed.*, S. P. R., II, 1884, 79.
8 Chevreul, *De la Baguette Divinatoire, du Pendule Explorateur et des Tables Tournantes*, 1854, 155.
9 Bertrand, *Deux Lois Psycho-Physiologique, Revue Philosophique*, 1884, I, 249.
10 Myers, *Automatic Writing. Proceed.*, S. P. R., 1885, 4.
11 *Proceed.*, 1882, 293.
12 Bertrand, *Deux lois psycho-physiologiques, Revue Philosophique*, 1884, I, 251.
13 Chevreul, *Op. cit.*, 158.
14 Gurney, Myers, and Podmore, *Phantasms of the Living*, I, 14.
15 *Ibid.*, 16.
16 *Proceed.*, S. P. R., II, 22.
17 Binet and Féré, *Archives de Physiologie*, 1st October 1887, 351.
18 On the history of the Fox sisters, Cf. Bersot, *Mesmer. Le Magnétisme et les Tables Tournantes*, 4th edit., 1879, 119.
19 De Mirville, *Op. Cit.*, 328.
20 Lafontaine, *L'art de Magnétiser*, 1860, 27.
21 Edmonds, *Journal du Magnétisme*, 1854, 90.
22 *Le Mystère de la danse des tables dévoilé dans ses rapports avec les manifestations spirituelles d'Amérique, par un Catholique* (M. de Richemond), 1853, 5.
23 *Ibid.*, 1.
24 *Instruction explicative et pratique des tables tournantes*, by Ferdinand Silas, 3rd edit., 1853, 14.
25 *Ibid.*, 20.
26 *Ibid.*, 21, 24, etc.
27 *Ibid.*, 28.
28 Allan Kardec, *Le Livre des Médiums*, 19th edit., 1870, 72.
29 Cf. Bersot, *Op. cit.*, 107.
30 Allan Kardec, *Op. cit.*, 196.
31 Bersot, *Op. cit.*, 123.
32 Gibier, *Le Spiritisme ou Fakirisme Occidental*, 1887, 170.
33 *Ibid.*, 220.
34 *Revue Spirite*, 1876, 136.

35 De Richemond, *Mystères de la Danse des Tables*, 1853, 15.
36 Allan Kardec, *Op. cit.*, 203.
37 *Ibid.*, 203.
38 *Journal du Magnétisme*, 1854, 92.
39 *Revue Spirite*, 1864, 148.
40 De Richemond, *Op. cit.*, 31.
41 de la Tourette, *L'hypnotisme et les états analogues*, 1887,, 476.
42 Philosophie spiritualiste, *Le Livre des Esprits*, containing the principles of the spiritist doctrine, on the immortality of the soul, the nature of spirits and their relationships with men according to the teaching given by higher spirits using various mediums, collected and put in order by Allan Kardec, 11th editi., 1864.
43 In 1864, there were ten notices in Europe, and in 1876, there were forty-six.
44 *Revue Spirite*, 1864, 4.
45 Tissandier, *Des Sciences Occultes et du Spiritisme*, 1866.
46 *Revue Spirite*, 1864, *passim*.
47 *Ibid.*, 123.
48 *Revue Spirite*, 1878, 71.
49 *Revue Spirite*, 1876, 42.
50 Cf. Gasparin, *Tables Tournantes*, II, 443.
51 Guldenstubbe, *La Réalité des Esprits*, 1873.
52 Summary article in the *Journal du Magnétisme*, 1854, 83.
53 Carpenter, *Revue Scientifique*, 1st May 1878.
54 According to Gasparin, *Op. cit.*, II, 508.
55 *Revue Spirite*, 1864, 310.
56 Gibier, *Op. cit.*, 125.
57 De Mirville, *Op. cit.*, II, 79 et *passim*.
58 *Revue Spirite*, 1878, 249. – The same fact appears in De Mirville, *Op. cit.*, 86, and many others.
59 Remarks by Father Bautain, reported by De Mirville, *Op. cit.*, 76.
60 Chevreul, *Op. cit.*, 224.
61 Gasparin, *Op. cit.*, I, 80.
62 According to Gasparin, *Op. cit.*, II, 76.
63 Myers, *Automating Writing. Proceed.*, S. P. R., 1885, 8.
64 *Revue Spirite*, 1878, 250.
65 Myers, *Op. cit.*, 20.
66 Myers, *Op. cit.*, 20.
67 *Journal du Magnétisme*, 1855, 164.
68 *Mystère de la Danse des Tables*, 21.
69 Allan Kardec, *Le Livre des Médiums*, 310.
70 De Mirville, *Op. cit.*, II, 84.
71 Myers, *Op. cit.*, 37.
72 *Ibid.*, 26.
73 Myers., *On a Telepathic Explanation of Some so-called Spiritualistic Phenomena. Proceed.*, II, 226.
74 According to Gasparin, *Op. cit.*, II, 508.
75 Wundt, *Spiritismus, Revue philosophique*, 1879, I, 666.
76 Allan Kardec, *Le Ciel et l'Enfer selon le Spiritisme*, 1869, 4th editi., *passim*.
77 *Ibid.*, 364.
78 De Mirville, *Op. cit.*, 76.
79 *Lettre de Gros Jean à son Évêque...* 1855, 4.
80 *Ibid.*, 5.
81 *Ibid.*, 7.

82 *Ibid.*, 9–11.
83 *Ibid.*, 21–22.
84 *Ibid.*, 22–24.
85 *Ibid.*, 44.
86 *Ibid.*, 43.
87 *Ibid.*, 31.
88 Liébault, *Du Sommeil et les États Analogues*, 1860, 249.
89 Cf. Myers, *Automatic Writing. Proceed…*,61.
90 Richet, *La Suggestion Mentale et le Calcul des Probabilités, Revue Philosophique*, 1884, II, 650.
91 Richet, *Les Mouvements Inconscients* in the homage to Chevreul, 1886.
92 Du Prel, *Die Philosophie der Mystik*, Vienna, 1884.
93 Hellenbach, *Geburt und Tod*, Leipzig, 1885.
94 Myers, *On a Telepathic Explanation of Some So-Called Spiritualistic Phenomena. Proceed…*, S. P. R., II, 217. *Automatic Writing. Ibid.*, 1885.
95 Baragnon, *Magnétisme Animal*, 1853, 375.
96 Silas, *Op. cit.*, 20.
97 *Ibid.*, 22.
98 De Mirville, *Op. cit.*, II, 97.
99 *Ibid.*, I, 405.
100 De Richemond, *Op. Cit.*, 15.
101 Myers, *Proceed.*, 1885, 32.
102 *Ibid.*, 9.
103 Charcot, *Maladies du Système Nerveux*, 1887, III, 228.
104 Silas, *Op. cit.*, 23, *Revue Spirite*, 1877, 141. Cf. Maudsley, *Pathologie de l'Esprit*, trans. 1883, 85.
105 *Revue Spirite*, 1864, 14.
106 *Revue Spirite*, 1864, 177.
107 *Journal du Magnétisme*, 1855, 143.
108 Myers, *Proceed.*, S. P. R, 1887, 216.
109 *Journal du Magnétisme*, 1855, 120.
110 Guldenstubbe, *Op. cit.*, 82.
111 Peladan, *Revue Spirite*, 1876, 191.
112 Perrier, *Journal du Magnétisme*, 1854, 79.
113 Chevillard, *Études Expérimentales sur certains Phénomènes Nerveux et Solution Rationnelle du Problème Spirite*, 1875, 19.
114 *Ibid.*, 31, 93.
115 *Ibid.*, 31, 93.
116 Lafontaine, *Op. cit.*, 31.
117 Allan Kardec, *Le Livre des Médiums*, 46.
118 De Mirville, *Op. cit.*, I, 64.
119 *Journal du Magnétisme*, 1855, 565.
120 *Revue Spirite*, 1879. Several articles, *passim*. 148, 271 et sq.
121 *Ibid.*, 157 et sq.
122 *Ibid.*, 159.
123 Cf. Bérillon, *La Dualité Cérébrale et l'Indépendance Fonctionnelle des deux Hémisphères Cérébraux*, 1884, 115.
124 *Ibid.*, 109. Cif Magnin. *Étude Clinique et Expérimentale sur l'Hypnotisme*, 1884, 157.
125 Cf. Chapter 3 of Volume 1.
126 Bastian, *Le Cerveau, Organe de la Pensée*, 1882, 149.
127 Myers, *Multiplex Personality. Proceed.*, S. P. R., 1887., 499.
128 Myers, *Automatic Writing. Proceed.*, 1885, 39.
129 *Ibid.*, 47 et sq.

130 *Ibid.*, 38.
131 Ballet, *Langage Intérieur*, 1886, 115.
132 Cf. Maudsley, *Op. cit.*, 363. – Ribot, *Maladies de la Volonté*, 75.
133 Luys, *Maladies Mentales*, 1881, 440.
134 Moreau (de Tours), *Psychologie Morbide*, 1859, 151
135 De Mirville, *Op. cit.*, II, 188, describes them very well, albeit by relating them, as always, to the devil.
136 Maudsley, *Op. cit.*, 288.
137 *Ibid.*, 334.
138 Michéa, *Médication Stupéfiante*, 1857, 12, Georget, *Maladies Mentales*, 1882, 22, etc. – II. Saury, *Études Cliniques sur la Folie Héréditaire, les Dégénérés*, 1886, 223.
139 "The subject," said Richet, describing roughly analogous facts, "finds that the suggestion was successful or not, and laughs at the spectacle he gives himself." *Revue Philosophique*, 1886, II, 325.
140 Tascher, *Lettres de Gros Jean*, 1885, 17.
141 Richet. *Homme et Intelligence*, 1884, 517.
142 Joly, *Sensibilité et Mouvement*, Revue Philosophique, 1886, II, 250.
143 *Ibid.*, 230.
144 Leuret, *Frag. Psychol. sur la Folie*, 1834, 259.
145 Maury, *Sommeil et Rêves*, 1878, 158.
146 Ellis, *Aliénation Mentale*, 1840, 200.
147 Ball, According to Paulhan, *Revue Philosophique*, 1888, 88, II, 119.
148 Cf. Ribot, *Psychologie de l'Attention*, 1889, 124.
149 Saury, *Op. cit.*, 63.
150 Michéa, *Op. cit.*, 14.
151 Moreau (de Tours), *Haschich*, 1845, 119.
152 Westphal, According to Ribot, *Psychologie de l'Attention*, 1889, 135.
153 Pinel, *De la Monomanie*, 1856, 41.
154 Marion, *Prophetic Warnings of Elie Marion*, 1707. – Gasparin, *Op. cit.*, II, 22.
155 De Mirville, *Op. cit.*, I, 241.
156 Luys, *Op. cit.*, 212.
157 Moreau (de Tours), *Haschich*, 354.
158 Ballet, *Op. cit.*, 64. – Other examples, Despine, *Somnambulisme*, 66, etc.
159 Max Simon, *Le Monde des Rêves*, 1888, 106.
160 Moreau(de Tours), *Haschich*, 330.
161 Cf. Wundt, *Psychologie Physiologique*, II, 1874, 433.
162 Moreau (de Tours), *Psychologie Morbide*, 147.
163 Binet has just published a study of this persistence of the association of ideas despite the disaggregation and the subdivision of the field of consciousness, a study that is so complete, that I am content to refer the reader to it. In this article (*The Alterations of Consciousness in Hysterics*, Revue Philosophique, 1889, I, 135), he demonstrated how all the former associations, even the slightest, between the currently subconscious tactile sensations and the still conscious visual images, all persist despite the division of personal perception. The experiences I had had for a long time, and which I have just summarized, had only related to the artificial associations produced by suggestion between the subconscious reference point and conscious hallucination; Binet has found that things happen the same way when it comes to natural associations between the touch of an anesthetic finger, for example, and the visual and conscious image of that finger. His extremely interesting observations, which seem to me to be very accurate, at least for the category of individuals who belong to the visual type, complete a point in my work that had obviously remained incomplete.
164 Deleuze, *Mémoire sur la Faculté de Prévision*, 1836, 148.
165 Bertrand, *Somnambulisme*, 1843, 233. – Cf. De Mirville, *Op. cit.*, I, 65.

166 Pigeaire, *Puissance de l'Électricité Animale*, 1839, 269.
167 Charpignon, *Op. cit.*, 414.
168 Moreau, *Haschich*, 337. – Cf. Ball, *Maladies Mentales*, 1890, 91.
169 Gasparin, *Op. cit.*, II, 60.
170 Richer, *La Grande Hystérie*, 1881, 825.
171 Maudsley, *Op. cit.*, 294.
172 Richer, *Op. cit.*, 811.
173 Deposition of Father Surin, according to Berillon. – *Dualité Cérébrale*, 102 cit. in Bérillon, *Hypnotisme Expérimental*, 1884, 102.
174 Cf. Regnard, *La Sorcellerie*, 1887, 40, 70 … *passim*.

Chapter 4

Mental weakness and strength

A phenomenon can be natural and, to a certain extent, not be absolutely normal. It can be seen as an abnormal modification produced by accidental circumstances, and yet not belong, at least in this form, to the regular and average existence of most people. The remarks of Claude Bernard in this regard have already demonstrated that even exceptional and unhealthy phenomena are not absolutely new, that they only present a development, in one direction or another, of natural forces and remain subject to the same laws. Before concluding, however, it is only right to consider to what extent the principal forms of automatism which we have examined are an unhealthy phenomenon and to what degree the will, normal and free (at least in appearance), differs from this mechanical and rigorously determined activity.

4.1 Psychological misery

Are hypnotizable subjects, as well as the spiritist mediums (since we know that they are identical), sick or healthy people? This question has given rise to the most vivid and perplexing controversies. Some only saw in these automatic phenomena the most distinctive manifestations of hysterical disease, while others thought that they were compatible with the most perfect health. For the former, somnambulism is a crisis of hysteria; for the latter, it is a form of natural sleep. Automatic writing itself has evoked the same opposing positions. While some see it as a form of madness and impulsiveness, others consider it quite natural. According to many English authors, "Some people write without being aware of it, in the same way that others hum a tune without paying attention to it."[1] This debate could only be settled by long medical studies and very precise statistics which we cannot present. We will only try, without generalizing, to point out the intermediate position to which our own observations have brought us.

A first point seems to us absolutely indisputable: that hysterical disease is by far the most favourable ground for the development of automatic phenomena. It is even difficult to understand how certain authors could have thought that hysterical manifestations made experiments more challenging. Undoubtedly, a hysteric can interrupt a study of hypnotism with contractures or a crisis. However, these crises are

DOI: 10.4324/9781003198727-4

in themselves phenomena of an extremely curious automatism, and it is very easy, when we know the mechanism of the subject well, to avoid them by taking a few simple precautions. In my opinion, the finest studies on somnambulism or successive existences, on suggestions, and subconscious acts or simultaneous existences, are done with hysterics. Furthermore, in order to provide clear and easy to study examples for this book, I have almost exclusively cited experiments with hysterical patients. I do not think I am much mistaken in saying that for most observers, the same is true. Undoubtedly, a number of scientists, I am not saying all of them, have been mistaken to describe the state of health of their best subjects and ignore the signs of hysterical disease. "Those who believe in hypnotism of healthy subjects have for criterion of hysteria the anterior convulsive crisis, and the permanent stigmas, amblyopias, anesthesias … are not investigated."[2] One of the main reasons for this error (I am even better suited to point this out because I was deceived myself at the start of my research), is that induced somnambulism replaces and, consequently, temporarily suppresses most of the hysterical symptoms. "We make crises disappear, when we replace them with somnambulism," magnetizers[3] have already said, "but always with this condition: as soon as we stop, the crises resume." "It is a curious thing," say the Moderns as well, "that induced somnambulism makes natural somnambulism disappear … as well as the crises of hysteria."[4] My observations are very clear on this point. Three sessions of somnambulism completely stopped Lucie's crises. Rose did not experience seizures when I hypnotized her, but they started again when I stopped. Even more impressive is Léonie, who, after a large number of magnetizations, lost all symptoms of hysteria and only retained somnambulism. But hysteria still remains latent, usually easily recognized by sensory disturbances. It is definitely ready to strongly manifest itself at the first opportunity, as happened for Léonie at the time of her menopause.

Conversely, a consequence that does not seem to me sufficiently known, but is still of great importance, is that when hysteria is healed completely, and not only in appearance, somnambulism and suggestibility disappear. Several authors have noted this fact. "The best sign of a return to perfect health," writes Despine, "is the cessation of the aptitude towards somnambulism."[5] "I must say that, as the patient returned to health, she became less and less susceptible to the means that I employed," says Baréty.[6] "As health returns," remark Fontan and Ségard, "the subject is less and less hypnotizable."[7] During my early studies with Lucie, I was completely ignorant of this law. I sought, in the interest of the subject and for the convenience of my experiments, to make the hysterical symptoms disappear, but I intended to keep somnambulism. I was therefore very disappointed when I realized that my experiments were no longer possible because the subject no longer manifested subconscious acts and could no longer be hypnotized. It cannot be said that I did not know how to put her to sleep, since, almost every day for a month, I had conducted all possible experiments with her. On the other hand, Lucie, who was accustomed to somnambulism, was very accommodating in allowing herself to be hypnotized. She consented to try all the procedures which I tried, and became quite tired without any result. The somnambulism that was so complete and so easy had absolutely disappeared with the last hysterical symptoms. Eighteen months later, she came complaining of some nervous disorders, migraines, nightmares, etc.; the anesthesia had returned and she was hypnotized in an instant. These troubles healed in a few days, and all somnambulism once again disappeared. Is this not a real case of "cross-experimentation"? Well, I have recently repeated this curious experiment with Marie. She remained ill for eight months, and, during this entire interval, was hypnotized irregularly, but frequently, by either Dr. Povilewicz or myself. She was therefore as accustomed as possible to hypnotic maneuvers. Now she is cured, at least for the time being, by the singular procedures which have been described, and it is impossible to put her to sleep or to give her the slightest hypnotic suggestion. Marie had never been exposed to Lucie's story; she is too easily influenced by all that she hears or sees, including everything I order her to do. If I insist on these facts, it is that they seem to me to have some importance and relevance in regard to the authors who would like to separate hysteria and hypnotism too completely.

Another fact, which it suffices to recall, since it has been continually pointed out in this work, is the identity between all hypnotic phenomena and all hysterical symptoms. Some authors have claimed that the hypnotic state and natural sleep are comparable. I cannot help but consider this a forced conclusion. Without a doubt, the subject in somnambulism can have the appearance of a naturally sleeping person. Léonie, if I make her believe that she is in bed, sleeps and snores during somnambulism in the most natural way. But what does that matter? A subject can take on the appearance of a drunk or a feverish person; shall we then say that somnambulism is a form of drunkenness or fever? If we put aside drowsiness, light sleeps, etc., produced by fatigue or boredom, in which we can encounter suggestibility as in the waking state, but which are not related to the hypnotic state, somnambulism is above all an abnormal state. During somnambulism, a new form of psychological existence develops, with sensations, images, and memories which are specific to it, capable, in some cases, of persisting in the background after waking and continuing beneath the awareness of the ordinary first existence. Sleep is above all a rest and a more or less complete interruption of the psychological existence. During sleep, and as it relates to this interruption, somnambulism can develop, just as during somnambulism, rests, disruptions, and sleep can intervene. But, in spite of these possible coincidences, somnambulism is not natural sleep.

On the contrary, hysterical phenomena are much more justly comparable to those of somnambulism. All attacks are identical, even in their varieties and details, to this or that form of complete somnambulism. Post-crisis attacks, contractures, or paralysis are comparable to posthypnotic suggestions. All the signs, anesthesia or various defects which persist between crises, are of the same nature as the characteristic signs of hemi-somnambulism. Moreover, crises are states which can be modified by mental influence, just as somnambulism itself and post-crisis contractures can be undone and posthypnotic suggestions erased. We can, by suggestion, change the nature of a crisis as we change that of a somnambulism. I replaced seizures with contractures and tremors with sweats. I suppressed Lucie's fits by telling her to fall asleep as soon as she felt the aura. Instead of rolling in convulsions, she lay down very quietly and remained motionless. If we spoke to her, she would reply, in a firm tone, "Don't bother me, Mr. Janet forbade me to move." This persisted as long as the crisis lasted. Moreover, seizures are naturally modified by imitation, as in somnambulism. Three hysterics whom I knew, who had very different crises from one another, had been brought together in the same room. I was astonished to see that they had confused their symptoms and that they now all experienced the same attack, with the same movements, the same delirium, and the same insults towards the same individual. Further, a new type of hysteria was forming in the room that we could have studied at another time as a natural hysteria.

It is not surprising that we find the memory of the crisis in certain somnambulisms, and that crises can even be completely replaced by somnambulisms, because they are absolutely the same kind of state. Ancient magnetizers have often expressed the thought, which is not lacking in truth: "People who have crises are imperfect somnambulists." And one can certainly consider hysteria as the most favorable state for the production of all these phenomena of automatism.

Should we stop there and argue that somnambulism is nothing more than a manifestation of hysteria? That would be an exaggerated opinion. First of all, hysteria is something very vague, an unpredictable disease, as we have often said, which can be found almost everywhere, and which does not shed much light on the conditions required for somnambulism. The symptoms of hysteria do not belong to a single disease, consistent in their origin and in their evolution; they are found in other completely different diseases. Contractures and anesthesias can be found in typhoid fever, in anemia, in syphilis (even in the secondary period, if Fournier is to be believed).[8] Certain poisonings such as alcoholism, lead poisoning,[9] or poisoning by carbon sulphide (according to very recent work),[10] bring on symptoms which can be confused with those of hysteria. There could be a complete medical study done on the ordinary illnesses that can be confused with hysteria. It is true that one sometimes meets with this facile objection: these attacks are only seen with subjects predisposed to hysteria itself by heredity and by their pre-existing pathologies, and ultimately alcohol or lead will only serve to awaken the neuropathic diathesis. Nothing could be more vague than this argument; Pitres, who accepts it when it comes to syphilis, refutes it when it comes to alcoholism or lead poisoning; it is a bit arbitrary. It would have to be demonstrated that in each determined case there was hysteria prior to the present disease. Without this, we risk seeing hysteria everywhere, because as the field of hysteria expands, the symptoms lose their precision. These are no longer crises: contractures are replaced by cramps, blindness by amblyopia, and, instead of anesthesia, mere distraction. If this were so, each month all women would be regularly hysterical, and all of us would go through periods of indisputable hysteria.

If one seeks to avoid this confusion, and if one limits the name of hysteria to a set of well characterized symptoms, it must be admitted that somnambulism, suggestion, and mental disaggregation exist outside of genuine hysteria. A doctor who also practised hypnotism pointed out to me how easily most consumptives enter into somnambulism. This is true, although not all of them have hysterical symptoms. Partial catalepsy, suggested movements, etc., can be achieved quite easily in typhoid fever, and, scruples aside, one could very quickly hypnotize these patients completely. Idle suggestions, miracle pills, and magnetized plates work wonders on chlorotic girls. The intoxication of alcohol, as we have shown in an interesting example, renders people more suggestible and more automatic than somnambulistic. Moreau (de Tours)'s studies on the intoxication of hashish are even more precise on this point.[11] Sleep, which is not by itself a hypnotic state, can be very favorable to suggestion and in the training of somnambulism.[12] Menstrual periods, as I observed with Lucie and Marie, cause women to become hypnotizable and suggestible again. Finally, impulses and fixed ideas are forms of mental disaggregation and suggestion, and they occur among a great number of individuals who are not neuropaths, in the specific sense of the word.[13] These remarks allow us to understand how certain doctors, experimenting in hospitals, where naturally the sick are found, have obtained many examples of somnambulism with subjects who, strictly speaking, did not deserve the title of hysteric.

Are we to conclude that somnambulism and the other phenomena are normal phenomena which exist in times of perfect health? By no means. How could we explain patients who are no longer hypnotizable after they have regained their health, or why so many people are resistant to hypnotism? As many observers have remarked, and as Despine put it so bluntly, "the effects of somnambulism on healthy people are nil."[14] What if we conducted a very simple experiment, if we took twenty people, preferably men between the ages of thirty and forty, physically and mentally healthy, having no hereditary or pre-existing neuropathic conditions, and, without including tiring procedures which lead to illness, and tried to induce a typical somnambulism or automatic writing? If we obtain these phenomena in only half of the subjects, we will submit quite willingly and we will recognize that somnambulism is normal. But the experiment not having been made, we still have great doubts about the outcome. We are ready to believe that the phenomena of automatism and disaggregation depend on a morbid state, but not one which is uniquely hysterical. This state would, on the contrary, be much broader than hysteria. It would include hysterical symptoms among its manifestations, but it would also be revealed through fixed ideas, impulses, anesthesia due to distraction, automatic writing, and finally somnambulism itself. "It is not hysteria which constitutes favorable ground for hypnotism, but it is hypnotic sensitivity which constitutes favorable ground for hysteria and for other illnesses."[15]

What is this morbid state? It is quite difficult to determine it exactly; we only have an approximate idea of it through reasoning and by observation. The results of our studies have been to reduce the varied phenomena of automatism to its essential requirements: most depend on a state of anesthesia or distraction. This state is connected with the narrowing of the field of consciousness, and this narrowing itself is due to the weakness of synthesis and the disaggregation of the mental composite into various groups which are smaller than they should normally be. These various points are easy to verify: the state of distraction, incoherence, disaggregation, in a word, states often observed in suggestible individuals. "We noticed," said Saint-Bourdin, speaking of a hysteric, "that, from time to time, she interrupted herself and began another topic, without remembering what had been spoken of earlier."[16] All the phenomena of impulsive madness, says Moreau (de Tours) so well, have their origins in a primordial fact which can be expressed in these words: "The vagueness, the uncertainty, the inconsistency, the mobility of ideas. It is a *disaggregation*, a true dissolution of the intellectual composite ... the separation, the isolation of ideas and molecules, whose union formed a harmonious and complete whole."[17]

But this author seems to me to express himself poorly when he connects the state of disaggregation itself to a state of excitement. "In order to explain the madness, it is necessary to accept an element of *excitation*, a basic element that is the generator of all the phenomena of delirium and of the molecular disaggregation of the intelligence."[18] It is only a question of wording, but I believe that it is important: disaggregation is not an excitement; it is a depression and a weakness. It is a natural mistake, when hearing a mad person shout and a hysteric babble, to believe them to be excited. But the rapidity of their ideas comes from their inability to coordinate them, from the weakness in which they indulge in all impressions, allowing all the images that the automatic game of association brings up successively in their minds to express themselves. It is a weakness of psychological synthesis which allows the ideas to disaggregate and group around several different centers. Some observations, in small numbers unfortunately, demonstrate the existence of a similar weakness in automatic individuals: these people manifest their weakness in a way that is visible, when it exists both physically and mentally. "Father Faria has already noted that weakness plays a role (in magnetic sleep) and that the extraction of a certain amount of blood made those who had no previous disposition to become epoptes (somnambulists)."[19] The first authors who described hysteria remarked that it is often produced by very heavy bleeding,[20] and Dr. Gibert told me of a very clear case in which profuse hemorrhages led to convulsive hysteria, which had not existed before. We can say together with Féré, "that hysterics are in a permanent state of fatigue, of psychic paralysis."[21] We then understand more easily that the pre-consumption state, typhoid fever, the secondary period of syphilis, and even certain intoxications bring on anesthesia, somnambulism, and automatism, not by injuring a particular nerve, but by depressing individuals from the psychological, as well as from the physical, point of view, and by rendering them incapable of sufficiently synthesizing their psychological phenomena.

Perhaps we could find a verification of this supposition in the phenomena which bring about the healing of certain automatic states, if we examine it from the other side. To cure hysteria and somnambulism, it is often enough to make the subject eat and sleep. We know that hysterics, like anemics, do not eat or digest. As can be observed in these vicious pathological cycles which occur frequently, it is both the principle cause and consequence of their ailment. But if, by indirect processes, we manage to make them eat and sleep, we can transform them. Rose, anesthetic and paraplegic and undergoing several attacks a day, was at the last stage of disaggregation and mental weakening. I had noticed that prolonged hypnotic sleep had a positive effect on her. "Hypnotic sleep alone is very restorative," said Beaunis.[22] "Magnetic drowsiness has undeniable sedative effects," wrote Despine. I then leave the subject asleep for four and a half days with the order to move her only to cat and to eat a lot. On the first day, she still had fits despite somnambulism, but without waking up; on the second day she was very calm; on the third day she regained the movement of her legs and part of her sensitivity. When I woke her up, she seemed almost healed. Unfortunately this renewed strength only lasted a few days, and the subject fell ill again, but less intensely. Following this line of reasoning and these observations, we can conclude that there is a particular mental weakness which consists of the powerlessness of the weakened subject to collect and condense her psychological phenomena, to *assimilate* them. A weakness of assimilation of the same kind has been given the name of physiological misery. We propose to call this mental ailment, psychological misery.

This state of psychological misery can exist in two forms. Sometimes it is constant and lasting, at least for a certain period of time. The mental force of the individual is not related to her age, to the number of sensations she experiences, and the number of images that her memory contains. It is a child's mind in a woman's body. But the child's narrow thinking allows her to coordinate her limited number of sensations and memories; it was narrow, but not inconsistent. The mentally disabled person also has a child's psychic strength, but also maintains only a small number of sensations and images; it is weak, but it is fairly orderly and regular. It is like a very mediocre administrator, to whom only a small capital has been entrusted, and who can hardly do much harm. The hysteric has subtle senses which are constantly being exercised, and a rich memory, in which all the images of the past and all the psychological systems organized in the past, live indefinitely. But at the same time, she has an organizing capacity like that of a child or one mentally disabled; so she does not know what to do with her fortune. She forgets, she throws out feelings and memories at random and lets them play out as they please. She is like a mediocre administrator at the head of a large factory, who forgets her duties and who leaves her employees without supervision, free to do what they want, and her machinery to run wild. In such a psychological state, all the attacks which we have described, and which are the consequence of automatisms of the psychological elements, become possible and occur frequently. But they have a particular character: they are extremely changeable. The same enduring state of psychological misery allows the automatic play of elements to take on all forms. Another characteristic trait, deriving from this weakness, is that it is very easy to artificially modify the nature of the attacks or the form the automatism takes on at any given moment. The mind of the subject has *extraordinary plasticity*.

To suppress the personal existence which the subject has at this moment and to replace it with another is not very difficult, since this form of existence is only a very unstable centralization of a small number of elements, taken almost at random, amidst a large number of others which are just waiting to act and to manifest themselves. This second existence or somnambulism can be produced in two ways. (1) Using fatigue to suppress the first current psychic combination – sleep, the chloroformic state, fatigue caused by a prolonged fixation – creates a good environment for the other elements (until then incoherent) to centralize somewhat and in turn take advantage. (2) Far more simply, it can be produced in subjects who have already had a second existence in some form (a dream, a crisis, or somnambulism) and excite one of the elements of this new state, which exists below the current consciousness. It is enough to mention a viper to Louis V, or frogs to a patient of Dr. Pitres, to bring about a hysterical crisis. It suffices to put Lucie's arms in a posture of terror to provoke a great crisis of hystero-epilepsy. This last example is all the more interesting since Lucie, who is anesthetic, does not consciously feel the position of her arms, and so it is the unconsciousness alone that is awakened and excited. It suffices to press the hysterogenic points, that is to say, to provoke a determined sensation belonging to the psychological phenomena of the crisis, to bring about the onset of convulsions. Likewise, it suffices to call some of the subjects (whom I have already described) by the name I gave them during somnambulism, to bring about a state of hemi-somnambulism, then complete somnambulism. Finally, when we wish, we can in turn awaken the elements that formed the normal waking state, and the individual will thus pass from one existence to another.

Thanks to this easy access to the subconscious parts of the mind, one can modify at will all the attacks of these automatic individuals. Is this a way to cure them? Yes, in a way; for suppressing a contracture or destroying a paralysis are, in some cases, relatively easy to do. But have we thereby suppressed the state of psychological misery which was the initial cause of the attacks and which, in a few months, or a few days perhaps, will bring on others? No, I do not believe so. The best proof that this state still exists is somnambulism itself and suggestibility. As long as you can heal the subject by suggestion, they are still sick. What explains this constant psychological misery? Very often it is heredity. It is not only in psychology that wealth and poverty are inherited. Sometimes it is a state of physical impairment that has occurred accidentally, such as in the recovery from certain illnesses, or maybe other mental causes that we are not yet familiar with. It seems to me that only in very rare cases can we manage to heal by suggestion the very state of psychological misery which is an essential condition for the execution of suggestions. But perhaps the progress of medicine and psychology, having now united, will make it possible to better understand and better treat this morbid state.

This state of psychological misery, the initial cause of disaggregation and fixed ideas, can present itself in another way and bring about slightly different results.

This state, instead of being constitutional and permanent, can be accidental and temporary. A woman who is normally strong and sensible can at times fall into a state of irritable weakness with characteristic distraction, systemic anesthesia, and suggestibility. A man who would ordinarily resist any false ideas can take on a narrow and suggestive mind when in a state of fatigue, sleep, or intoxication. Exhaustion following great efforts of attention and prolonged intellectual work often has this result. One of the most curious and frequent causes of momentary psychological misery is also emotion, the nature of which is still so little understood. Emotion, as we know, makes people distracted; moreover, it sometimes renders them anesthetic, either temporarily or permanently. Hack Tuke repeatedly quotes individuals who have become blind or deaf as a result of a strong emotion.[23] I myself have observed that among recovering hysterics, all sudden emotion brings back anesthesia. In a word, emotion has a dissolving effect on the mind, decreasing its synthesis and making it, for the moment, miserable.

What will be the results of this accidental misery? They are very different according to the circumstances. If, during this unhappy period, the patient was not influenced by any abnormal sensation, if they were not struck by any specific and dangerous idea, they will heal without any difficulty, will preserve little or no memory of this accidental state, and will remain, during the rest of their life, perfectly free and reasonable. How many people have had opportunities to go mad that they did not take advantage of? But if, unfortunately, a new, specific, and dangerous impulse is impressed on the mind at the moment when it is unable to resist, it takes root in a group of abnormal phenomena; it develops there and does not fade. It is in vain that, when the unfortunate circumstances disappear and the mind tries to regain its accustomed power, the fixed idea, like an unhealthy virus, has already taken root in them and developed in a place of their person that they can no longer reach. It acts subconsciously, disturbs the conscious mind, and causes attacks of hysteria or madness. A seventeen-year-old girl was brought to the hospital who had begun having attacks of terror because she had been followed at night on the streets by a stranger at the time of her menstruation. It was in the same condition that Marie did the foolish things that left such a strong mark on her life. Examples of this kind are innumerable. Here are some which are more rare. "A forty-year-old clergyman," says Erasmus Darwin, "found himself one day in a social situation, drinking wine ... Being completely drunk, he swallowed the seal of a letter. One of the guests jokingly said to him, 'Now your guts are sealed.' From that moment on he became melancholic and, after two days, he refused to take any food, either solid or liquid. He stated that nothing could pass, and he died as a result of this false idea."[24] Likewise, the impulse to cut someone's throat with a razor, which had never entered his mind before, came to the young man of whom I spoke before, when, in a fit of disaggregation and mental weakness, he had the misfortune to touch a razor. So it is that the fixed ideas of these unfortunate people are related to their profession, to the books they have chanced to read, or the words they overhear in their moments of weakness. "It is present events which decide the forms of madness, because it is the current circumstances which provoke them. But these ideas do not create madness nor the predisposition to madness. They do not explain this nervous state, this physical and mental hyperesthesia which heredity has deposited in the depths of their being and which ends up sooner or later taking away reason and consciousness."[25] In explaining the invasion of madness, Moreau (de Tours) has best described the role played by this primordial state of momentary psychic weakness. "The fixed idea, repeats itself constantly but does not occur without a reason. It is the result of a profound, radical modification of the intelligence. It is a great mistake in psychology to confuse it with error ... The madman is not mistaken, but acts in an intellectual sphere different from ours that one cannot remedy, any more than *the waking state can remedy dreams ... The fixed ideas are the detached parts of a dream state which continues in the waking state ... It is a partial dream."*[26] *"The fixed idea is the result of this intellectual decomposition, a result which persists, even though in many respects this decomposition has ceased and the intelligence has somehow been reconstituted. It is the main idea of a dream that survives the dream that gave birth to it."*[27] It is impossible to better express that which seems to us to be the truth, and we only hope, by our studies on mental disaggregation and on the persistence of ideas in a subconscious state, to contribute to clarifying and to strengthening the theories of this great alienist psychologist.

Another characteristic of these fixed ideas, the result of a non-permanent but temporary disaggregation, is that it is much more difficult to reach and modify them. You affect the consciousness of a hysteric however you want, because she is *currently* in the state of psychological misery which makes her manageable. You do not modify an insane person in the same way, because you usually only study them during the period when their delirium is organized and when their intelligence has returned to a state of stable equilibrium, which cannot be disturbed. We would have to explore whether we could bring the individual back to the psychological state in which delirium originated. Thus, I would have tried to intoxicate Erasmus Darwin's patient for a second time, in order to find out if we could not, in a new intoxication, have more power over the fixed idea. We could also sometimes look for periodic states that bring back the initial conditions of the delirium. In any case, we realize that we are up against a great many other challenges. However, I still believe that pathological psychology, which in the last few years continues in its infancy, holds unforeseen relief for the insane.

We wondered, after all our studies on automatism, if these phenomena were absolutely created by disease. We can now reply that they do not belong to a particular or in some way specific disease, but are simply the result of a kind of weakness that we call *psychological misery*. Whether these individuals manifest their illness in a thousand different ways; whether they make the tables talk and evoke the soul of Gutenberg, whether they open a hospital for sick dogs or give lectures against vivisection, whether they contract their limbs or contort them in a sort of muscular delirium: all this does not change the illness and does not create new psychological phenomena. It is always because of the same weakness, the same fatigue, that they abandon themselves without resistance and allow this or that group of sensations and images to develop indefinitely.

4.2 Lower forms of normal activity

If the phenomena of automatism are only due to weakness, they must exist in healthy people as well as the ill. But instead of being isolated, as with the former, the latter are obscured and surpassed by more complex phenomena. The rich already have the poor man's bread and water, but they also have something more. The healthy person has the ill person's automatism, but with the addition of other higher faculties. Let us quickly look at experiences in everyday life analogous to those which we have studied, which seem to be subject to the same laws.

Although the field of consciousness is usually quite large and allows us to bring together in a single personal perception a fairly large number of conscious phenomena, there are times when it is restricted to the point of putting us in a state analogous to that of the suggestible and hallucinable individual. The mind goes through a period of inevitable natural narrowing when it disappears in complete sleep, or when it re-forms after sleep. It is the moment *of dreams*, when each image which is born in isolation in consciousness clarifies itself somewhat, yet not enough to be manifested by a complete movement in persons who are not accustomed to stir their limbs by images of this kind, but enough to appear outwardly and objectively, as in hallucinations. Like the suggestible somnambulist, the dreamer is not surprised or in doubt of what he sees. He undergoes without resistance the automatism of the elements to which his mind is reduced. A slight noise, a glimmer of light, a fold in the sheets, the position of the body: all serve as suggestions. The arrangement of bodies in this or that position, expressive of an emotion or a passion, gives the dream its general direction, and everything happens as in a regular automatism. Even during normal waking, psychological phenomena occur which escape us entirely. One could include the physiological functions among these acts, which take place outside of personal perception, the intelligence of which no one disputes, even though it is not understood to what being this intelligence of the organs should be attributed. Perhaps there is, as Liébault has said, "an unconscious remembrance for each vital function: the heart has learned to beat and the lungs to breathe."[28] "Perhaps within us, there are a large number of spinal or ganglionic units susceptible to habits and learning which direct each of our physiological functions."[29] "There may be within the marrow of the backbone, real spiritual beings, which are of greater spiritual worth than the soul of the frog."[30] Although these hypotheses seem likely to us, as they relate to experimental psychology, they go beyond the scope of our observations. We will content ourselves with pointing out commonly known realities which personal consciousness leaves to automatic development, the phenomena *of distraction, instinct, habit, and passion.*

We say that a person is distracted when they do not see or hear something that they should see or hear. Or when someone unknowingly performs an action which they would not have consented to had they been aware of it.

A preoccupied person will chase a fly from their face without feeling it, answer questions they have not heard, or, like Biren, Duke of Courland (who used to put parchment in his mouth) destroy an important trade treaty without having examined it.[31] Who has not heard stories of people who, as they are talking at the table, continue pouring water until they have soaked the guests or continue to add sugar to their cup to the point of filling it? There are countless anecdotes similar to these.

Systematic anesthesia and subconscious acts are the two characteristics which we have reported among patients. Only distraction can arise in healthy people, for different reasons. Sometimes it is due (as with patients) to a narrowing of the field of consciousness caused by fatigue or to half-sleep: "Day of misery and extreme despondency," writes Maine de Biran in the curious journal in which he studies experimental psychology on himself, "I had dinner with the Chancellor. I found myself in a state of disorder, of embarrassment, of *momentary deafness* … I am *like a somnambulist* in the midst of this cheerful and light world, dissatisfied with others because I am with myself."[32] But the same distraction may be due to an excessive concentration of thought, or on the other hand, to a significant focus of attention, which *without narrowing the actual thought*, displaces the field of consciousness. The same author writes, referring to Deleuze when he spoke about somnambulism, "I am almost always connected with myself and I see too much within to see well without."[33] But, in both cases, a certain number of psychological phenomena are left to themselves and develop according to the laws of their own automatism.

As soon as phenomena are isolated in this way, either by extreme attention or by distraction, they bring about reverie, sometimes even hallucination. We hear chanted words in the ringing of the bells, we see the people we are thinking of, or make abrupt gestures and speak out loud. All these psychic reflexes have been studied elsewhere, when they were isolated and magnified. It suffices to recall that they also play a considerable role in the attitude and physiognomy of very normal persons. These kinds of activities account for the instinctive acts which play an important role in animals, although they are quite rare in humans. It is impossible to suppress consciousness in instinct and to make it a pure mechanism, but neither can it be made into an intelligent and voluntary act. Lemoine says it is likely something intermediate between the movement of raw matter and that of the human will.[34] Instinct is very similar to acts caused by suggestion and, just as these were only the manifestation of a phenomenon of perception, we can say that instinct is activity directed by perceptions which are clearly conscious in the animal and even forming the whole of its mind, whereas it is almost always subconscious in people whose minds are filled by higher phenomena.[35]

In humans, automatic activity has become concentrated in the phenomena of *habit or memory*. As we have pointed out before, we are not looking to see if our memories subsist in a conscious manner within us, which is not improbable, for this goes beyond our experience.[36] We only recognize that our habits and our memories lead to acts, connections of ideas that we witness beyond what we actually generate, which are often outside of our consciousness and always outside of

our will. Conscious phenomena are not suppressed, because we can regain consciousness of things that we hold in memory or that we do out of habit, but consciousness is neglected, as if these phenomena can be sufficiently exercised when
they are harmlessly left to their own devices. Jouffror rightly says, "Habit seems to
dull the organ, or it sharpens it. But the fact is that it neither sharpens nor dulls it,
the organ remains the same, the same sensations are reproduced. But when these
sensations are interesting for the soul, it applies itself and becomes accustomed to
disentangling them. When they are not, it becomes accustomed to neglecting them
and does not disentangle them."[37] These ideas, entrusted to memory and habit,
are sometimes sharper than those of consciousness itself. To find the spelling of
a word that we have forgotten, we let our pen write automatically, almost in the
way mediums interrogate their spirits. This forgetting of the phenomena given
over to automatic memory allows us to consciously think of something else while
they are independently carried out with perfect consistency. "I remember," wrote
Erasmus Darwin, "having seen a pretty, young actress, rehearsing her singing
part with great taste and delicacy while she accompanied herself on the pianoforte
under the eyes of her master. I saw on her face an emotion for which I could not
divine the cause. At the end, she burst into tears. I saw then that during all the
time she had been singing, she had been watching her canary, whom she loved
very much, who seemed to suffer and who, at that moment, fell dead in its cage."[38]
As for simultaneous intelligent actions, I do not include, as the author does, the
beating of the heart and the movement of the breath, which continued during all
this time. Yet this person sang, accompanied herself on the piano, likely played
different notes with both hands, and still used all her conscious intelligence to follow the stages of agony of her canary. Neither mediums nor somnambulists have
shown us anything this complicated. This aptitude, which habit gives us to perform intelligent acts without personal perception, allows us to make new progress
and to use our intelligence for greater things. This psychological automatism is
the necessary condition of our progress.

   The study of habit leads so naturally to the notion of automatic and subconscious acts, which many authors can only describe by using the hypothesis of two
simultaneous personalities. Condillac's description is especially interesting for
us. "Thus," he says, "there are, as it were, two selves in each person: the habitual
self and the reflective self. It is the first which touches, which sees. It is the one
which directs all the animal faculties. Its object is to accompany the body, to
keep it from harm, and to watch continuously over its conservation. The second,
leaving all these details to the first, focuses on other things. It occupies itself with
adding to our happiness, its successes multiplying its desires … The former is
responsible for that which makes an impression on the soul: ideas, needs, and
desires, which establish in the body the corresponding actions necessary for the
conservation of the animal. The latter is excited by all things, which, by stirring
our curiosity, multiply our needs. Although each has a specific purpose, they often
act together. When a surveyor, for example, is very busy with the solution of a
problem, objects still continue to act on his senses. The habitual self therefore

obeys its impressions. It is the one who crosses Paris and avoids obstacles, while the reflective self is entirely devoted to the answer it is looking for... The habitual self is sufficient for needs which are absolutely vital for the conservation of the animal ... The measure of reflection that we have beyond our habits is what constitutes our reason."[39] In this context, this description undoubtedly has only the truth of a metaphor, because the conscious phenomena which develop automatically in habit are not grouped and synthesized in the average person so as to form a second self, as in hemi-somnambulism. However, in our previous discussions, which are impossible to reiterate here, we learned that, despite this exaggeration, there is more truth in this description than in most common opinions, which describe automatic and habitual phenomena as simple physiological movements.

The most curious manifestation of psychological automatism in the average person is *passion*, which resembles, much more than one generally imagines, suggestion and impulse, and which, for a moment, lowers our pride and reduces us to the level of the insane. Passion, strictly speaking, that which drives people in spite of themselves, thoroughly resembles madness in its origin, in its development, and in its mechanism. Everyone knows that passion is not dependent on will and does not come when we want it to. For example, to fall in love, it is not enough to simply want it. On the contrary, the voluntary effort that we might try to make, the reflection and the analysis in which we might engage, far from bringing love itself, irresistible and blind, would infallibly move away from it and produce completely opposite feelings. Likewise, it is in vain that one might try to evoke in oneself feelings of ambition or jealousy. No matter how much you declare these passions useful or necessary, you would not experience them. Another characteristic, which seems to me to be less known and less analyzed by psychologists, is that passion can only emerge at certain moments, when we are in specific situations. It is commonly said that love is a passion to which we are always exposed and which can surprise us at any time in our life, from the age of fifteen to seventy-five. This does not seem correct to me. A person is not all their life, at any time, likely to fall in love. When someone is in good health and in good spirits, they have complete and effortless possession of all their thoughts; they can expose themself to the circumstances most capable of giving rise to passion, but will not feel it. Desires will be reasonable and voluntary, leading a person only as far they want to go and disappearing as soon as they want to be rid of them. On the contrary, if someone is mentally ill, whether it is as a result of physical fatigue or excessive intellectual work, or else after violent tremors and prolonged grief, if they are exhausted, sad, distracted, reserved, unable to gather their thoughts, in a word, depressed, they will fall in love or take on the seed of some passion at the earliest and most futile opportunity. Novelists, when they are psychologists, have understood this. It is not in an instant of gaiety, boldness, and good mental health that love begins. It is in a moment of sadness, languor, and weakness. Anything is sufficient – the sight of anyone, a gesture, a word that would have left us completely indifferent a moment before – to strike us and become the starting point for a long love affair. Even more so, an object which had made no impression on us at a moment when our healthy mind was immune and produced an insignificant memory can reappear in a moment of morbid receptivity. That is enough. The seed is now sown in favourable soil; it will develop and grow.

First, as in any virulent disease, there is an incubation period; the new idea goes back and forth in the vague reveries of the weakened consciousness, and then seems to disappear for a few days and let the mind recover from its transient disorder. But it has accomplished its underground work; it has become powerful enough to unsettle the body and cause movements whose origin are not within personal consciousness. What is the amazement of a man of intellect when he finds himself standing pitifully under the window of his beauty, where his unsuspecting, wandering steps transported him, or when, in the middle of his work, he hears himself continuously murmuring a name, the same one, over and over! Let us add that every idea brings about expressive modifications throughout the body which are not always appreciable to others, but which the tactile and muscular senses transmit to consciousness. How great then, must the nervous irritation of the mind be, which constantly feels its rebellious organism initiating actions which it has not been ordered to do! Such is genuine passion, not idealized by fanciful descriptions, but reduced to its essential psychological characteristics.

In fact, we find these same characteristics in all kinds of passion. Taking a more liberal interpretation, let us look at a very specific and well-known passion: that of fear. When you are healthy, reasonable, and in good spirits, you are not fearful, and the things that are said, the dangers that surround you, are evaluated by you with calmness and composure. You defend yourself, you take precautions: this is reasoning and not fear. However, when you are weak, sorrowful, and ill, you now feel your legs preparing to flee, the beating of your heart, your face turning cold. You find yourself, like the famous coward of Toppfer, looking under your bed or checking the lock for the twentieth time. It is then that you feel the anguish of dread and an indomitable fear. If we turn to another far lesser passion, the smoker's passion for tobacco, we find in an article by Delbœuf a confession which has all the merit of a psychological document: "The tobacco jar sits at some distance from me, in its usual place; I feel its pull. Suddenly, I get up and unconsciously walk towards it. I perceive my weakness; I sit down and resume my reading. Now my hand mechanically plunges into my pocket and pulls out my cigarette case. Irritated with myself, I violently return the case to its place, etc."[40] As with suggestion, fixed ideas, or impulsive madness, passion is not an error; for an error exists entirely in the personal mind and can be fought and destroyed by it, while passion has its origin outside the personal mind and cannot be suppressed by reasoning. No matter how irrefutably we are shown that this love is absurd, that this fear is ridiculous, we remain convinced of it, and we will remain in love or frightened. Passion is sometimes cured when it is satisfied, when the fixed idea has definitively brought about the act to which it corresponds, is exhausted, and disappears. It can also be cured by a new shock which once again upsets the layers of consciousness and allows us to reclaim the ideas that had been separated.

Is this brief description of passion not the exact reproduction of what we have observed so many times among the insane or the hysteric after having received a suggestion? With them too, a state of momentary weakness of consciousness has made it possible to sow a foreign idea which is not integrated into their judgment and their will. The ideas develop independently, in spite of themselves, and cause them to perform acts of which they are sometimes unaware, but which, in some circumstances, they accept and continue. They may occasionally somewhat resist them, but, in any case, they always remain foreign to them. We really do not need to take hashish, as Moreau (de Tours) did, to know for ourselves what madness is, for who can boast of never having been mad?

The subconscious action of certain ideas during passion is so evident and clear to see that it has given rise to a quantity of moral expressions known throughout time. The battle of "two men" which share our heart has been described in all religions and all philosophies. A charming author, during the moments of rest that his great "Voyage around his room" leaves him, has drawn such a perfect description of the "system of the soul and the beast" that I cannot resist the pleasure of recalling it here.[41] "I realized," he says, "through various observations, that man is made up of a soul and a beast. These two beings are absolutely distinct, but so embedded in one another, or on one another, that the soul must have attained a certain superiority over the beast in order to make the distinction ... One day last summer, I was on my way to go to court. I had painted all morning, and my soul, taking pleasure in meditating on the painting, I left it to the beast to transport me to the King's Palace. Painting is a sublime art, thought my soul, happy; it is the one that the spectacle of nature has touched ... While my soul was making these reflections, *the other* was going on, and God knows where it was going! Instead of going to court, as it had been ordered to do, it drifted far to the left, so that by the time my soul caught up with it, it was at the door of Madame de Hautcastel, half a mile from the Royal Palace. I leave it to the reader to think what might have happened, if it had itself come upon such a beautiful lady ... I usually give my beast the care of the preparations for my lunch; it is the one who toasts my bread and slices it. It makes wonderful coffee and even makes it quite often without my soul getting involved, unless it chooses to watch the beast work ... I had laid my tongs on the coals to grill my bread; and some time later, while my soul was wandering, a flaming piece of it rolled onto the hearth. My poor beast put its hand to the tongs and I burned my fingers." Here one should recall the whole episode of the portrait of Mme de Hautcastel. "My hand had automatically seized the portrait of Mme de Hautcastel and *the other* amused itself by removing the dust which covered it. This occupation gave it a quiet pleasure, and this pleasure made itself felt in my soul, although it was lost in the vast expanses of heaven ... Her whole figure seemed to be reborn and to emerge from nothingness. My soul rushed from the heavens like a falling star. It found *the other* in an ecstasy of beauty and succeeded in increasing it by sharing in it." And elsewhere still: "Joanetti (his domestic) is a perfect, honest man. He is accustomed to the frequent journeys of my soul, and never laughs at the inconsistencies of *the other*. He even directs it sometimes when it is alone, so that we could say that it is led by two souls. When it gets dressed, for example, he warns me with a sign that it is about to put on its stockings inside out, or its coat before its jacket. My soul has often amused itself to see poor Joanetti running after the madman, beneath the supports of the Citadel, to warn it that it had forgotten its hat, or, another time, its handkerchief or its sword." What better summary could I have made of the automatism of our thoughts in distraction, habit, or passion? To describe these phenomena further would be to repeat studies already carried out, so close are they to the phenomena observed during illnesses and somnambulism.

4.3 Judgment and the will

What separates the normal person from these weak-minded individuals is that they have other actions in addition to the automatic activity which they both share. For suggestible people, who are in a state of psychological misery, automatism influences all aspects of their life. It only exists within us in certain inferior acts, which are habitual or passionate. It is then completed and taken over by the will. It is not necessary to study the higher or voluntary activity itself; we only have to demonstrate its existence and show how it differs from the previous activities.

It is very difficult to explain the nature of the will, not to mention recognize and describe a voluntary act, because psychologists are far from agreeing on the signs which characterize it. A very simple initial definition is frequently quoted. "The difference between voluntary movement and involuntary movement of the leg," Spencer says, "is that, while involuntary movement occurs without any prior awareness of the movement to be made, voluntary movement occurs only after it has been represented in consciousness."[42] "The subjective characteristic of voluntary movement," writes Wundt, "is that it is preceded, in our conscious-ness, by some sensation which seems to us to be the internal cause of the move-ment."[43] Similarly, many physiologists, like Bastian, say that a voluntary act is simply preceded by the idea or representation of the kind of movement to be performed. If we accept this definition, all the possible movements executed by a living being will be voluntary movements. All our studies have shown that there is no action even among somnambulists or cataleptics which is not either preceded by or accompanied by the representation of the act to be performed, because it is precisely this representation which brings about the action and the movements.

Shall we say, like Romanes in his work on the intelligence of animals, or like Delbœuf,[44] that there is a greater interval of time between the idea and the act which follows it, when it is a voluntary act rather than an automatic act, and should the will be made to consist solely in hesitation? It suffices to say then that certain clearly automatic acts, like those which we have suggested to som-nambulists, will be carried out very slowly because of the resistances which they encounter. The hesitation arises simply from the struggle of several ideas which oppose one another before the strongest one has triumphed, and this struggle can exist in mechanical and other types of action.

Many psychologists make use of the well-known theory of the feeling of effort. There is in us, they say, a particular feeling, that of the effort, which exists in voluntary action and which does not exist in any other. "If it was a foreign cause which gave movement to my arm," Rey Regis, in the eighteenth century, is already quoted as saying, "I would not feel more *influence or effort* on the part of my soul than if someone, with my consent, amused himself by moving it. Now, I appeal to experience. If someone moves my arm or if I move it myself, do I not feel something quite different, especially if I hold a heavy body in my hand?"[45] We know that Maine de Biran and, later, a very large number of philosophers founded a whole philosophy on this particular sensation of effort. For my part, I do not believe that there is yet any reason to debate this theory after William James made his study (*The Feeling of Effort*), which I do not consider to have been refuted. The particular feeling which Rey Régis speaks of is a set of muscular sensations which exist in all voluntary or non-voluntary movements, but which are specific to when we carry the weight of our own arm and especially when we add the weight of an object.

But, it is said, this effort is required before the act. "No matter how sincerely I want my arm to move, no matter how much I repeat my volition, however insistent and strong it is, my arm will remain inactive until I apply the driving force myself by a particular effort."[46] This amounts to saying: each individual sets their arm in motion with specific images, muscular for one, visual for another. If they are successful, in a manner which remains quite vague, in representing the movement of their limbs with different images, there will be no real movement, at least not in the limb they are thinking of. A hysteric who can only move her legs by using kinesthetic images is paralyzed when she loses these images. If she represents this movement by visual images, she will have movements in her eyelids, eyes, chest or arms, etc., but not her leg. In a word, if the idea of a movement is represented in a precise way and by the appropriate images, this movement will be carried out in the same way, whether it is a voluntary act or an automatic act.

Since the voluntary act cannot be inserted between the idea and the movement, which are always indissolubly united, it is in the idea itself, in the intellectual phenomenon proper that it must be sought. "What makes it possible to establish tangible differences between the forms of will is the undisputed fact of their correspondence with the forms of representation. These are much more distinct than the former, or rather they alone are distinct. It is those which give their colour to actions, which are themselves indeterminate."[47] Automatic acts are presented to us with two degrees of perfection corresponding to two degrees of intellectual phenomena, whether they are the expression of simple sensations or isolated images, or they correspond to perceptions already more complex and variable. In order for there to be acts elevated above these last automatic acts, there must be, in the intelligence, phenomena of knowledge superior to perceptions themselves.

For our part, we are disposed to believe that *judgments* or *ideas of connection* are, in the intelligence, phenomena different from sensations, images and perceptions, which are simply groups of images associated with one another. The idea of resemblance, for example, is not a sensation, or an image, for it is neither red, nor blue, nor warm, nor acoustic; neither is it a group of images, for an addition of this kind would form a new image and the resemblance cannot in any way be represented. This idea arises in relation to terms presented by the senses or represented successively by association and memory, but it does not seem to be of the same nature. The image I think of when I see Peter and Paul is not an exact representation of either Peter or Paul. Truth, beauty, morality are, in my mind, something different from objects themselves about which I have these conceptions: aesthetic judgment is not the same as a mosaic of pleasant sensations given side by side. Whether we call these new phenomena reflections, as Maine de Biran does,[48] or apperceptions, as Wundt calls them (following Leibniz), or simply judgments, it does not matter, as long as they are not confused with psychological phenomena. I make no pretense of addressing the theory of judgment, which forms, in my opinion, the key point of contemporary psychology and which most separates psychologists today. I am simply repeating the conclusions which have already been brilliantly supported by several authors, particularly Rabier. I only wish to point out that if we erase this distinction between judgment and image, we thereby eliminate any possible separation between voluntary acts and automatic acts, for voluntary acts are precisely those which are determined by judgments and ideas of connection.

We perform daily acts which are absolutely identical to those which we made our somnambulists perform by means of suggestion, and yet we say that our acts are voluntary and theirs are automatic. There was something more in our mind than in theirs at the time that the act was executed. Like them, in our thoughts we have the representative image of the act to be carried out, but they enact it only because they have the image in mind. We perform it because we also *judge* whether it is *useful* or *necessary*. The subject automatically copies the movement of my arm while I voluntarily copy a drawing: the subject does the act solely because she thinks of the image of this act and without judging that she is doing an action similar to mine. I copy while thinking of the *resemblance* and because of it. "Instead of acting similarly in similar cases," said Fouillée, "by a pure automatism, like an animal, without any awareness of similitude, he will act similarly in similar cases with awareness of similitude, that is to say with a feeling of resemblance strong enough to be reflected upon and pictured."[49] The subject utters such words simply because they pass through their mind in the absence of any others; we speak thus because we judge it to be *true*. In short, without worrying about the nature of judgments or how they determine action, we are saying that there is only voluntary activity when it occurs.

How does judgment determine activity? Is it in the same way that images and perceptions, necessarily translate themselves to the outside by a particular movement? That hardly seems intelligible. The idea of resemblance, beauty, or truth is, in reality, not linked with any determined movement. Indeed, it should not be said too easily, as certain authors do, that the idea of a connection is related to the movements of articulation of a certain word. If this were so, an idea of connection could never provoke acts other than words, and we know that it can determine any act. Besides, speech is determined by the visual or auditory images of the word "resemblance" and not by the idea of connection that it expresses. It seems to me more correct to say that ideas of connection are not driving forces in themselves, but that they stop and unite in the mind; in a word, that they synthesize in a new way a certain number of real images which themselves have the driving power. Voluntary effort would consist precisely in this systematization, around the same relationship of images and memories, which will then be expressed automatically. The weakness of synthesis which we have recognized in patients, does not even allow them the elementary syntheses which form personal perceptions, and more particularly it does not allow them the higher syntheses which are necessary for voluntary activity. The authors who have made quite a complete study of the mechanism by which attention is developed and maintained have perhaps not sufficiently insisted on the role of judgment in attention, for it is that intervention which, in our opinion, characterizes true voluntary attention. In short, it does not seem to us that there is reason to establish any great differences between voluntary activity and voluntary belief. On either side, intelligent judgment, because it brings them together strongly, serves to keep in the mind different images which will then be expressed, in one case by action, in the other by simple words.

Whatever the case may be with this mechanism of voluntary activity, determined by judgment, it possesses certain characteristics. First it presents a unity and a much greater harmony than the automatic activity. In fact, the latter, coming from a rather weak synthesis which brings together only a small number of images, does not maintain its focus for long. It manifests one perception, then another which has no relation to the first. It seems, as a whole, very uncoordinated and variable. Has anyone ever successfully given a somnambulist a suggestion, the execution of which was delayed for fifteen days? On the contrary, there is nothing more common than a voluntary resolution, such as writing a book or establishing a successful business, that will last for years. Moreover, one of the principle judgments that we apply, rightly or wrongly, to our own psychological phenomena is that of unity. We notice our unity and we increase it because we have noticed it. While automatic activity leads us through several different psychological existences, voluntary activity tends to make unity reign in our mind and make real the ideal of the philosophers: the soul, one and the same.

As long as the action is determined only by images, it is necessarily individual and self-serving, because a perception, an image, is always a specific individual phenomenon, which has no existence or value outside of itself. One who yields "to the vertigo of representation"[50] produces an action whose nature is both narrow and personal, just like the sensation which gave rise to it. But ideas of connection are something else. They alone are susceptible to generality, for they can remain the same and yet apply to many different terms. The activity determined by such ideas broadens. Although composed of elements, which in themselves are distinct phenomena, in its form it has the common direction imposed on all these movements, a meaning and a general scope. Just as each syllable which an orator utters is a specific phenomenon while their sentence is a universal conception, so the action which brings about a scientific discovery or creates a work of art participates in something universal. An automatic act has no value outside of itself; a voluntary act can become beautiful, true, and moral, and "in its highest degree," as one of our great philosophers has said, "merge with the will of the universal and with morality."[51]

Finally, the automatic act is rigorously fixed, because it is a sudden expression, without any modification, of the phenomena which currently exist in the mind of the subject. Whether it depends on a single isolated image or whether it is the result of a large number of phenomena, of a whole psychological situation, it has various degrees of complexity. Nevertheless, it is just as fixed and can be just as easily calculated. But when it is the consequence of a judgment and a general idea, it acquires real independence. Without doubt, it is always the translation of the judgment itself, for the movement is never independent of the idea, since they are two identical things, or better yet, the same thing considered from different points of view. But this judgment itself was not contained in the previous images and in the given psychological situation. Here is a new and unexpected phenomenon resembling consciousness itself, appearing in the midst of the phenomena of mechanical movement and in relation to them. It is something indeterminate and free. It is because the act is intelligent, universal, and moral that it becomes free. There is nothing more free – I do not say this in an absolute way, which would be meaningless, but as it relates to reason and to human science – than what cannot be foreseen, that for which the outcome is beyond our comprehension.

A great scientific discovery which upsets science cannot be foreseen by current science, since, by definition, it does not yet exist. A discovery of this kind is something original, new, something which did not exist before. It is, if not in its substance, at least in its form and in the new synthesis it imposes on the elements, a real creation *ex nihilo*. Now this idea only exists when it is realized in a book, or in a work of art, or an intellectual act. It is an illusion of the weak-minded to believe that they feel, deep in their heart, sublime ideas which they cannot bring to realization. If their idea was determined, if it really existed, their limbs would move on their own to carry it out. Is not the act of a person of genius the freest in the world? Insofar as someone is capable of conceiving a personal idea which is not given in the sensations he receives, and in the associations previously made, he approaches genius and freedom.

4.4 Conclusion

How could a psychologist like Moreau (de Tours) write this astonishing sentence: "By becoming a mental degenerate, a subject goes through a psycho-cerebral state which, by continuing to develop, will make him a man of genius."[52] How could he have believed that diseases of the nervous system, and even insanity itself, strongly favoured the development of intelligence?[53] It is probably because of this word "excitement", that he frequently uses to designate madness. No, whatever the similarities of external circumstances, madness and genius are at the two extreme and opposite ends of all psychological development. The entire history of madness, as argued by Baillarger, and after him many alienists, is but the description of psychological automatism left to itself, and this automatism, in all its manifestations, depends on the present weakness of synthesis which is mental weakness itself, psychological misery. Genius, on the contrary, is a power of synthesis capable of forming entirely new ideas which no previous science has been able to foresee, and is the supreme degree of mental power. Ordinary people oscillate between these two extremes. They are more determined and automatic when their mental strength is weak. They are more worthy of being considered free and moral beings to the degree of mental strength they possess, although we are unaware of how it grows.

Notes

1 Myers, *On a Telepathic Explanation of Some So-Called Spiritualistic Phenomena*. Proceed., S. P. R, 1884, II, 224.
2 de la Tourette, *Hypnotisme*, 1887, 55.
3 Dupau, *Lettres Magnétiques*, 1826, 178.
4 de la Tourette, *Op. cit.*, 173, 285.
5 Despine, *Somnambulisme*, 1880, 242.
6 Baréty, *Magnétisme Animal*, 1887, 4.
7 Fontan and Ségard, *Médecine Suggestive*, 1887, 37.
8 Cf. Pitres, *Des Anesthésies Hystériques*, 1887, 151.
9 *Ibid.*, 149.
10 Marie, *Hystérie dans l'Intoxication par le Sulfure de Carbone*, Semaine Médicale, 11 Nov. 1888.
11 Moreau (de Tours), *Haschich*, 1845, 141, 117.
12 Cf. Hack Tuke, *Le Corps et l'Esprit*, 1886, 159; – Moreau (de Tours), *Op. cit.*, 256, 234. – Cullère. *Les Frontières de la Folie*, 1888, 211.
13 Moreau (de Tours). *Op. cit.*, 106.
14 Despine, *Op. cit.*, 131.
15 Ochorovicz, *Suggestion Mentale*, 1887, 255.
16 Bourdin, *Traité de la Catalepsie*, 1841, 93.
17 Moreau (de Tours), *Op. cit.*, 36. – This author has already used, in this context, the term disaggregation, which we have borrowed from him.
18 *Ibid.*, 96.
19 de la Tourette, *Op. cit.*, 20.
20 Cullerre, *Nervosisme et Névroses*, 1887, 61.
21 Féré, *Sensation et Mouvement*, 1887, 21.
22 Beaunis, *Somnambulisme*, 1886, 211.
23 Hack Tuke, *Op. cit.*, 109.
24 Erasmus Darwin, *Zoonomie*, 1811, IV, 77
25 Moreau (de Tours), *Psychologie Morbide*, 1859, 126.
26 Moreau (de Tours), *Haschich*, 1845, 123.
27 *Ibid.*, 98.
28 Liébault, *Du Sommeil et les États Analogues*, 1860, 137
29 Philips, *Cours de Braidisme*,1860, 104.
30 Lotze, *Psychologie Physiologique*, 1876, 144. – Cf. Lewes, Maine de Biran, *Œuvres Inédites*, II, 13. – Hartmann, *Inconscient*, I, 1877, 75. – Colsenet, *Inconscient*, 1880, 141, etc.

31 Garnier, *Facultés de l'Âme*, I, 1852, 325.
32 Maine de Biran, *Journal Intime*, 242.
33 *Ibid.*, 145. – Cf. Ribot, *Psychologie de l'Attention*, 1889, 115.
34 Lemoine, *Habitude et Instinct*, 1875, 137, 150.
35 Cf. Espinas, *L'Évolution Mentale chez les Animaux*, Revue Philosophique, 1888, I, 20.
36 Cf. Colsenet, *Op. cit.*, 229.
37 Jouffroy, *Mélanges Philosophiques*, 1833, 229.
38 Erasmus Darwin, *Op. cit.*, I, 332.
39 Condillac, *Traité des Animaux*, Œuvres Complètes, 1798, III, 553.
40 Delbœuf, *Le Sentiment de l'Effort*, Revue Philosophique, 1882, II, 516.
41 De Maistre, Xavier, *Voyage autour de ma chambre*, Chapters VII–VIII, 1794.
42 Spencer, *Psychologie*, 1870, 1, 539.
43 Wundt, *Psychologie Physiologique*, 1886, I, 23
44 Delbœuf, *Revue Philosophique*, 1881, II, 516.
45 According to Paul Janet, *Revue Philosophique*, 1882, II, 370.
46 Rey Regis, *Revue Philosophique*, 1882, II, 372.
47 Espinas, *L'Évolution Mentale chez les Animaux*, Revue Philosophique, 1888, 1, 20.
48 Maine de Biran, *Œuvres Inédites*, II, 1839, 225.
49 Fouillée, *Sensation et Pensée*, Revue des Deux-Mondes, 15 July 1887, 409.
50 Renouvier, *Psychologie*, II, 1876, 360.
51 Fouillée, *Liberté et le Déterminisme*, 1884, 228.
52 Moreau (de Tours), *Psychologie Morbide*, 71.
53 *Ibid.*, 463.

Conclusion

We encounter notable difficulties and we expose ourselves to great risk when we try to draw general conclusions from these long experimental studies. The strange facts that we have reviewed and the alluring theories that we have glimpsed about this or that problem, seem to confront us with the most adventurous hypotheses of philosophy. Do not the speculations of the old hylozoist authors on universal life and consciousness, which are widespread everywhere, and the more modern theories on the persistence of ideas in memory and on the indestructibility of thought relate very closely to our experiences with catalepsy, therapeutic suggestion, and subconscious acts? But to engage with these assumptions, however attractive they may be, would be to depart entirely from the method that we are committed to follow and follow through with, as the old logic says, from one genre to another. Although it may seem strange to say so, one of the great merits of these new studies of psychology is that they are susceptible to error. We can rigorously demonstrate the unintentional inaccuracy of this or that observation or the error of this or that interpretation, and we have done so for many of these studies. In this there is both merit and advantage. There is a satisfaction for the mind to note when one is wrong on a certain point, because it gives the hope of being able to glimpse the truth on another point. The general assumptions of philosophy are not susceptible to disproof. Who has refuted or will ever be able to refute spiritualism or pantheism, so as to dismiss the hypothesis as useless? This is why we should not engage in these theories which are by their nature above and beyond any precise discussion.

However, since the summary is the main merit of intellectual work, it is necessary to synthesize all the studies contained in this book. General hypotheses are simple summaries, symbols which more or less represent the momentary state of a question and the point at which one stops in the interpretation of phenomena. Although the few propositions which we are going to propose seem plausible to us, they should only be considered as hypotheses, and therefore transient and momentary.

When the study of psychology began, philosophers insisted on the following generally correct and perhaps necessary point: the radical separation of the mind and the body. This conception had its justification in being very useful at a certain

DOI: 10.4324/9781003198727-102

time, and it contributed powerfully to the foundation of the study of psychology. But it also had its exaggerations and its dangers. The drawbacks of this hypothesis first manifested themselves in metaphysics, and the difficulty of explaining the reciprocal action of soul and body forced philosophers to construct the most bizarre systems. Faced with the difficulties and sometimes the absurdities of these theories, philosophy gradually modified its primitive conception and, under the influence of Leibniz, and then under that of Kant, singularly brought together the two natures which it had believed to be irreconcilable. This movement is quite natural and is perfectly linked to the general laws of intelligence. To understand things, we have to begin by separating them: *discrimination* is the first step of science. However to separate is not to understand; it is then necessary to unite, to synthesize, the different terms that have been distinguished and to establish a unity in diversity, which is properly the work of the human mind.

This progress, which has been more or less effected in the metaphysics of soul and matter, does not seem to me to have been as complete as possible when it comes to the science of mind and body. In fact, within science the separation had been as complete between the two categories of psychological and physiological phenomena as it had been between the two types of entities distinguished by metaphysicians. This separation had taken a particular form. Instead of being the opposition between thought and extension, it was the antagonism between ideas and feelings on the one hand, and the physical movement of organs on the other. However, difficulties did not take long to arise, and they forced psychologists, as with Cartesian philosophers in the past, to invent all kinds of intermediaries between the facts that had been separated. Scientifically speaking, the theories of the motor faculty, of muscular effort, and even of the will appear to me, to be absolutely parallel to the famous hypotheses of the plastic principle, of occasional causes, or of pre-established harmony, which exist in metaphysics. These intermediaries, however, were not sufficient, and increasingly we see the role of activity and even movement in thought, and reciprocally the role of thought in movement. Can we today present a theory of physical activity, instinctive, habitual, or voluntary, without endlessly involving all the theories of intelligence? Can we talk about intelligence, perception and attention, without constantly involving the notion of bodily movements? A theory of pure intelligence, independent of organism and movement, is no longer possible today, and soon a theory of a purely mechanical organism, without the intervention of consciousness will also be untenable. We can no longer consider psychology and physiology as independent. We cannot make one an insignificant appendage to the other. It must be admitted that between these two sciences there are particular connections which do not exist between any other, and that, by taking different points of view, they both create parallel descriptions of one and the same thing.

By limiting this general question, and rather than studying all the organs, only studying the movements of the limbs and the relevant organs, we have made our contribution to the establishment of this modern theory. We have tried to show the complete union, the absolute inseparability of the phenomena of feeling and thought and the phenomena of physical movement in organized beings. On the one hand, we have shown that any movement of the limbs in a living being, however simple this movement may be, was accompanied by a phenomenon of consciousness. Whether it concerns poses of the limbs, postures, convulsions in certain states of crisis or illness when the subject seems insensitive and reduced to the state of a machine, or whether it concerns involuntary movements or persistent contracture in a subject who is currently conscious of something else and who maintains that they are unaware of anything else, we can always legitimately suppose and sometimes demonstrate the existence of phenomena of consciousness, simple no doubt, but real, lasting as long as the movement itself. On the other hand, we believe we have demonstrated that, if we cause any psychological phenomenon whatsoever, a sensation, a hallucination, a belief, or a simple or complex perception, to be born in the mind of a person, we infallibly provoke a corresponding bodily movement which is as varied in complexity as the psychological phenomenon itself.

Conversely, if we examine, or if we produce, various suppressions of movement, when subjects, for example, become incapable of carrying out a particular determined act or of saying a certain word, or when they are affected by a complete paralysis, we find that there is at the same time a particular void in the consciousness, an amnesia or the loss of an image, or an anesthesia or the loss of a sensation. Finally, whatever modifications the exterior movement seems to experience, whether it becomes precise or vague, complex or uncoordinated, regular or variable, there is always a corresponding modification in the mind. Instinctive activity corresponds to sensations and perceptions; habitual activity should not be separated from memory; voluntary activity does not exist without judgment. In short, whatever point of view one takes, there are not two faculties, one of thought, the other activity. There is, at each moment, that one and the same phenomenon always manifesting itself in two different ways.

How is this unity, despite the apparent diversity of these two things, possible? I believe that current theories of knowledge and science clearly give us the reason for this. It is the same thing, which is known and studied in two different ways. A phenomenon which I consider externally, thanks to my sensory organs, and which I interpret by the rules and habits of my thought, cannot have the same appearance if I consider it internally with my consciousness. The difference in points of view, in procedures, in methods of investigation is so great that it suffices to explain the apparent differences which had led us astray. No doubt these differences should not be suppressed, since they result from a genuine opposition between our processes of knowledge, and the physiological study of external movement should not be identified with the psychological study of thought which accompanies it. Each one of these studies has its role and its significance, and, according to the issues with which one is concerned, one or the other of these sciences has the greater advantage. Who would think of creating the psychological theory of digestion or the physiological theory of syllogism? But this does not prevent these sciences from being parallel and from having connections between them that no other science can have, because they study the same object from two different points of view. It is certain that the knowledge of humanity in an ideal science, would not be complete unless each psychological law found its counterpart in a physiological law. In the journey towards this ideal, the two sciences are of mutual help to each other and, depending on which is further advanced on a particular point, one of the two sciences can give indications and directions to the other. In the study which occupies us, that of the movements of connection, it seems that, for the moment, it is psychology which has preeminence. It must be emphasized that the physiologists themselves believed that they could explain the acts of the somnambulists they observed only by appealing to psychological laws.

Let us therefore put aside the physical phenomena. Let us move on to pure psychology and seek in its laws the explanation of the particular and automatic activity that we set out to study. Things seem to happen as if there were two different activities in the mind which sometimes complement each other and sometimes hinder each other: let us consider each of these activities separately.

As the ancient philosophers said, to be is to act and create, and consciousness, which is in the highest degree a reality, is therefore a vital activity. This activity, if we seek to represent its nature, is above all an activity of synthesis which brings together more or less numerous given phenomena in a new phenomenon, different from its elements. This is a genuine creation, for, no matter what point of view one takes, "multiplicity does not contain the reason for unity,"[1] and the act by which heterogeneous elements are brought together in one new form is not given in its elements. At the moment when, for the first time, a rudimentary being brings together phenomena to create the vague sensation of pain, there is in the world a true creation. This creation is repeated for every new being that succeeds in forming a consciousness of this kind, for, strictly speaking, the consciousness of this being which has just emerged did not exist in the world and seems to have come out of nothingness. Consciousness is, therefore, in itself and from its beginnings, a synthetic activity.

It is impossible to say which are the first elements that are combined by consciousness in this way. Just as physiology finds organization in all the elements of the organized body, so psychology already finds an organization and a synthesis in all the elements of consciousness which it can trace. But what is certain is that there are increasingly complex degrees of organization and synthesis. The small elementary syntheses which are constantly repeated become the elements of other, superior syntheses. Being more complex, these new syntheses are much more varied than the previous ones; although always remaining units, they are units which have different qualities from one another. Just as beings composed of a single cell are all alike and beings composed of several cells begin to take on distinct forms, vague consciousnesses of pleasure and pain gradually become definite sensations of different kinds. Each sensation is thus a whole, a compound, in which elements of consciousness corresponding themselves to very simple movements have been combined. It should not be said that once a child has learned to feel a particular sensation, they then learn to do the corresponding complex movement. The child learned both things at the same time, and the coordination of movements was done at the same time as the organization of the elements of sensation.

These sensations in their turn organize themselves into more complex states which may be called general emotions. These unify and form, at each moment, a particular unity called the idea of personality, while other combinations will form our different perceptions of the outside world.

Certain minds go beyond, further synthesizing these perceptions into judgments, general ideas, and artistic, moral or scientific conceptions. Doubtless, we are then struck by the creative activity of the mind; we do not believe that the high scientific syntheses made by some geniuses were given to them in the elements furnished by the sensations. We know well that generations of people have possessed these same facts, these same elements, and have not succeeded in coordinating them, and we say that the genius is the creator. But the nature of consciousness is always the same, and children, who, for the first time, have built in themselves the weakest of artistic or religious emotions, have also made a discovery and a creation on their own account. "Perception is not something different from association," said Fouillée, "It is always the introduction of a higher current of irresistible force which subordinates all the rest and carries everything in its own circle."[2] How, by what slow progress, does consciousness make such syntheses, in what order does it pass from one to the other? These are things that we have not researched in this book, because we have always assumed that this primary activity had already done its work, and we have always studied the consequences of this work.

In fact, there is in the human mind a second activity which I cannot better designate than by calling it a *conservative* activity. Syntheses, once built, cannot be destroyed; they last; they keep their unity; they keep their elements arranged in their original order. As soon as one places oneself in favourable circumstances, one observes the sensations or the emotions, with all their characteristics, maintaining themselves as long as possible. Even better, if the previously accomplished synthesis is not completely given, if there still exists in the mind only a few of its elements, this conservative activity will complete it, and will add the missing elements in the order and in the manner necessary to remake the primitive whole. Just as the previous activity tended to create, this one tends to conserve, to repeat. The greatest manifestation of the former was synthesis; the most significant characteristic of the latter is the association of ideas and memory. "It is the mental counterpart of the great law of mechanism, the conservation of force. This law, in fact, dictates that every mobile object should persevere in its movement, as long as another force does not divert it from it, and that it always follows the line of least resistance. An early experience brought together the flame and being burnt in the child's mind, and thus produced a certain direction of thought as well as action; we thus have, in favour of the flame-burn direction, a positive force and no other in opposition."[3]

It is the consequences of this general law of conservation and reproduction that we have examined in this work. We have seen the sensations last and maintain the elements which constitute them. We have seen the emotions reproduce themselves and maintain the movements and facial expressions which made up their constituent parts. One element of a particular memory and complex personality being given, all memory and all personality is reproduced. When one brings in the elements of such and such a previously constituted synthesis, one alternates between consciousnesses and personal existences. Finally, once the subject has grasped the meaning of the words and understood the language formed, one evokes past syntheses, all the actions, all the thoughts, and one generates all the psychological phenomena in a regular and easy to predict order. Those who only want to see one side of the mind can obviously stop at this automatism which we have described in detail. But, for us, this automatism is only the consequence of another quite different activity, which, acting in the past, made it possible today and which, moreover, continues almost always to accompany it.

In fact, these two activities usually subsist together as long as the being is alive; the health of the body and the soundness of the mind depend on their harmony and balance.

Just as in a political state, innovative activity and conservative activity must regulate and limit each other, likewise, in the mind, the current activity, capable of understanding new syntheses and adapting to new conditions, must balance this automatic force that wants to keep the emotions and perceptions of the past immutable. When the mind is healthy, it abandons to automatism only certain inferior acts which, the conditions having remained the same, can be easily repeated. However, it is always active in carrying out new combinations at all times, which are constantly needed to keep in balance with the changes in the environment. This union of the two activities is, then, the condition of freedom and progress.

But if the creative activity of the mind, after having laboured from the beginning of life and accumulated a quantity of automatic tendencies, suddenly ceases to act and rests before it is finished, the mind is then completely unbalanced and left without counterweight to the action of a single force. The phenomena which arise are no longer brought together in new syntheses, they are no longer seized to form the personal consciousness of the individual at each and every moment. They then naturally return to their old groupings and automatically bring about the combinations which had reason to exist in the past. Doubtless, if minds of this kind are carefully kept in an artificial and invariable environment, if, by suppressing any change of circumstances, one saves them the trouble of thinking, they would be able to remain for some time weak and absent-minded. But whether the environment changes, whether misfortunes, accidents, or simply change occurs, requiring an effort of adaptation and new synthesis, they will fall into the most complete disorder.

It is all these disorders, small or large, which are the result of the predominance of an old automatism over a very weak present synthetic activity which we have studied in the second half of this work. We have seen that the strangest disturbances can be boiled down to a few simple laws and that psychology is not powerless to explain them.

The general ideas that we have laid out and which, moreover, are found in part in the work of several philosophers today, seemed to us a simple way of summarizing and synthesizing the phenomena that we have described. They should only be considered as probable conjectures. Their imperfection or even their falsity would not alter the accuracy of any particular laws or facts which are always, in our eyes, the central point in this essay on experimental psychology.

Notes

1 Boutroux, *De la Contingence des Lois de la Nature*, 1874, 9.
2 Fouillée, *Sensation et Pensée. Revue des Deux-Mondes*, 15 July 1884, 47.
3 *Ibid.*, 417.

Appendix

In this appendix we have provided several references relating to the disease and the principal character of several subjects who have played an important role in this work. We do not think it necessary to present a great deal of detail. Typically, the state of mental health of these subjects is very similar, and so it has almost always been described as it relates to the individual subject, along with our observations.

Be   Young woman of twenty-five. A healthy father, a nervous irritable mother with no specific attacks, an insane maternal uncle. Around the age of fifteen, she had various hysterical attacks, a few fairly severe, with loss of memory, contractures, and attacks of pseudo-peritonitis. She was hypnotized at this time quite frequently. Since then, she has not had any well-defined nervous attacks and has not been put into somnambulism. Today, she is in good health and *does not present any kind of anesthesia.* On the contrary, when we examine each of her senses separately, she has an extremely fine sensitivity everywhere. The only abnormal characteristic is a very strong tendency towards distraction, a very visible narrowing of the field of consciousness which prevents her from focusing on two things at the same time. She has only been studied from one perspective: that of suggestibility in the waking state, which is quite extraordinary with her.

Blanche   Eighteen-year-old girl. A healthy mother, a nervous, strange father, an insane maternal aunt. She is the last of fifteen children, nine of whom died at an early age, all before the age of three; the survivors are quite healthy. In her childhood up to the age of three, she had frequent seizures, and a manifestation of epilepsy, which was almost exclusively on the left side. She has remained in all respects very under-developed, almost mentally defective, very small, weak, has not begun menstruation. She has bulimia, steals food and especially bread, when she can, and eats until she chokes. This triggers a seizure, similar to those of her childhood, with convulsions limited to the left side and she foams at the mouth; but these attacks are now very rare. Sensitivity is about normal on her right side, although reduced, but almost nil on her left side. Obscure intelligence, although she has received some education. She was studied from the same perspective as the previous subject for suggestibility in the waking state and automatism, which she presents to the highest degree.

D   Young man of twenty-four years. A case of impulsive madness, the observation of which was reported in this work.

G   Seventeen-year-old girl. Hysterical mother, no information about the father. In recent years, she has had attacks of minor hysteria, which occur very frequently for periods of two to four weeks, then disappear for a while. Extremely variable anesthesia on the left side, which disappears in periods of good health. Familiar with the state of hypnotic sleep, which, in this subject, quite easily replaces seizures and temporarily suppresses them.

H   Young man of twenty-eight. Healthy father, hysterical mother (convulsions and paraplegia). He exhibits no characteristics of hysteria and his sensitivity is intact, although he is distracted and emotional. He is easily put into a state of minor hypnotism with forgetfulness upon awakening; however, rather singularly, he almost always recovers the memory of hypnotism the next day, after a normal night's sleep. He presents a particular sensitivity to the magnet, which evokes contractures in him.

Lem   Young man of nineteen. Healthy father, hysterical mother, hysterical maternal aunt. For the past two years, he has presented fairly infrequent attacks of hystero-epilepsy. Complete tactile and muscular anesthesia, except in his right leg. Had hysterical contracture of the muscles of the abdomen and chest for six weeks following a shock. Very hypnotizable.

Léonie Forty-five-year-old woman, who has been described and studied many times. Healthy mother, epileptic father and paternal grandfather, other paternal relatives likely insane. Has had seizures since early childhood, but has been extremely altered by magnetizers who have studied somnambulism in her. When I first studied her several years ago with Dr. Gibert, she no longer exhibited any distinct hysterical features; however, since last year, following violent hysterical attacks which occurred during her menopause, she has retained complete and unchanging anesthesia on her left side. The story of this very interesting woman should be related in more detail and I would do so if it were possible to collect the notes of Dr. Perrier, a doctor from Caen, who studied her for over ten years.

Lucie   A young woman of twenty, whose observations I have already presented several times in articles published in the *Revue Philosophique*. Healthy mother, hystero-epileptic father who died during an attack. She had convulsions throughout her childhood, an attack of blindness (likely nervous) about the age of nine. Following a scare, experienced around that time, she resumed very particular hysterical attacks, which at first were very short, grew little by little, and lasted, at the time I met her, at least five hours; she was a complete anesthetic, had significantly impaired hearing and sight. Induced somnambulism suppressed the hysterical attacks within a few days, then within a month's time, all other symptoms of hysteria had disappeared, and, in its turn, somnambulism disappeared as well. Lucie remained in good health without any incident for eighteen months. Then her nightmares and natural somnambulism resumed. A few sessions of hypnotism made these symptoms disappear, and the subject once more ceased to be hypnotizable. Lucie then remained a year without incident, she then had a few minor seizures which were again suppressed by a somnambulism session.

M   Twenty-three-year-old woman. Healthy father, hysterical mother, maternal grandmother, and aunt. Quite rare attacks of minor hysteria, incomplete anesthesia of the left side.

Marie Nineteen-year-old girl. Nervous irritable mother, no information about the father. From her childhood she presented true tantrums followed by choking. We have related in this volume the singular circumstances in which she lost the sight in her left eye at the age of six, and how a poorly chosen comment on the part of an adult at the time of her first period brought about fits, convulsions, and delirium much later. She now seems fully recovered and is no longer hypnotizable.

Mi   Seventeen-year-old girl. Seizures of minor hysteria, irregular plaques of anesthesia.

N   Thirty-year-old woman. Rather rare attacks of minor hysteria, anesthesia on the left side. The somnambulism of this subject has been described in this work.

P   Forty-year-old man. Taken to the hospital for an attack of subacute alcoholic delirium; towards the end of this attack presented a great suggestibility.

R   A young man of twenty, dismissed from his regiment because he had seizures which were considered to be epilepsy. Left side anesthetic, easily induced hypnotic sleep.

Rose   A woman of thirty-two, belonging to a family in which almost all the members of the maternal side, maternal grandfather, mother, aunt, nephews, are convulsive hysterics; her brother is also likely hystero-epileptic. Since childhood she has presented all of the most severe attacks of hysteria: from the age of eight, persistent anesthesias and contractures lasting for several months, hysterical blindness at fifteen, periods of major attacks of lethargy lasting for several days, etc. Did not begin menstruating until the age of twenty. She had eight children, all of whom died within the first few months of infancy.. A year ago, following her last childbirth, she had an attack of false hysterical peritonitis, then, when this disappeared, a contracture of both legs, in extension. Complete anesthesia in the lower limbs, soon spreading over the whole body, complete dyschromatopsia of both eyes. Moreover, the state of sensitivity in this subject often varied during her long stay of seven months in the hospital. Some of these variations have been described. This woman exhibited, when hypnotized, many varieties of cataleptic or somnambulist states, and in some of these states, when she recovered sensibility, she could move her legs freely. The cure of the contractures has been extremely difficult, but has, however, been obtained, in an apparently complete manner, by suggestions made under certain conditions and by prolonged somnambulisms. However all the hysterical symptoms were not gone, and, in particular, the hypnotic sensitivity and the state of suggestibility were still strong when this person left the hospital. Healing did not last for more than two or three months, and now the paraplegia and contractures have returned in much the same way.

V   Twenty-eight-year-old woman. Parents who had no nervous incidents. V is the youngest of twelve children and was born a twin. She always remained weak and frail. Following a period of intellectual study in preparation for examinations, she had, at the age of fifteen, natural delusions or somnambulisms, during which she constantly recited her *History of France*. In good health for ten years, at twenty-six she had a single major attack of hysteria following a strong emotion, and, during this crisis, began again to recite the chapters of her *History of France*. At twenty-seven, she suffered an attack of natural catalepsy caused by a thunderstorm. When she was twenty-eight, she had tonsillitis and was put on bed rest, but when the illness was over she found herself paralyzed in both legs. The patient's family history, the current state of almost general anesthesia, the existence of ovarian pain and numerous hysterogenic points, make the existence of diphtheria paralysis very unlikely. The study of this very interesting subject, which I was able to carry out, is recalled elsewhere. I could not resolve the paralysis at first, because V, even in somnambulism, claimed that it was impossible. I convinced her of my ability by causing her to see several different hallucinations; I could then easily restore the movement of the legs. I then suggested that she sleep motionless all night and the next day she had no anesthesia or hysterogenic points. The symptoms of hysteria have not returned for a year.

These few observations, which have been graciously communicated to me by the doctors who have treated these patients, are doubtless far from being complete, but they may provide some useful information on topics that have been studied in this book from new points of view.

Index

For Product Safety Concerns and Information please contact our EU
representative GPSR@taylorandfrancis.com
Taylor & Francis Verlag GmbH, Kaufingerstraße 24, 80331 München, Germany

9 781032 056890